HITLER:
THE PATHOLOGY
OF EVIL

HITLER:
THE PATHOLOGY
OF EVIL

George Victor

BRASSEY'S

Washington

Library of Congress Cataloging-in-Publication Data

Victor, George
    Hitler : the pathology of evil / George Victor
        p. cm.
    Includes bibliographical references and index.
    1. Hitler, Adolf, 1889–1945—Psychology. 2. Heads of state—Germany—
Biography. 3. Heads of state—Germany—Psychology. 4. National
socialism—Psychological aspects. 5. Germany—Politics and government—
1933–1945. I. Title.
DD247.H5V48 1998
943.085'092—dc21   97-35632
                                                             CIP

ISBN 1-57488-228-7 (alk.paper)

Printed in Canada on acid-free paper that meets the American National
Standards Institute Z39-48 Standard.

Brassey's
22883 Quicksilver Drive
Dulles, Virginia 20166

10 9 8 7 6 5 4 3 2 1

Dedicated to a victim and friend
Wolfgang Ludwig Brandt

CONTENTS

FOREWORD

The Third Reich with all its hideous cruelties so bewildered the world as to stimulate an outpouring of popular and scholarly work. Nonetheless, little of the horror has been explained satisfactorily. For me—as for George Victor—this is largely because scholars as well as ordinary people have erected barriers. One has been to deny that Hitler was an abused child. A victim of abuse deserves sympathy, but, since Hitler is thought of as a heartless monster, deserving no sympathy, he could not have been a victim. People still fear that explaining his personality could lead to forgiving him or condoning the atrocities of the Third Reich. This is certainly not the effect of Victor's comprehensive explanation.

The research underlying *Hitler: The Pathology of Evil* is thorough, the analysis is deep, and the results are of compelling interest. History accounts for the conditions that allowed a madman to seize power. But to understand Hitler's rule of Germany—his tortuous motives, driving obsessions, and charismatic power—requires probing the mind of the man who, in my opinion, was the most evil in history. For this task, more is necessary, and Victor has drawn on child development, experimental and social psychology, psychoanalysis, sociology, and anthropology. His blending of these social sciences with history is masterly, resulting in a deeper penetration than any work I know.

From the beginning, Victor challenges illusions about Germany. He notes that it was not a nation with a predatory past, as is so commonly thought by Americans and others. The simple truth of history is that Germans were the victims of many invasions. That contributed to Hitler's success in building up their sense of outrage and thirst for vengeance into a self-righteous eruption of killing.

Hitler: The Pathology of Evil is most impressive in its scholarship—both historical and psychological—and in the richness of its insights. It ranks very high among the tens of thousands of books about Hitler. Victor uses Karl Schleunes's phrase "The Twisted Road to Auschwitz" to describe the steps by which Hitler gained absolute power and systematically used it to transform Germany into a killing machine. He ends by pointing out that genocide, as practiced in the Third Reich, resulted from condoning government crime—a subject yet to be studied in depth. This is a message that the present generation and the next ignore at their peril. We want no further "twisted roads to Auschwitz."

John Laffin
Canberra, Australia

PREFACE

The words leave us the task of working out what to think and what could prevent a similar slaughter. The human toll of Hitler's war and genocide has been estimated at forty million dead with even more wounded and made refugees. Germany's defeat limited the deliberate killing of civilians to about thirteen million. Hitler's main plan called for killing another eleven million Jews and another thirty million Slavs; a second plan involved killing far more Slavs. A substantial but unknown number of Germans—Jews and non-Jews—committed suicide on learning they were wanted by the Gestapo or that they were to report for shipment to camps. Millions who survived had been deliberately starved, beaten, and mutilated.

When these events were happening, what to think and do were clear to a tiny minority in and outside Germany. Risking their lives, Oskar Schindler saved twelve hundred Jews and Raoul Wallenberg saved twenty-five thousand. And hundreds of thousands of others—mostly unknown—saved Jews and other victims. Many of Germany's senior military officers, as well as civilians, plotted Hitler's overthrow or assassination. But most people, myself included, did not know what to think or do.

During my childhood I had heard Hitler was an anti-Semite and, since I was a Jew, that was enough to turn me against him. But racism was rather common, and I did not see anything strange about Hitler. Then he annexed Austria and part of Czechoslovakia and invaded Poland, launching World War II. Again, from the history I was taught in school, expansion and war were normal national pursuits, and I could not understand why people said Hitler was insane. At twelve years of age, I read his book *Mein Kampf* and did not find it all that strange. Then I began to hear about Germany's death camps, and outrage led to my first publication when I was fourteen—a letter in the *New York Post* in 1942. I proposed that for every person killed in Hitler's concentration and death camps, the Allied governments should threaten to kill a German and, after the war, carry out the threat. In condemning a group—in proposing to kill Germans randomly—my thinking was like Hitler's, although I did not realize that. Like him, I believed that victims and people who identified with victims were entitled to outrage and vengeance.

1

After World War II, I thought much less about what had happened, avoiding information on the Holocaust. Becoming a psychologist, I was impressed with how often people allowed themselves to be harmed, embraced the position of victim, felt outraged, and took vengeance—a pattern that wrecked their lives and the lives of their families. Later, the lesson helped me understand the Third Reich.

Germany was seriously harmed after World War I—a victimization to which its leaders and people submitted, although Germans remained highly conscious of the victimization and outraged over it. Even more important, however, was Germany's long history of victimization. While Americans have thought of Germany as a warlike, predatory nation, its history was the opposite. Until the nineteenth century, what is now Germany was a collection of independent cities and principalities—small units, defenseless against nations around them. Germans were the victims of many invasions, some of which decimated the population. That history made Germany a fertile soil for Hitler's message of victimization, outrage, and vengeance.

I stopped avoiding the Holocaust in 1991 and made a painful visit to the Dachau concentration camp—to the museum and memorials there. My worst shock was a large wall with nothing on it but the names of the camps. For half a century, I had thought there were between ten and twenty concentration camps—thirty at most—but the wall listed 355 names. This simple number is a reminder of how hard it is to comprehend fully Hitler's destructiveness. And the 355 names identify only a fraction of the camps.

Back home, I began to read about Hitler and the Third Reich, trying to understand what had happened. Although much has been written on Germany's history and character, particularly on its circumstances after World War I, there was little to explain why things happened. Those biographers who addressed Hitler's madness grasped only pieces of it. Others omitted the topic, declaring him normal and explaining his acts by political and military considerations. My impression was that Hitler's madness had been at the heart of his destructive rule—an impression that led to writing this book.

The Holocaust was conceived by bizarre people, but most of those who carried it out—many of whom found it repugnant—were reasonably normal. And those who helped, as well as those who knew and did not try to stop it, were ordinary people. Moralizing about people who perpetrated the Holocaust has been so intense that the idea of understanding them remains offensive. Many fear understanding could lead to sympathy for the perpetrators and even to condoning their acts. According to Hannah Arendt, to write a biography of Hitler or to interpret history in the light of his personality "could only result in [his] falsifying promotion to respectability . . ."[1] According to a reviewer of books on Hitler, a growing number of people concerned with the Holocaust believe explaining him is "obscenely immoral" for:

> any attempt to understand Hitler inevitably degenerates into an exercise in empathy with him. To understand all is to forgive all, and . . . even the first steps down the slippery slope to understanding are impermissible.[2]

Nevertheless, the way to learn from the Holocaust is to understand how and why it happened. Far more than most historical events, it came from the mind of one man. And understanding does require empathy. Readers of this book, however, will neither find Hitler made respectable here nor his actions condoned.

The question of Hitler's sanity has been widely argued, but he has proved hard to diagnose by biographers and even by physicians he consulted. Although his physicians knew he was a hypochondriac plagued by psychosomatic illnesses, most of them said he was mentally normal. His false beliefs that the nation had been betrayed by its government in World War I and was dominated by Jews were not thought to be delusions because they were widely held. His physicians also considered him normal because he was the ruler, and paranoid and psychopathic traits are commonly ignored or excused in rulers. Biographers described him as paranoid, psychopathic, or depressed, depending on what struck them. He was all those, and also compulsive and phobic; his symptoms went beyond any familiar diagnosis.

During the 1950s, people with such a variety of symptoms were diagnosed as pan-neurotic schizophrenics. This meant that, although their symptoms were largely neurotic, there were so many that a psychosis was thought to be hidden under them. Hitler suffered breakdowns when he was twenty and twenty-nine. Today, the first would be called a major depression; the second, schizophrenia. Considering his breakdowns and the variety of his symptoms after he recovered, the contemporary diagnosis that best describes him is borderline personality disorder. It means a person shows symptoms of a variety of disturbances but little or no sign of psychosis, and is considered on the border, neither fully psychotic nor simply neurotic.

A biographical study provides a fuller picture than a diagnosis. Hitler's life—his suicidal and homicidal drives, his inability to hold a job, sustain a friendship or love relationship, manage his eroticism, or even take adequate care of his basic needs to eat and sleep—shows he was extremely disturbed.

In explaining Hitler's personality and actions and people's response to him, making broad use of behavioral science enabled me to explain more than adhering to a single theoretical approach. My analysis is a mixed one, combining data and concepts from sociology, child development, behaviorism, experimental psychology, psychoanalysis, and social psychology.

The idea that Hitler, as an absolute dictator, controlled everything done under his administration, is far from true. While overcontrolling in many ways, Hitler also gave his subordinates free rein. Sometimes he had more than one person or agency deal with a matter and encouraged them to compete with each other toward a resolution he did not decide in advance. But Hitler's loose direction did not apply to the Third Reich's war against the Jews nor to military decisions and understanding them requires seeing events through his eyes.

Besides Jews, people of many groups were persecuted and killed, with the goal of partly or fully exterminating them. Gypsies were subject to racial laws directed against

Jews, while not always mentioned in those laws. Gypsies were also sterilized involuntarily without benefit of law. And about a quarter million were killed by death squads, while others were killed in death camps—perhaps a half million in all. Hitler also persecuted and killed Slavs, Blacks, Catholics, Jehovah's Witnesses, Freemasons, Communists, Social Democrats, and homosexuals. About fifty thousand men were convicted of homosexuality; about fifteen thousand were put in concentration camps and some in death camps. All these groups shared the fate of the Jews, but the extent to which they did has not been ascertained fully and is only touched on here.

"Nazi Party" is used here instead of "National Socialist German Workers Party," which is not only cumbersome but also less familiar. No connotation is intended in using "Nazi." The same applies to "Aryan." History does not justify calling Germans "Aryans" (and Gypsies had a better claim to Aryan ancestry), but a name is needed for the distinction Nazis made between some Germans and others. To use "German" in place of "Aryan," as Nazis often did, would perpetuate the racist idea that German citizens of Jewish, Gypsy, Slavic, or Black descent were not really Germans.

I am grateful to the following people for suggestions, encouragement, and manuscript criticism: Gisela Bock, Wolfgang Brandt, Kathryn Deguire, Bud Feder, Gerald Friedman, Robert Goggins, William Gordon, Herman Huber, Edward Lawson, Charles Maguire, Franklin Margiotta, Benno Müller-Hill, Algernon Phillips, Mario Lo Presti, Terence Ripmaster, Cheryl Roth, Joseph Schulman, John White, and my nephews Alan Feltus and Peter Feltus. For recounting his experiences in Vienna and Nuremberg, giving me his scarce German edition of *Mein Kampf,* and helping with translations, I thank Erich Wolf especially. For very patient and extensive help, I am grateful to Rudolph Binion and John Diaz. For the most help, for accompanying me to Dachau and sharing the pain there and at other points along the way, and for the joy in my life, I thank my wife, Marian Victor.

CHAPTER 1

THE ENIGMA

The enormity of the crimes . . . How could one of the chief centers of the civilized world have become a torture chamber for millions of people, a country ruled by criminals . . . ? [And] how did intelligent, well-intentioned, educated, principled people . . . become so caught up in the [Nazi] movement, so captivated by Hitler's magnetism that they could accept everything—the secret police, the concentration camps, the nonsensical rhetoric of Aryan heroism and anti-Semitism . . . ?[1]

—Eugene Davidson

The Third Reich was the greatest failure of civilization . . . Germany represented one of the farthest advances of the culture, yet the Third Reich profoundly perverted the entire heritage of Western civilization.[2]

—Lance Morrow

A half century after Hitler led it in a convulsion of destructiveness, Germany has recovered from the ravages of war and the hatred that led up to it. While Nazism is resurgent among a small minority, anti-Semitism is illegal and ethnic violence is repudiated by the great majority. Hatred of France and Russia, the old enemies, is also largely gone. But the question remains of how a highly civilized nation became perverted, wreaking unprecedented destruction, despite the outpouring—approaching one hundred thousand—of serious articles and books on the Third Reich.

The historical background of Hitler's rise to power—particularly Germany's situation after World War I—has been amply described:

- Political instability with no end in sight: coups and attempted coups, private armies wandering the country, street fighting, and domination by France, which arbitrarily marched in troops and stripped the industrial center in the Ruhr valley containing 80 percent of Germany's coal and steel.

- Worsening economic disaster: war reparations and a skyrocketing inflation in which "It was cheaper to burn marks than coal," as the currency went in five years from four to the United States' dollar to 130 billion. And then, when inflation was brought under control, giving Germans hope, despair returned with the Great Depression.

- Rapid social changes: decline of the aristocracy, impoverishment of part of the middle class, and a movement for women's equality that was more advanced in Germany than in its neighbors.

- Fear of communism and paranoid distrust and resentment of leaders believed to have sold out the country by surrendering when many Germans thought they were winning World War I.

The chaos was more than enough to make Germans eager for a dynamic leader—a savior—but fails to explain why Hitler was the one chosen. Dozens of extremist would-be leaders promised solutions, as desperation gave rise to a multitude of tiny parties and political organizations—seventy-three of them racist. But only one, the Nazi Party, would grow into a major force. What set it apart from the rest was Hitler's charismatic power, which has been only partly explained. While his pathology alarmed some Germans, for most, it added to his appeal. His fantastic, mystical message struck a response in the Romanticism and nationalism resurgent in Germany since the nineteenth century. To understand the destructiveness of the Third Reich requires understanding that Hitler was widely admired and even adored. To his followers, he was omnipotent, omniscient, and infallible, acclaimed as the greatest leader in history and as a god. The attraction between him—the alien—and the tiny party empowered both. It foreshadowed the fateful relationship that would develop between Hitler and the nation.

When he joined the Nazi Party in 1919, Hitler was a homeless, lost person—a dreamer trying to hang on to his tenuous identity as a soldier for a country of which he was not even a citizen. Born in Austria, he was at first an apt and obedient pupil who received good grades. But he became hostile to his teachers and irregular in his homework, getting low grades, failing courses, repeating a year of high school, and dropping out. Yearning for a career as an artist, he became increasingly alienated. After the death of his mother, to whom he was very close, and his failure to gain admission to an art academy, he cut himself off from family and his one friend. For six years he lived marginally, often depending on charity and guidance from strangers to survive. He had grown up unable to study or work, unable to sustain an intimate relationship, and beset by inhibitions, conflicts, and imaginary diseases. He was incapable of ordinary living. The details of Hitler's pathology are crucial because they—not political and social conditions—were behind the most destructive programs of the Third Reich. His good intentions, perverted by his demons, ruled Germany.

Unable to manage his own life, unimpressive to look at, and given to wild proposals, Hitler was not taken seriously by the nation at first or even when he became chancellor (prime minister). People looked past him, saying he was a tool of the military, of industry, of conservatives, or of monarchists. When the extent of his regime's destructiveness was revealed, Nazis defended him, saying Hitler did not initiate or even know about the worst. They argued that Goebbels, Göring, Himmler, or Bormann was mainly responsible and had manipulated Hitler. The evidence against that conclusion is overwhelming. The outline of the destructiveness to come was already in Hitler's mind when he wrote *Mein Kampf* in 1924, before Goebbels and the others played their parts. The motives— the cravings for revenge, for war, and for extermination of Jews—were Hitler's.

Despite widespread anti-Semitism, conditions for Jews were improving in Germany. In itself, anti-Semitism does not explain the Holocaust. The Nazi Party was virulently anti-Semitic, but even that does not explain actions repugnant to most Nazis. They refused to believe stories about extermination and were horrified when they eventually accepted them as true. The key was Hitler, a leader exceptional in setting out to transform society totally and to conquer the world and in his determination to pursue the extermination of a people.

The contrast between his ineffectiveness on reaching manhood and his later success puzzled even those who worked hardest to understand him—his biographers. In 1952, Alan Bullock published what was for years the foremost biography of Hitler. In 1958, after new personal information about Hitler became available, Bullock made an extraordinary confession:

> For my part, the more I learn about Adolf Hitler, the harder I find it to explain and accept what followed.[3]

That a person of so little promise became a historic figure on a par with Caesar and Napoleon seemed against all reason. As the century drew to its close, Hitler towered as its dominant figure, yet the puzzle remained.

> No one has adequately explained how a man of such insecurity and personal weakness could generate national confidence with such terrifying results.[4]

John Lukacs, a specialist in the Third Reich, wrote:

> Fifty years later we in the English-speaking world have not yet been able to come to terms with the historical figure of Hitler . . .[5]

People in the German-speaking world and elsewhere have also failed. Eberhardt Jäckel, who became a historian to understand the phenomenon of Hitler, wrote:

> . . . Hitler's accession to power . . . seems to be obscured rather than explained by the very mass of information and by the innumerable interpretations . . . We know much but understand little . . .[6]

Hundreds of books have been written about Hitler, but he remains an enigma. This is partly a result of his secrecy and deceptiveness. He had records of his childhood and early adult years removed from public access and had some of them destroyed. He had people who knew personal details about him killed. He invented a past for himself, even changing his birthplace and ancestry. He became a poseur in public and among his associates and gave misleading reasons for destructive acts of state. Unfortunately, the reasons he gave were accepted at the time and even today are widely believed.

An enduring puzzle is Hitler's sexuality. Determined to keep it a secret, he was aided by the reticence of people who knew him. The writings of his authorized biographers and most of his associates omitted Hitler's sex life. Except for sensational books and articles, only limited descriptions of Hitler's sexuality have been given and have hardly been used in explaining his actions and influence. We are left with wild speculations and a mystery. One associate of Hitler said he was a Don Juan who fathered forty children. Another said he never touched a woman. Many perversions were attributed to him, while some of his physicians and biographers insisted he was perfectly normal. Bullock touched lightly on Hitler's sexuality, saying it would "only have a place in a study of Hitler's career if it can be shown that his relations with women affected his political judgment and decisions."[7]

Hitler's sexuality did affect his political judgment and decisions, and crucially so. Because of his needs and inhibitions, he meddled in the personal lives of most Germans, especially in their marital, sexual, and reproductive activities. He established restrictions on intercourse among adults and over thirty restrictions on marriage, while urging unmarried adolescents to get pregnant. He established a breeding program that included kidnapping women. He had hundreds of thousands sexually mutilated by sterilization procedures and experiments. And he tried to exterminate the people he saw as the personification of demonic sexuality—Jews. In short, the most personal reasons were behind steps that led from the sterilization law of 1933 to the death camps. In addition, his repressed affection and eroticism came out in his oratory, contributing to his appeal, to the adoration of him that swept Germany.

Hitler's sterilization of about four hundred thousand people has been described as a regrettable instance of eugenic policy, which was common in the western world during the 1930s. But in Hitler's plan, control of hereditary diseases was only a first step toward racial "purification," toward eliminating Jews and even other Germans who were not tall, blond, and blue-eyed—most of the population. During the war, he had a staff working in super secrecy on a method to sterilize millions of Germans without their knowledge.

Anti-semitism, destructiveness, and sexual obsession are not rare. Many people hate and wish to destroy, and some wish to control the sexuality of others. They are held back by customs, morals, personal inhibitions, and social controls, as was Hitler during his early years. But he found a way to free himself and his followers. Once he achieved power, he expressed his hatred and sexuality with amazing wantonness. A key to understanding the Third Reich is Hitler's success in freeing himself and others.

Why the pessimism of Bullock and others about understanding Hitler, and why the lack of progress after fifty years? Some difficulties in understanding him have been mentioned; another is that key pieces of his story are offensive. That he was a sadist is accepted, but that he was also a masochist—equally important in his acts of state—is not. Particularly difficult is the matter of his victimization in childhood. For many people, seeing him as a victim—a figure calling for sympathy—is unacceptable. In addition, writers have been careful about offending Jews by suggesting that Hitler's anti-Semitism was linked to his identification of himself as Jewish. His ethnic ancestry was German, probably also Czech, and possibly also Jewish. No more can be established, but there is ample evidence that Hitler thought of himself as Jewish in the core of his being—in his "poisoned" and "diseased" blood. Still another difficulty in explaining Hitler is concern that understanding him may lead to forgiveness, to condoning actions of the Third Reich, and to weakening bulwarks against another such destructive convulsion. Taking the opposite position—that understanding is the best protection against a repetition—an attempt is made here to give the fullest possible description of Hitler's personality in order to explain the destructiveness of the Third Reich.

The most crucial mystery about Hitler was the source and nature of his obsession with Jews. Page after page of *Mein Kampf* refers to them, as does his dying *Testament*. Friends said he could not talk for ten minutes without bringing them up. When he was withdrawn and torpid, mention of Jews invigorated him. They and the fight against them were his life. And when he became chancellor, his obsession became Germany's political program.

Hitler's hatred of Jews has been explained by the anti-Semitic literature he found in Vienna and read avidly, but that explanation is incomplete at best. Few people found the literature absorbing or even acceptable. Like any obsession, Hitler's anti-Semitism had personal roots, which his secretiveness made hard to uncover. As recently as 1991 Lukacs wrote, "His main obsession was with Jews. We do not *and will never know* the source of that deep obsession."[8] (Italics added.) Once Hitler's obsession is understood, many of his acts of state take on a new meaning.

Three blunders by Hitler are often cited as causing Germany's defeat—letting the British forces escape at Dunkirk, not invading England, and invading the Soviet Union. These decisions were not blunders, however, for Hitler's goals were not what they seemed. The decisions were calculated risks taken to further a secret goal—the launching of the Holocaust—which was more important to Hitler than military victory. Although they led to disaster, from his viewpoint they were the right decisions because they enabled him to carry out the Holocaust. His conduct of the war, costing forty million lives, is extreme when viewed as an event in geopolitics and militarism. But when understood as a cover for getting rid of Europe's Jews, it is even more chilling.

PART I:

THE DEVELOPMENT OF A CHARISMATIC LEADER

Rarely has an epoch been shaped so strongly by one person. Hitler's personality—especially his pathology—ruled Germany, casting a shadow over much of the world. Part I is a biography of his formative years, designed to provide the widest possible base for explaining his motives, his charisma, and his acts of state.

CHAPTER 2

THE PHANTOM JEW

These people must not be allowed to find out who I am. They must not know where I came from and who my family is.[1]

—Adolf Hitler, 1931

An unused key to Hitler's personality is an obscure prohibition he enacted in 1935, the most innocuous of his anti-Semitic measures. Never explained by the government and hardly enforced, the prohibition has been ignored by biographers and historians because it had no context or apparent source. But behind it were the reasons for Hitler's dedication to exterminate Europe's Jews—the goal for which he sacrificed Germany.

The prohibition—that Jews were not to employ Aryan women under the age of forty-five as maids—was part of what became known as the Nuremberg Laws, the keynote of his racial program.* The first of the Laws took from Jews their German citizenship and the rights of citizens. The second prohibited Jews from marrying or engaging in sex with Aryans. To this, the prohibition on Jews having Aryan maids was attached.

Taking away Jews' citizenship and barring them from marrying and engaging in sex with Aryans were part of Hitler's and the Nazi Party's known position on establishing Germany as a racial state, but the employment prohibition was not. Included because it had the most personal meaning for Hitler, it points back to the beginning of the story of his life—back to a mystery, a century-old secret, which, more than any other single event, shaped Hitler's thinking and his measures leading to the gas chambers. For years before the Nuremberg Laws, Hitler had been seriously troubled by the rumor that his paternal grandfather was a Jew. Political opponents had used it against him and so had a blackmailer. He had the rumor investigated over and over and reportedly took measures to destroy evidence supporting it. The ethnicity, religion,

---

* The word "Aryan" was used by racists to distinguish those regarded as true Germans from Jews, Gypsies, Slavs, and Blacks. "Aryan" had a positive meaning to racists, but their use gave it a negative one. Aryan is used here simply to refer to Germans who were not Jews, Gypsies, Slavs, or Blacks. Less value-laden alternatives—"non-Jewish, non-Gypsy Germans"—have more disadvantages than advantages.

or even the identity of the grandfather cannot be established, but there is no doubt the allegation haunted Hitler.

Some parts of the story are clearly established. Maria Schicklgruber, Hitler's paternal grandmother, like other known members of his family, came from a poor section in northwest Austria near the Bavarian border known as the *Waldviertel* (Forest Quarter). All were Catholics. A single woman, Maria was working as a maid when at forty-one she became pregnant. As a result she returned to Strones, the village where she grew up, to have her baby. Reportedly, her family turned her away, and she found shelter with a local farm couple named Trummelschlager, giving birth to Alois, who would become Hitler's father. He was her only child, and she lived with him at the farm for five years. The Trummelschlagers became Alois's godparents.

When Alois was five, Maria married Johann Georg Hiedler, a shiftless man, and the three lived together. Had Georg acknowledged Alois to be his son, Alois would have become legitimate, that being the only legal requirement. But Georg did not acknowledge him, and Alois remained illegitimate, bearing the name Schicklgruber. With the marriage's failure, Maria and Georg separated after several months, and Alois's care was taken over by Georg's more responsible and prosperous brother, Johann Nepomuk Hiedler, a farmer in the village of Spital.

Thus Alois's first years were marked by neglect and loss. His father, whoever he was, failed to acknowledge Alois as his son. And before he was six, Alois also lost everyone he knew—his mother, his godparents, his stepfather, and whatever playmates he had in Strones. One can only infer the effects of these losses on Alois, for there is no record. Presumably during his first years, he became very attached to his mother. Outcasts, they had no one but each other, and such circumstances foster exceptional closeness. Why Alois was separated from her is unknown. The cause of her death five years later was given as tuberculosis, a slowly developing, highly contagious disease. She may already have been too infirm to care for Alois, or they may have separated to protect him from catching tuberculosis. Whatever the reason, he was too young to understand why he lost her.

During the following years, Alois was old enough to realize that his situation was strange and unfortunate. At the time, rural Austrians rarely moved far; children grew up in the villages where they were born. Unlike other children in Spital, Alois had not been born there; he was an outsider. Nor did he have a clear position in the Hiedler family. Probably during this period, he became aware that he bore his mother's name and was illegitimate. Somewhere he had a mother and somewhere a mysterious father. Somewhere, too, were other relatives—Maria's family and his mystery father's family—but he was estranged from them all. So he was not clearly an orphan or without family, but he lived with a foster family as if he had no kin. He may have called Nepomuk Hiedler "Father" and Nepomuk's wife "Mother," but they had three children of their own and he was not one of them. Village children probably asked him why he was named Schicklgruber while the rest of the household was named Hiedler. They probably asked where his parents were and why he did not live with them, for that is what children ask. And Alois would not have known what to answer. He would have felt embarrassed—that there was something wrong with him—for that is what children in his situation feel. Probably there was gossip in the village about who Alois's father was, including the rumor that he was a Jew.

Alois lived with Nepomuk's family until he was thirteen, when he left for Vienna to be apprenticed to a shoemaker. Some people said Alois ran away, but there is no evidence of harsh treatment that might have made him flee. More likely he left by mutual agreement, with the apprenticeship arranged for him by his foster family. Some such plan was required in his circumstances. Alois had to make his way in life, and remaining in Spital offered no prospects. For poor farm boys, an inheritance was the only way to acquire land, and Alois could not expect one. As far as he knew, his mother and stepfather had left him nothing, his mystery father was not going to leave him anything, and Nepomuk's estate would go to his own children. Alois was on his own.

Of Adolf Hitler's ancestors, Alois was the first known to have been ambitious and to enter the middle class. None of Nepomuk's children received more than a minimal education, but Alois felt the lack more keenly than they. The others were girls; all they needed for a start in life was a dowry. To Alois, trying to advance himself in Vienna, lack of education was a handicap. He decided to teach himself and learned enough by age eighteen to leave the shoemaker's trade and enter the civil service, first as a border guard and then in the Customs Service. There he would stay until retirement, rising to the highest position open to a man without a diploma.

The outcast who had grown up without a home he could call his own had found a place in the civil service—a place he valued above any of the homes he later established. And he had found an ideal father, Emperor Franz Josef, whom he admired, whose moustache and sideburns he copied. Also like the emperor, Alois wore almost everywhere the elegant uniform that came with his job—at home, at social events, and in town. Returning proudly to visit his foster family, as a customs officer his status was above that of the villagers. In Spital he was now a hero. When transferred by the Customs Service to Braunau, he moved to that town and later lived in a series of villages in the *Waldviertel,* where his job made him a leading citizen.

On the job Alois was hardworking and proper; he won the respect of superiors and peers. His subordinates, who at times smarted under his strictness, also had a good word for him.

Apparently to advance his career and perhaps to acquire a bit of wealth, at thirty-six he married fifty-year-old Anna Glasl-Hörer, the daughter of a higher government official. But his love life was not as successful as his career. Before marrying, he had been a Don Juan, and marriage did not change him. When Anna became sick, he brought his "niece" Klara Pölzl to stay at the inn in Braunau where they lived to take care of Anna. Klara, who was to be Adolf Hitler's mother, was a granddaughter of Nepomuk. Of a younger generation than Alois, she called him "Uncle" and he called her "Niece." Soon, Alois was having affairs with Klara and with a maid at the inn named Franziska Matzelsberger. Alois was thirty-nine, Klara sixteen, and Franziska fifteen.

Alois then took the action that compounded the mystery of his birth. Illegitimacy was common enough in Austria, and there is no evidence that it slowed Alois's advancement. Rumors that his unknown father was a Jew probably did not reach Vienna, but returning to live near Strones exposed him to embarrassment over his paternity. Alois decided to legitimize himself, probably to counter the rumors and to erase the stigma of bastardy. (The German word *Bastard* has two meanings—illegitimate and mixed breed—and both applied to him.) He had three distant relatives of Georg Hiedler go to the priest who kept Alois's birth record and swear Georg had confided to them he was Alois's father. Biographers have pointed out the legitimization was a fraud. Identifying an illegitimate child's father for official purposes could be done only while the father was still living, and Georg was long dead. The use of fraud contributed later to disbelief of the witnesses' statement.

Nonetheless, their testimony was accepted at the time, and Alois became legitimate and officially the son of two Catholics. The late Georg Hiedler was recognized as his father and he was entitled to give up the name Schicklgruber and take the name Hiedler. He took it but, for an unknown reason, used the spelling "Hitler." (In English the names Hitler and Hiedler look different, but in German they are similar; Hiedler is pronounced "Heatler.") He also received a new baptismal certificate, which he gave to his superiors in the Customs Service.

Here we come to the first important controversy about Adolf Hitler's background. Most of his biographers concluded the relatives swore falsely and behind their deception lay the identity of Alois's true father. Their skepticism is supported by the fact that Georg not only never acknowledged Alois publicly but also seems to have shown no interest in him before marrying Maria or afterward. Many concluded that Alois's foster father, Nepomuk, was his true one. Nepomuk also did not acknowledge Alois as his son publicly, and no witness has said he did so privately. The reason advanced for his not doing so is consideration of his wife. Either she was not to know he had been unfaithful and fathered a son, or she had agreed to accept the situation provided it was kept secret. If so, Nepomuk could have acknowledged Alois as his son after his wife's death, which preceded the legitimization by three years, but he did not. What he did do, according to those who advance this explanation, was leave money in his will to Alois, of whom he was fond and proud. Supposedly Nepomuk wanted his name carried on and, since his recognized children were daughters, he made a condition of his bequest that Alois take the name Hiedler. But no such will was found. Another problem with the explanation is that Alois had no recognized children and Anna, now fifty-three, was not going to bear him any. (Alois reportedly had a daughter out of wedlock from whom he was estranged. She would not have been affected by his legitimization.) And as a Catholic, he could not divorce and remarry. At this time, Nepomuk could not reasonably have expected that Alois would become widowed, remarry, and have children.

That Nepomuk and Alois were attached to each other is supported by the fact that they kept in touch; Nepomuk seems to have been the only person who could be considered family with whom Alois had substantial contact. The evidence for the theory is that Alois seems to have been more prosperous after Nepomuk's death, as if he had come into money. That is inferred from Alois then buying property. The theory is supported by no direct evidence—no witness, no document—and does not explain that, after the death of his wife, Nepomuk still failed to acknowledge Alois. It may be true, but it rests entirely on conjecture.

The third conclusion is that Alois's father was a shadowy Jew—a man whom no witness had seen. The only person in the family who would have met him was Maria, and she had died thirty years before Alois's legitimization. The conclusion was supported by a book in which the author claimed to have been a member of the Gestapo, Germany's secret police, and to have learned in the course of his duties that Alois had been fathered by a Jew for whom Maria had worked as a maid.[2] The authenticity of the book was questioned, however. Several spurious books on Adolf Hitler were published at the height of his fame, and this may have been one. A more authoritative report came from Hans Frank, a lawyer for the Nazi Party and later an administrator in the Third Reich. While awaiting execution after his conviction at the postwar Nuremberg trials, he wrote a memoir that included the following account.[3]

In 1930, he was called in by Hitler and shown a blackmail letter from his nephew Patrick Hitler about Hitler's ancestry. Frank was asked to investigate the allegation, did so, and reported back to Hitler that Maria had become pregnant while working as a servant in Graz for a Jewish family named Frankenberger. Her pregnancy resulted in her leaving the job with an arrangement that the Frankenbergers would send monthly support until the child was thirteen. The money came with letters that referred to a nineteen-year-old son of the Frankenberger family as the father of Maria's child. Frank said the letters had been saved by a relative of Maria, but he did not make clear whether he had seen them or only been assured they still existed in 1930.

According to Frank, Hitler confirmed his report in all respects but the crucial one. Hitler said Maria had become pregnant by Georg Hiedler, but the couple had been extremely poor, and Maria had pretended the father was a Frankenberger to extort money from the family.

Hitler's version is doubtful on its face. It implies Maria was engaging in sex with Georg and the Frankenberger youth at the same time. If so, she could not have been sure who the father was, and Hitler could not have been sure, although he said he was. His version may have been an invention simply for Frank's benefit; Hitler apparently never mentioned it to anyone else. But Hitler's comments supported most of Frank's report, and he showed that he took it very seriously by sending one confidential investigator after another to check it and by measures he took as ruler of Germany.[4]

Hitler refused to give money to Patrick, who then spread the story of the Jewish grandfather. The result was a confrontation between them, and it was then Hitler reportedly said, "These people must not be allowed to find out who I am. They must not know where I came from and who my family is." Patrick agreed to keep silent, and Hitler found him a job.

The story of the Jewish grandfather, although accepted by some biographers and mentioned by others who rejected it, has hardly been used in explaining Hitler's racism. It was understandably offensive to his admirers, and detractors seem to have been careful not to offend Jews by explaining his anti-Semitism on the basis of Jewish ancestry. Here it makes no difference whatever who his unknown grandfather was, but who Hitler thought he was is vital

By the time he was an adult, Hitler hated his father, and with ample reason. That hatred, along with self-loathing, ruled his life. He believed Alois was evil and that his evil came from mixed ancestry—from Alois's Jewish father. The prohibition against Jews marrying or engaging in sex with Aryans was meant to prevent someone like his father from being born ever again. And the obscure prohibition against Jews employing Aryan maids during their childbearing years covered the exact situation in which his father had been conceived, as Hitler understood it. Hitler's government officially designated forty-five as the end of women's childbearing years.[5]

The story of his father's conception became Hitler's model of how evil spread. He spoke venomously of the government leader Matthias Erzberger—"the bastard son of a servant girl and a Jewish employer"—as Germany's worst villain and traitor.[6] Erzberger was Catholic, but Hitler considered him a Jew, saying his mixed parentage was the cause of his evil nature. Hitler was also fascinated by a similar story about President Tomas Masaryk of Czechoslovakia, another villain in his mind.[7] In addition, he imputed partial Jewish ancestry to Franklin Roosevelt, Winston Churchill, Joseph Stalin, and other leaders, whose evil he explained by that ancestry. *The arch-villains he singled out were not full Jews but men he thought were part-Jews.*

The idea of evil coming from a Jewish father also provided an explanation for Hitler's own troubles. Growing up filled with self-loathing—"rotten to the marrow" were his words—Hitler found the cause in his ancestry, which he believed had poisoned his marrow. He had come to believe Jewish blood dominated Aryan blood—the offspring of a Jew and an Aryan was always a Jew.[8] Therefore, Alois was a Jew, and Adolf Hitler himself came from the same kind of mating that had produced his father. Repeating the circumstances of his birth, Alois had used Hitler's mother as a maid and impregnated her. The Nuremberg Laws also served to prevent someone like Adolf Hitler from being born. Hitler was undoing the circumstances he thought had produced his wretched self.

The idea that he carried Jewish blood obsessed Hitler, leading to increasingly bizarre and destructive measures. In addition to the Nuremberg Laws, he enacted thirty restrictions on marriage according to how much Jewish ancestry people had. Believing Jewish physicians seduced Aryan women and girls who were their patients, he prohibited Aryans from consulting them. As an ultimate protection for Aryan women, he considered sterilizing all Jewish men. To prevent relationships with Jews, he stopped Aryans from shopping in Jewish stores, from going to the same schools as Jews, and from living in the same apartment buildings as Jews. He went on to require Jews to have "Jewish names" so they could not fool unsuspecting

Aryans and have intimate relationships with them. And his comments about the extermination of Jews made clear that it was meant to end forever their mating with Aryans.

Coming back to Alois, his beginnings are the only clues to his personality development. As an adult, his wanderlust was striking. He came from a culture in which many men lived their lives in the villages where they were born, sometimes in the same house, but circumstances made that impossible for him. By the time he was thirteen, he had been moved three times. Later, when the decision was his, he moved far more, sometimes as a result of increasing prosperity, but not always. "Actually he often moved from a decent dwelling into a poorer one. The house was not the important thing; rather the moving."[9] In addition, he took many trips, living apart from his family at times. Some were required by his job, but others were entirely voluntary.

"The need to magnify themselves, to bestir themselves, is characteristic of all illegitimates."[10] Although the offense causing illegitimacy was committed by parents, children were the ones who bore the stigma, who had something to prove, something for which to make up. Illegitimacy was probably a spur to Alois's ambition. Another factor was the abandonment he had suffered. He had a craving for acceptance.

Whichever story of his father is true, Alois was abandoned by both parents. If his father was Georg, Alois was abandoned during his first five years, lived with him for several months, and was abandoned again. If his father was Nepomuk, again Alois was abandoned during his first years. And if his father was the shadowy Jew, Alois never knew him. Probably he did not know who his father was. By the time he was old enough to ask, his mother was gone. And being abandoned by her was the severest loss.

Many people who grow up without a mother or father search for their parents. Some do it purposely, others unconsciously and aimlessly, wandering from place to place, from person to person, as if asking, "Is this where I belong? Are you the one?" Alois's early experience could explain his wandering and philandering.

Boys grow up to be Don Juans for various reasons—inability to love, distrust of women and hostility toward them, a need to make intimate connections without real intimacy, and a need to prove themselves and be accepted. Alois's childhood fostered all of these. Abandonment—especially repeated abandonment—makes children fear involvement. A common effect is wariness and distance; relationships are limited. Abandonment also generates intense anger for which no outlet is possible except on scapegoats.

There is no evidence that Alois loved anyone in his adult life. His hunger to find a new woman was usually greater than his interest in building a relationship with the one he had. Apparently he enhanced his sense of worth by the number of his conquests. For a Don Juan who has lost his mother in childhood, the chase is also a search; the hidden hope is that each new woman may turn out to be the ideal woman—the lost mother. Then each one proves to be a disappointment, for none can live up to her romanticized image.

Thus Alois's beginnings provide a basis for understanding his personalit extraordinary ambition, his wanderlust, and his cruelty to women and his sons (

ter). The resentment he accumulated as a child had no direct outlet. He was respectful to authority and behaved properly on the job. At the tavern, he was reportedly quick to anger but not violent. His scapegoats were women and children.

As noted, marriage did not stop his philandering, nor did legitimacy. Anna apparently had tolerated his infidelities, but at Braunau she stopped. Perhaps the fact that he was having affairs with Klara and Franziska under the roof he shared with Anna was too much for her. Unable to divorce him, she obtained a separation and moved away.

Alois then installed Franziska, who was pregnant by him, as his common-law wife, and Klara was sent away. Franziska gave birth to a son, Alois, Jr., and was soon pregnant again. On Anna's death, Alois married Franziska, legitimizing his son and making his second child Angela legitimate at her birth. But then Franziska fell sick, and to care for her and the babies, Alois again sent for Klara and again began an affair with her.

Klara became pregnant at about the time of Franziska's death, which opened the way for her and Alois to marry. But a papal dispensation was needed because they were "related." By claiming Georg Hiedler as his father, Alois had officially become Klara's second cousin.

Klara's child, born after they married, died in infancy. So did the next two. Klara's fourth child, Adolf, was her first to survive and he, too, seemed sickly. Alois vented his frustration on Klara, "So you have failed me once more! Is it impossible for you to bear me a healthy child?"[11] The words typify the hostile, blaming attitude members of the family saw.

Yet, Alois may have been reasonably satisfied with his life. The most important part to him was his career, and he rose to a position equal to the rank of army captain. He achieved legitimacy, respectability, and the courtesy of having men tip their hats to him. He enjoyed his daily visit to the tavern, where his opinions on politics carried weight. His marriage to Klara proved to be a lasting one, and many people said it was a happy one. To him, it may have been, for Klara was obedient, dependable, and loyal, and did bear him more children. At fifty-eight he retired, tried his hand at beekeeping, failed at it, and gave it up for a life of ease.

By community standards, Alois was a success—a hard worker who supported his family, a solid citizen, and a person of prominence. (His drinking, affairs, and roughness with his family hardly counted against him. That was what men did.) He had come a long way from being a penniless waif.

Unfortunately, his success was at a heavy price, which was paid by others. The circumstances of his birth set off a chain of events, bringing suffering to Klara and his sons and leading on to the tragedy of the Third Reich. His cruelty caused Adolf's self-loathing and craving for revenge. In turn, they led to failures in school and work and to the desperation in the call Adolf felt to become a hero. The story of Alois's mystery father was the source of Adolf's ideas that he himself was the victim of Jews and that his blood was Jewish. The phantom Jew may never have existed, but in Adolf's mind he was a powerful figure, standing behind the morbid obsession that drove him to bleed himself with leeches and, after he identified himself with Germany, to bleed the nation.

CHAPTER 3

THE BIRTH OF A CHAMPION

... the bride is without means and it is therefore unlikely that she will ever have another opportunity of a good marriage.[1]

—Alois Hitler, 1884

What every young girl hopes and dreams about in marriage was not granted to me. But does such a thing ever happen?[2]

—Klara Hitler, 1905

By the time Adolf Hitler became Germany's leader, he was convinced he had been chosen supernaturally to save his nation and the world. His egocentrism and grandiosity began early in his childhood and grew until he saw himself as virtually divine. Although he grew up anti-Christian and a near atheist, he said after a brief visit to Berlin:

... the luxury, the perversion, the iniquity, the wanton display and the Jewish materialism disgusted me so thoroughly that I was almost beside myself. I nearly imagined myself to be Jesus Christ when he came to his Father's Temple and found the money changers.[3]

He said about himself and his followers, "We are few, to be sure, but once a man rose in Galilee, and today His teachings rule the world." On coming to power, he ordered a new chancellery built for him on so grand a scale that visitors would sense they were in the presence of "the Master of the World," and he had prayers and songs rewritten, putting himself in God's place.[4]

The origin of Hitler's grandiosity and yearning to be a savior was the suffering in his mother's life. Hopeless about bettering her own situation, she put her energies into raising a special child who, in turn, wanted to become her champion.

Less is known of Klara's childhood than her husband's, perhaps because it was not dramatic. She came from an intact family, probably a wholesome one, and seems to have grown up without mental disturbance. She showed remarkable strength in dealing with the stresses and tragedies of her life. Alois was driven by the traumas of his childhood, which he overcame to the extent of outward success. Klara grew up a gentle person with little ambition, with nothing personal to overcome. The misfortunes that shaped her life came from poverty, from her culture and the condition of women in it, and from disease.

Alois was short with a wide head and flat nose, stubborn and hard to get along with, cruel and destructive. He was twenty-three years older than Klara—forty-eight and balding when they married. Klara was tall and slender with a shapely figure and striking eyes, said to be particularly attractive. She was dutiful and kind, admired as a good person by all who remembered her with one exception—her stepson Alois, Jr. She was a nurturing, adaptable person with whom it was easy to get along. Klara had become acquainted in childhood with Alois. To her he was a former member of her grandparents' household from far away who visited occasionally. By the time she married him, Klara knew Alois reasonably well, especially his infidelity. Today, a century later, her choice of a husband may be puzzling.

Because Spital was such a poor village, goodness and looks counted little toward a girl's future. Klara came from an especially poor family. Her sister Johanna was a hunchback, unlikely to marry or even to hold a job. She would probably need to be supported by the family all her life. For Klara, there was hardly a dowry; her chances of marrying a local peasant were poor. And without an education or a marketable skill or craft, she had no way to a better life in a town or city. If she did not marry, her main prospect was to enter domestic service. Probably these concerns were on her mind when Alois first called her.

Why she accepted Alois's offer to go to care for his first wife is not reported. It eased the burden on her family and provided an opportunity to leave her poor village for a prosperous town. Perhaps she thought she might meet a man there with sufficient wealth not to need a substantial dowry—one who might accept her for her goodness and looks. And Alois knew single men in the Customs Service. Klara was sixteen; it was time to do something about her future.

In becoming involved with Alois, Klara may have hoped to succeed his sick wife, but when Anna moved out, it was Franziska who took her place. Forced to leave, Klara did not return to her family. Perhaps she did not want to burden them or perhaps there was talk in Spital about her relationship with Alois, further reducing her chances of finding a husband there. She moved to Vienna, where she took a job as a maid.

When Alois called Klara a second time, her situation was no better. She was wiser and more defeated, the dreams of her childhood even further out of reach. As a servant and no longer pristine, she might have found, as Maria Schicklgruber had, that only a Georg Hiedler would marry her—a shiftless man who would not provide for her or for her children, if she had any. Probably she thought she had nothing to lose by returning to Alois.

In his petition for a dispensation to marry Klara, Alois wrote that she had little chance for a good marriage except with him. His words may sound pompous; unfortunately, they were true. As Klara knew, despite his character defects, Alois was an outstanding catch. Even though the marriage brought Klara depression rather than happiness, she seems never to have thought, or at least said, that she made the wrong choice. Her situation long ago is still the situation of women in many countries. She was not being foolish. In her circumstances, the alternative to marrying Alois was life as a servant.

Some people who knew Klara after her marriage thought her mildly retarded, but she was not. She adapted to middle-class life in one community after another. She took care of Alois's children and her own, and ran the household with little help from her often-absent husband. Her dullness was a sign of depression and resignation to a dreary life. Klara was described as a quiet, isolated woman. Except for family, a crony of Alois, and friends of the children, visitors did not come to her house. People she met on errands in the village found her friendly and liked her but noted she cut these contacts short to hurry home. Despite her limited circumstances until her marriage, despite the misfortunes that followed, and despite the cancer that painfully ended her life early, people said she did not complain.

Klara had achieved the best for which she could reasonably hope. Her husband was a good provider; through him, she rose from poverty and even had the help of a housemaid. Her one known personal indulgence was fancy dresses; whether to please herself or her husband is not reported.

But things did not go well. Alois, the only man to whom her looks might have mattered, grew increasingly distant. His job-related trips became more frequent, and he developed a hobby of keeping bees. Since they had no suitable space, he kept them at the farm of a friend so far away that it required overnight trips to tend them. Then the trips lengthened into stays of a week or two. And when he was transferred for a year to the city of Linz, instead of moving the family, he went to live there without them. According to a friend of his, "Alois hardly saw his family at all."[5] Given his history, it would have been only logical for Klara to assume he was having affairs. When with the family, Alois went daily to the tavern, often returning home in a bad mood. And some time during the marriage, he reportedly began to beat her.[6]

Klara became resigned to the situation and devoted herself to the house, to Alois, Jr., and Angela, and to the children she quickly bore, but here, too, matters got worse. In the fall of 1887, Klara's newborn son died; then her two-year-old first-born son and her one-year-old daughter died. Within several months she lost all her children. Adolf was conceived a half year later and born April 20, 1889—Holy Saturday.

In rural Austria many babies died; it was to be expected. But Klara's losses were extreme and compounded by her husband's blaming attitude. Commonly, the loss of a baby is traumatic, causing depression in women. Klara did not become clinically depressed; she did not take to her bed or neglect her work. She became sad and dull-looking. The loss of a child also fosters superstitious ideas. When women who have lost one or more become pregnant again, the usual effect is extravagant hope and dread. Thoughts of having a specially talented child mingle with fears of a miscarriage, a stillbirth, or a sick baby, and the newborn is often perceived to be sickly or defective. When women's fears are extreme at the end of pregnancy, their bodies transmit chemicals to the fetus induce subnormal appearance—a condition called fetal depression. Such a chain of events may have caused Adolf to be born subnormal. In any case, Klara perceived him as sickly. Fetal depression usually disappears within a few days, but perception of a newborn as sickly or defective often endures, fostering preoccupation with the infant's health.

Klara believed Adolf had a weak constitution and never stopped believing it. Because she was his caretaker, her perception affected him strongly. Adolf's health became her constant concern. She overprotected and overindulged him and favored him over her stepchildren and her children born after him. Her belief that he was sickly and in need of special treatment would lead to letting him drop out of school on the basis of a supposed lung disease. It would also foster the hypochondria he would suffer from throughout his adult life.

Klara's perception was disputed by others. The Hitlers' housemaid said Adolf was a healthy, lively baby, and he himself said toward the end of his life, "I was never sick." His boast, although exaggerated, was supported by medical evidence. Eduard Bloch, the family physician for years, including the time when Adolf dropped out of school, said he was thin and frail-looking but in excellent health, and the lung disease was nonexistent.[7] In middle age, Adolf consulted many physicians who found him to be in good health and without a trace of disease in childhood. Their findings are striking because he took poor care of himself. His diet was unhealthy, he slept poorly, and he did not exercise except for walking. In addition, for years he regularly used many drugs and in large doses, which associates said finally ruined his health. The one he used most, for his chronic stomach pain, contained strychnine and belladonna; it was a dangerous drug. Furthermore, as leader of the Nazi Party and of Germany, he was subject to enormous stress. He developed a variety of symptoms, including tremor and paralysis in his limbs, but the opinion of most of his physicians was that, like his stomach ailments, they were psychosomatic. The medical evidence is that he was born with a strong constitution.[8] Nonetheless, Klara's overconcern with Adolf's health persisted. When he was an adolescent, she said Adolf had been a very weak child, and she had always lived in fear of losing him.[9] Her devotion to him was extreme.

There were other reasons for her special closeness to Adolf. Besides Alois's lack of interest in her, when home he was rude and abusive. Disappointed in her marriage and resigned to it, she had no expectations of happiness in her own life. Her hopes became centered in Adolf, whom she saw as a child of special promise. And from birth, Adolf resembled her more than Alois. By adolescence, with his long face, large, staring eyes, and prominent nose, he resembled her even more. Probably the resemblance heightened her sense of closeness to her special child. Reportedly Klara caressed him often and breast-fed him longer than her other children and, when Alois was away, took Adolf into her bed. Her intimacy with him was obvious to relatives and acquaintances. Bloch said, "I have never witnessed a closer attachment," and "One thing is certain: he idolized his mother . . . !"[10] Klara's attachment to Adolf remained extreme until her death; his attachment to her remained extreme until his death thirty-seven years later.

The usual effect on a child of intense parental devotion is precocity—rapid learning, exceptional performance, and often the development of artistic or other special talent. Other effects, especially when devotion is combined with overprotection and indulgence, are self-importance, egocentrism, and the expectation that all one's needs will be met by others. The toddler feels special and valuable and has no need to restrain impulses, to look before leaping. The watchful parent is there to catch the child before harm occurs; the indulgent parent is there to prevent consequences of impulsiveness and disobedience.

Overprotection also has drawbacks. As an adult, Adolf would say he needed adversity "to tear him away from the emptiness of an easy life, to pull the mama's boy from his tender eiderdown,"[11] for:

> A mother's love is too great to keep her from constantly making every effort to help the boy, to pamper him, look after him, and even do his thinking for him . . .

> A boy who grows up entirely in his own home, or surrounded only by sisters and their girlfriends, is like a hothouse plant. Later on he trembles at every harsh word, recoils from another's attack, and has a nervous breakdown if fate administers a good thrashing.[12]

> The spoiled mother's darling, the fellow who knows that things will never go wrong for him: he will never confront life like someone who is thrown back on himself.[13]

(After his older half-brother left home and his younger brother died, Adolf had only sisters.) The overprotected child gets limited experience in self-reliance and tends to feel weak, vulnerable, and defective—incapable of managing without help, dependent on others for rescue from predicaments.

The effects of devotion and overprotection were soon evident. Adolf was a bright boy, learning rapidly—the only child in the family to grow up highly intelligent, talented, ambitious, or grandiose. He also grew up extremely insecure.

There were changes during his first years, but Adolf seems to have been insulated against them. When he was three, Alois was transferred from Braunau to Passau, on the German side of the border, and moved the family there. Adolf's world, centered on his mother, was hardly affected. When Adolf was five, Alois left his family for a year. Again Adolf suffered no apparent loss.

Lively and quick, he did very well upon entering school then. An obedient student, his grades were excellent, his teachers liked him, and Klara was proud of him. Probably the first seven years of his life were the best years of her adult life.

When Adolf was five, Klara gave birth to Edmund. To an only child or a child who is the center of attention, the arrival of a sibling is usually disturbing. Adolf was an only child to the extent that for five years he was Klara's only child of her own, and he was certainly the center of her attention. Nonetheless the birth of his brother seems not to have changed Adolf's position significantly. He remained the center of Klara's attention; presumably his baby brother was the loser.

When Adolf was seven, his sister Paula was born. Again there is no indication of a significant change in Adolf's situation. Having lost three children, Klara probably worried about Edmund's health, and she did worry about Paula's—a concern increased by Edmund's sickness and death a few years later. But it was Adolf about whom she worried most.

Alois died when Adolf was thirteen, leaving the family well provided for and easing tensions, but the relief lasted only a few years. Klara developed breast cancer and, despite a mastectomy and painful chemical treatment, her decline was rapid. Her last year of life was spent as an invalid, in much physical pain and in worry about her special son. To Bloch she said, "You know, Herr Doctor, when all is said and done, Adolf is still too young . . ."[14] As Bloch pointed out to Klara, Adolf at eighteen was already grown, while his sister Paula was only eleven. But Klara knew Adolf was a dreamer—*mondsüchtig* she called him—moonstruck. She thought of him as talented but out of touch and therefore facing a troubled future, and she was right. He was not prepared for life.

During the interlude between Alois's death and her ordeal with cancer, Klara reflected on her life. With Adolf's friend August Kubizek, the only person to whom she is known to have unburdened herself, she spoke of a life of suffering and commented sadly that the dreams of her youth had come to nothing. Her victimization and suffering were the source of her special son's calling to become a savior.

CHAPTER 4

THE TURN TOWARD NIHILISM

Our poor father cannot rest in his grave because you will flout his wishes. Obedience is what distinguishes a good son, but you don't know the meaning of the word. That's why you did so badly at school and why you're not getting anywhere now.[1]

—Klara Hitler, 1905

In *Mein Kampf* Hitler wrote that "excessive emphasis upon purely intellectual development and the neglect of physical education . . . leads to the premature onset of sexual fantasies."[2] Under his rule, Germany took the extraordinary steps of cutting education, persecuting intellectuals, burning books, and destroying art. Hitler was determined to raise German education and culture to a higher plane but, by the time he became chancellor, hate overshadowed his creativity, crippling a superb educational system. Academic hours in public schools were shortened as physical training increased, and less time was required to graduate. The number of college students soon fell to 40 percent of what it had been, and eventually most colleges were closed. Anti-Semitic and other oppressive policies caused a third of Germany's college teachers to leave the country, many of them fleeing for their lives. Twenty-four Nobel Prize winners—six of them Jews—were lost.

Determined to create a more just society, Hitler perverted Germany's legal system. Preaching a return to traditional values, he attacked the churches and undermined family structure. Without realizing it, he had become a nihilist.

Under his mother's tutelage, Adolf had been a reasonably good boy and more—an idealist and a budding artist. It was a shaky start in life, with grandiosity masking his sense of inadequacy, but a start in a positive direction before he got caught up in events that warped his moral sense. The changes began when he was seven.

Alois's return from Linz and retirement increased the problems of his wife and children. He bought a farm, moving the family and establishing his bees there. Now he was in and around the house much of the time, and the first major development was deterioration of his relationship with Alois, Jr. Alois had shown little interest in Adolf until this time; of his children, Alois, Jr., was his favorite, the important one for whose future he made plans. Perhaps the fact that, like himself, Alois, Jr., was born illegitimate and lost his mother early had fostered a special closeness on Alois's part. For Alois, Jr., the circumstances were also conducive to special closeness. When they lost their mother, he was two years old and Angela was only one. Both were too young to have remembered her but old enough to have suffered from losing her. Angela found compensation in becoming attached to Klara, calling her "Mother," but Alois, Jr., grew up thinking of himself as having only one parent. If there is any truth to Alois, Jr.'s, complaint in later years that Klara was against him or even if he believed it without foundation, he was especially dependent on Alois and probably felt abandoned whenever Alois went away.

An insecure child is hurt and develops resentment when the parent to whom he or she is attached goes away even for a day. The resentment is usually expressed after the parent's return in disobedience. After Alois's return from his year in Linz, Alois, Jr., was particularly disobedient and showed no interest in the civil-service career toward which his father was directing him. A strict father, Alois was intolerant of disobedience, and he was moodier than before, perhaps because the part of his life that had provided the most satisfaction—his job—was gone. The result was an intense clash of wills. Alois often beat Alois, Jr., and, on catching him in truancy, choked him and nearly killed him.[3] It was then that Alois, Jr., left home—running away, according to his siblings; being forced out by his father, according to his own account.

We now come to the second important controversy—the question of whether Alois beat his sons, particularly Adolf. While most biographers accepted the story that Adolf was beaten severely, some said he invented it as part of the myth with which he surrounded himself. Some of them said Alois did not use violence on his sons, and others that he simply spanked Adolf as fathers commonly spanked their children. The idea of Adolf as an abused child, calling for sympathy, continues to offend people. But what actually happened is crucial to understanding him.

The story of the beatings came from Adolf and his sister Paula and was supported by Alois, Jr.'s, report of being beaten. The contrary version came from Josef Mayrhofer, Alois's best friend, who said Alois never struck Adolf. If true, that would have been rare for a culture in which fathers ordinarily punished their children physically. But Mayrhofer had not been present during the times of the alleged beatings and was stating only his belief.[4] The evidence is on one side.

Earlier, Adolf had escaped his father's brutality, but now, with Alois at home during the day and Alois, Jr., gone, Adolf became the target of his father's hostility, which was more intense than ever. The loss of his favorite son—another abandonment, added to those of his childhood and the losses of two wives and three children—exacerbated Alois's resentment. According to Paula, he now carried a whip in the house, terrifying the family.[5]

Overindulged, Adolf was unaccustomed to dealing with either frustration or punishment, let alone destructive anger. His siblings said he grew up determined to have his way. He had learned he could overcome his mother's objections by brightness, persuabornness, or tantrums. But none of these worked with Alois. Adolf was now d by someone as egocentric, willful, and stubborn as himself, and dangerously

important
-Hitler learns from his father
that you may hurt because of what you are
instead of ~~you~~ what you do.

HITLER: THE PATHOLOGY OF EVIL   29

violent—someone who carried through life a sense of having been deprived and was easily moved to rage. For the first time, Adolf's omnipotence was challenged seriously and his weakness exposed. And it remained exposed, for Klara did not protect him from his father.

Apparently, there were no major issues between Alois and Adolf at first. Adolf was beaten mainly because Alois harbored rage, which he took out on his family, particularly on his sons. Adolf was old enough to realize he became the goat when the first goat, Alois, Jr., was no longer available. He learned scapegoating by example and painfully, being beaten for what he was, not necessarily for what he did.

As Adolf began to dream of a career as an artist, Alois objected and pointed him toward the civil service, making career choice an issue between them. Sympathetic to Adolf and his wishes, Klara nonetheless accepted Alois's argument that art was impractical. She would never resolve the issue in her own mind.

For Adolf, a background issue was emerging also. As a small child, usually in bed when Alois was home, he may have been unaware of his father's abuse of his mother, but now he was in a better position to see it. Given his adoration of Klara, her victimization presumably disturbed him badly. The usual reaction of a boy who sees his father beating his mother is fear, an impulse to intervene, and shame about failure to do so. As an adult, Adolf reportedly would have a recurrent nightmare in which a Jew menaced a woman and Adolf failed to intervene, feeling humiliated.[6] Recurrent dreams ordinarily come from a childhood trauma.

Klara's resignation to her situation was evident; she was not going to save herself. A boy who is close to an abused mother tends to become her champion—to have fantasies about standing up for her, rescuing her, and providing a better life for her. As the child grows up, the fantasies often turn into the ambition to become a champion of the people. A psychoanalyst developed this idea at length to explain Adolf's political career—an explanation supported by much evidence and bearing especially on the measures by which Adolf would try to save all Aryan women from all Jewish men.[7] At this point in Adolf's eighth year, it helps to explain his emerging opposition to his father. And Klara, while openly supporting Alois's authority, may subtly and unintentionally have encouraged Adolf to stand up to him, for that is common in the circumstances.

Adolf became very stubborn with his father and, according to his sister Paula, provocative. Probably the repetition of what had happened with his first son was too much for Alois. Paula said he beat Adolf daily and severely.[8] Then, at ten, Adolf too decided to run away. On discovering this, Alois beat him so badly he went into a coma.[9] For days the family did not know whether he would live.

Frequent or severe punishment conveys to children that they are evil. Being nearly killed by parents conveys that they are unworthy to live. Adolf began to experience himself as evil and worthless—feelings he would describe in middle age and be troubled by until his death.

Lebensunwürdige Leben

Psychological Aspects

—Living things unworthy to live.

Many abused children accept their situation and what it implies about them until they reach a position from which they can abuse others—usually their own children. Adolf would never have children, partly because of his belief that he was too defective to father healthy offspring. But he would become the *Führer* and judge millions of his subjects to be *"lebensunwürdige Leben"*—living things unworthy to live—and have many beaten, mutilated, and killed.

Adolf never again tried to run away, and outwardly he accepted the beatings. For the rest of his life, except when referring to his father as a drinker, he would voice no disrespect toward him. But Adolf would voice hatred of things associated with his father—the middle class, the Austro-Hungarian government, and especially the civil service.

Parents are expected to protect children, and being harmed by them is a betrayal of trust. Adolf's beatings were behind the sense he would carry through life of having been betrayed, a victim entitled to revenge. And he would enact over and over the experience of trusting men and finding himself betrayed.

While his sense of betrayal came largely from his father, his mother also contributed. For seven years she gave him extraordinary protection, but when he was beaten—when he most needed it—she failed to protect him. As an adult, while speaking adoringly of his mother, he would distrust women, including Eva Braun, who was extremely devoted to him.

Adolf's sense of power—which survived being nearly killed by his father—did not rest on physical strength. He would later say he was inspired by a feat of his hero Old Shatterhand, a fictional cowboy. Old Shatterhand dealt with enemies who held him prisoner and tortured him by resolving that, no matter how bad the pain, he would not cry out. By force of will, the hero became superior to his oppressors. Adolf resolved to do the same with his father. No matter how severe the beatings, he no longer cried. By this feat, he considered himself the winner in their confrontations. And not crying may have helped with his father; Alois stopped beating him. This was the beginning of Adolf's self-training in will power, which would become a key part of the sense of omnipotence he would carry into adulthood. The inspiration of Old Shatterhand fitted the main example set for him at home—Klara's submission to abuse from his father. She accepted it without complaining. Her stoic submission may have become associated in Adolf's mind with her moral superiority over his father.

A child who hates a parent nonetheless imitates and takes in aspects of the parent. Adolf began to sneak into Alois's room, put on his uniform, and shout commands.[10] In middle age, he would wear a uniform on unofficial occasions, as his father had, and carry a whip and snap it to impress and intimidate people. He would strive to become a man of ruthless violence. And he would become an abuser of women. Most crucial for the fate of millions, Adolf would apply to Jews and others the lesson in scapegoating he had received from his father.

Identification with a hated parent contributes to self-loathing, fostering a need to hate parts of oneself that are reminders of the parent. Adolf would grow to hate the

Adolf becomes powerful from his father's brutality

traits in himself he associated with his father—traits he came to think of as Jewish—and try to purge himself of them. From adolescence on, he would deny being a member of the middle class; later, he would deny even having come from it, and reject its values contemptuously.

Values develop from what a child is taught, from examples provided, and from conditioning. For Adolf the combined effect was confusing in the extreme. Klara and Alois taught Adolf values consistent with their religion and culture, but the examples he got from them were contradictory. His mother conducted herself according to those values, but his father did not. The more he learned about Alois, the more confusing would have been Klara's attitude toward him. Even though Alois was a childbeater, a wifebeater, a drunkard, and a Don Juan, Klara submitted to him and exalted him as head of the family. And Alois was treated as a solid citizen in the community.

Adolf's own beatings probably had the greatest impact on his values. He was beaten when he obeyed the rules as well as when he broke them. No matter what he did, he was bad in his father's eyes. Klara also contributed to his confusion by rewarding him when he broke the rules as well as when he obeyed them. Her indulgence meant he was good no matter what rule he violated. Moral precepts were of little use as guidelines to behavior; the consequences of his actions from both parents showed the precepts to be irrelevant.

When no reasonable pattern can be found in the consequences of a child's acts, understanding of causation is hindered and superstition fostered. Events are thought to be controlled by invisible, mysterious forces, and fatalistic, magical, or paranoid explanations develop. Such explanations would be prominent in Adolf's thinking as an adult. As Germany's leader in World War II, he would increasingly neglect material considerations and rely on superstitious factors for victory.

Adolf's grandiosity from being his mother's favorite was increased by the fact that he could get away with almost anything. No matter what rule he broke, he hardly had to deal with consequences—not from his mother because she did not punish him, and not from his father because he was beaten even if he had not broken any rule.

Since consequences from his parents were hardly related to his actions, whether something was worth doing depended on immediate, practical effects. If a sweet was enjoyable, it was worth eating. If evading a chore enabled him to do something pleasant, evading it was worthwhile. His conditioning favored immediate gratification over working toward long-range goals.

Adolf did not understand that his moral training was being undermined, but he knew that he violated more and more of the rules he had been taught. This added to his self-loathing. As his values became confused, he sought new ideals by which to live. At eight, he decided to become a monk, and during adolescence he adopted socialist principles. But by then his morality was strict only in condemning other people, as he rationalized his own lapses. Nonetheless, it would not be until middle age that he could violate his moral code freely.

Meanwhile, the abuse he suffered fostered depression and a pattern of behavior called learned helplessness. Depression comes from the accumulation of pain and anger without an outlet, from the impossibility of escaping an oppressive situation, and from a sense of being worthless. At first Adolf's grandiosity masked his depression and sense of worthlessness, but they would emerge during adolescence in failure to take care of himself and in self-destructive tendencies. As an adult, he would be suicidal when things went wrong, and finally he would kill himself.

Learned helplessness is a pattern of maladaptive behavior found in people and animals after they are given indiscriminate punishment—punishment unrelated to what they do.[11] Even a brief period of indiscriminate punishment impairs future learning and performance by reducing effort. Subjects given a task make limited efforts to complete it. Rather, they direct their energy to controlling their feelings. Human subjects conclude that whatever they do has no effect on the outcome. Therefore, instead of trying to solve a problem set for them, some make random efforts; others make no effort at all. Instead they focus their energy on bracing for the expected punishment so they will feel it less. This is what Adolf did in dealing with his father.

Learned helplessness is a barrier to new learning and recurs particularly with difficult tasks and in stressful circumstances. When combined with depression, it results in periods of torpor, with inability to choose or act. Adolf's problem with making decisions and his periods of inactivity would begin in adolescence and soon reach a peak. Except during his army service, they would persist for the rest of his life.

Alois's retirement also led to moves from one village to another, which meant frequent changes of school for Adolf. He was again and again the new boy in the class and had to win acceptance by an already established group. Adolf lacked the patience to win it gradually and he needed more than acceptance. His growing sense of worthlessness fostered striving for superiority. Wherever Adolf went, he tried to be the leader, relying on knowledge, cleverness, and stubbornness. Often he was successful, but he did not get to rest comfortably in the leader's position, for he did not stay in a group long. Over and over he struggled for leadership, and the intense competitiveness he developed would be lifelong. Even after achieving supreme power, he would be insecure in his status and keep strengthening his position and weakening others' positions. He would have people he saw as potential challengers killed, remaining highly sensitive to imaginary as well as real threats to his position.

Teachers vary in their methods and the order in which they take up topics. Therefore, changing schools requires extra adaptations and puts a child in the position of being unprepared on topics for which the rest of the class is prepared. Despite Adolf's precocity, keeping up became difficult.

Resentment of his father, displaced onto teachers, compounded the difficulty. When eight, Adolf began to neglect his homework and tease his teachers and play pranks on them. The decline leading to his dropping out of school had begun. He annoyed teachers by writing sexual remarks on the blackboard, bested them in clever exchanges he provoked, and locked one in a room. When in his fifties, he would still boast about how he had tormented them, and his favorite story was:

> Father Schwarz had a huge, blue handkerchief . . . You could hear [the dried phlegm] crackle when he spread it out. One day he had dropped it in class. During break, when he was talking with some other teachers, I went up to him holding the handkerchief at arm's length . . .[12]

Adolf said his mock-helpful gesture, drawing attention to the phlegm-filled handkerchief, caused much laughter at Father Schwarz's expense. Teachers tolerated Adolf's pranks because he was bright, reinforcing his experience of being able to get away with breaking the rules.

While Adolf's schoolwork fell off, his skill in drawing and painting increased, and he became determined not to enter the civil service but to become an artist. (One expression of animosity toward teachers was drawing caricatures of them.) His wish aroused strong opposition from Alois. Adolf later said he did poorly in school in order to thwart his father's plan of having him prepare for a civil service career. Probably this was true, but there were many reasons for the decline in his schoolwork.

To the above stresses were added increasing academic demands over the years, and brightness was no longer enough for success. In addition, when Adolf entered high school in the city of Linz, the family was living in the village of Leonding. Feeling out of place and unaccepted, Adolf concluded city children looked down on rural ones and treated him as a country bumpkin. He also got less interest and attention than he was accustomed to from teachers. His morale and effort weakening, he failed his first year and had to repeat it. The next year, he made a strong effort, earned good grades, and won some acceptance as a leader from his peers. And he began to lecture them on political and military topics—the beginning of his harangues, a lifelong pursuit that would lead to success in politics. But in high school, moderate success was not enough to overcome his discontent. In his third year, his effort slackened and he failed again. That summer he studied, took a makeup test, and was given credit for the year, but on the condition that he not return to the school. The combination of poor scholarship and hostility to teachers had made him unwanted. A teacher in the Linz school would later say, "He was notoriously cantankerous, willful, arrogant, and bad tempered . . . He reacted with ill-concealed hostility to advice and reproof . . ."[13]

For Adolf, school had become misery, and Alois's death encouraged him to think about dropping out. His rejection by the Linz school increased the hope that he could, but Klara continued to insist he finish high school and entered him in one in the town of Steyr. Adolf was very unhappy, calling Steyr "purgatory."

He performed poorly at school once again. As he was gaining more confidence about pursuing a career in art, he considered high school a pointless ordeal. When asked what he wanted to be, Adolf answered, "A great artist." He tried to persuade Klara that formal education was unnecessary for an artist, but she continued to follow her dead husband's plan for Adolf, partly out of a sense that a wife should and partly out of concern that art was an impractical choice.

That year, Adolf developed a cough, which led to resolution of the conflict. Convinced he was sick, Klara let him drop out of school temporarily, although he was not confined to bed. And once he was out, she failed to get him to return. The resolution cost him a diploma, which limited his future options, but that seemed no loss for he felt sure he would succeed in art.

As an adult he would rationalize dropping out of school:

> Our teachers were absolute tyrants. They had no sympathy with youth . . . If any pupil showed the slightest trace of originality they persecuted him relentlessly, and the only model pupils I ever got to know have all been failures in after life.[14]

Actually, his teachers had indulged Adolf. The absolute tyrant, the one who persecuted him relentlessly, had been his father. Adolf's statement, that all boys who submitted to the tyranny of school became failures, need not be taken literally. Psychologically, it was an important truth; had he accepted his father's authority, he would have been accepting the latter's implied judgment of him as unworthy to live. In maintaining his brittle self-esteem, he opposed all authority. Hatred of his father, never expressed directly, had turned into hatred of teachers. It had led to failure and the end of his formal education. Eventually, it would lead to fierce anti-intellectualism, even though he himself was an intellectual.

Now sixteen, at home while boys his age were in school or working, Adolf was doing little. He had grown increasingly introverted and isolated as well as depressed. No longer interested in games and playmates, when old enough for real friendship he had little desire for it. Rather, he looked down upon his peers and avoided them. And he was highly contemptuous of adults and their institutions.

His half-sister Angela had married when Alois died, and her husband Leo Raubal took a fatherly interest in Adolf. When Adolf dropped out of school, Leo offered him guidance in getting a job. Like Alois, Leo was in the civil service and urged Adolf toward such a career. That was too much for Adolf; he talked about Leo with "pronounced hatred" while "his face assumed a truly threatening aspect." And "Whenever he heard the words 'civil servant' . . . he fell into a rage."[15]

Despite his isolation, during adolescence Adolf did form a close friendship —the only one of his life. With August Kubizek, a would-be musician who worked in his family's shop, Adolf shared enthusiasm for the arts, isolation from their peers, and lack of overt interest in girls. Another key was August's good nature. He was sympathetic and patient, tolerating Adolf's moodiness and angry outbursts and listening to his harangues. Adolf dominated August, who went along with his plans and obsessions even when he considered them unrealistic. They were sensitive to each other's feelings and went out of their way to help each other, becoming very close, sharing the most personal experiences. For a few years, they spent a good part of most days together.

That did not stop Adolf from criticizing his friend or trying to make him over. Adolf objected to his name, refusing to call him August. Instead he gave him the name Gustav—the name of Adolf's brother who had died before Adolf's birth. This was one proposal August did not accept. They settled on the diminutive Gustl, used for boys named August and Gustav.

Probably his rejection of his friend's name came from his unhappiness with his own name and identity, both of which he later changed. "Spoiled identity" is used to describe enduring feelings of shame, guilt, or defectiveness associated with one's identity—feelings that increasingly plagued Adolf. At this time, he began to alter the way he wrote the *A* and *d* in his name so that *Ad* resembled *W*. In later years he would call himself Wolf, sometimes as his first name and other times as his family name. The idea of calling himself Wolf probably came from his own name; Adolf is derived from Adelwolf (Noble Wolf). Another probable source was German mythology, which he began to read at this time. The Teutonic god Wotan, who was associated with wolves, would become Adolf's role model. As an adult, Adolf would use the name Wolf when being playful and as a cover when in hiding or perpetrating crimes.

Adolf had already become highly conscious of family names to distinguish Austrians of German descent—the good people—from those of Czech or other ancestry. In this vein, he objected to his friend's name—Kubizek, of Czech origin—which he said was an "unfortunate name" for a German to have. By adolescence, he had rejected his Austrian identity and saw himself as a German, and Czechs became the first ethnic group he hated. His own Czech ancestry is something Adolf never mentioned, and he would deny it in an authorized biography by the gratuitous statement that his ancestors had "kept absolutely clear of any Slavonian admixture."[16]

Adolf's distant ancestors are unknown. The names Schicklgruber and Pölzl are German; it is the name Hitler that people took to be Czech. "Hitler" was a modern spelling of an old family name and provides no clues in itself. Some biographers said it was derived from the Czech name Hydlarcek, which cannot be proved. But an early spelling of the name, Hüttler, is a better clue to its derivation. It probably came from the German word *Hütte,* meaning cottage or foundry.[17] Another name in the family, however, was a clearer sign of Czech ancestry.

The ancestor most obviously of probable Czech descent was Johann Nepomuk Hiedler. Johann Nepomuk was the name of the patron saint of Bohemia (part of Czechoslovakia). In Austria, the name Nepomuk was used to refer to Czechs in general, often derisively. A person of Czech ancestry was sometimes called a Nepomuk, and a Czech whose name was unfamiliar might be addressed by the name, as in "Hey, Nepomuk, come here!" Johann Nepomuk Hiedler may not actually have had Czech ancestry, but his name declared that he did. Given Adolf's strong interest in names as clues to ancestry, he is unlikely to have missed the meaning of the name Nepomuk.

While Johann Nepomuk Hiedler is not proven to have been related to Alois, there is no doubt he was Klara's grandfather. Thus Adolf was probably of Czech descent and had reason to be aware of it. His comment that Gustl was unfortunate in having a Czech name probably reflected problems with his own identity.

Adolf's friendship with Gustl seems to have helped him emerge from his depression and into more activity. Gustl's interest in the arts and his support of Adolf's ambition to be an artist were boosts, as was Gustl's admiration for him. Adolf attempted to develop his skills on his own by sketching and painting, and won Klara over to a plan of entering the Academy of Fine Arts in Vienna, perhaps the best state school in the Austro-Hungarian Empire. To prepare for admission, he reportedly took a class, received private instruction in art briefly, and became an avid reader, which compensated for his lack of formal education. But he also spent much time idly, daydreaming when alone and drawing Gustl into his fantasies when they were together. Continuing suggestions by relatives about his getting a job now provoked Adolf's disdain—an artist did not need to hold an ordinary job. Despite the confidence he expressed in becoming a successful artist, he put off applying to the Academy. The procrastination that would hamper him the rest of his life was already well established.

At times Adolf embarked on new projects with striking enthusiasm. He joined a society for the improvement of the theater in Linz and drew architectural plans for a new building to house it. (The society decided to repair the old building instead.) He decided to study the piano, and his mother got him one. He wrote poetry; he began an opera, stories, and plays, the plots drawn from German mythology. He worked on architectural plans for rebuilding much of the city of Linz. Except for poems, he failed to complete the projects, always returning to sketching and painting, to his dream of becoming a great artist.

Adolf and Gustl loved opera and went often. For Adolf there was only one important composer, Richard Wagner, whose operas were mostly drawn from myths of the Teutonic gods and godlike heroes. But the opera that stirred Adolf most was *Rienzi,* about a reformer who led a revolt against a corrupt Roman government and as a result incurred the enmity of the Christian church. According to Gustl, Adolf was strangely silent after the performance, in "a state of complete ecstasy and rapture."[18] Then he spoke of a mandate he would one day receive from the people to lead them out of bondage.

Adolf viewed the Austrian government as an oppressor, probably because of its association with his father. The Catholicism of his childhood was turning into hostility to the Church, the clergy, and religion generally. Thinking of himself as a German patriot, he longed to be the hero of a fight against the combination of Austria and Catholicism, which he saw as oppressing the German people of Austria. The patriot Rienzi, fighting a government and religion that oppressed the people, was an ideal hero. Years later, when chancellor of Germany, he would tell Gustl, "In that hour it began," linking his vocation as a political leader to the inspiration of *Rienzi.*[19] Perhaps that was when he first seriously saw himself in such a role. But the inspiration soon faded from his mind.

Along with his decision to enter the Academy, Adolf decided he and Gustl would live together for life. The idea obsessed Adolf; he drew detailed plans for a house to be built for them and outlined the life they would lead—a life of two bachelor artists, without a place in it for women or children. To finance it, Adolf bought a lottery ticket, confident of success. Losing the lottery struck Adolf as a personal betrayal by the Austro-Hungarian government, in which he had placed his trust. Gustl wrote:

> I have rarely heard him rage so madly as then. First he fumed over . . . this officially organised exploitation of human credulity, this open fraud at the expense of docile citizens. Then his fury turned against the state itself, this patchwork of [ethnic mixture], this monster built up by Hapsburg marriages.[20]

The conclusion that he had been betrayed was to become his usual reaction to disappointment. Adolf's limited resilience was near the breaking point.

During the next few years, he was often in a rage at the "Philistine world," according to Gustl, and, "Wherever he looked, he saw injustice, hate and enmity."[21] Occasionally, his fury erupted in assaults on strangers. His rages were an adolescent version of children's tantrums, and worse. A tantrum is over quickly, but a belief that one has been betrayed may evolve into a new, paranoid understanding of what is "really" going on and to thoughts of vengeance.

Probably Adolf's devastation over losing the lottery had roots in his greatest disappointment, his betrayal by his parents. The reference to Hapsburg marriages creating an ethnically mixed monster suggests his own family history.

The dream of life as an artist with Gustl had provided direction, but losing the lottery took it away. No longer tied to the structure of school or even to a plan, stymied by indecision and procrastination, Adolf was adrift. His position at home as an unemployed youth depended on progress toward becoming an artist, but he was not making progress.

Gustl was an only child and had grown up very close to his mother. Adolf had been reared by his mother somewhat as if he were her only child and had grown up extremely close to her. And Gustl's and Adolf's fathers had been distant. The key difference was that Gustl's father had not been abusive. Having a highly punitive father intensifies a boy's shame over closeness to his mother, and the shame carries over to relationships with girls and women. The usual effect of closeness in such circumstances is precocious eroticism followed by inhibition. In Adolf's childhood there is one sign of unbridled sexuality. When twelve he was disciplined by his school for molesting a girl, although the record gives no details of the offense. His inhibition set in early and was severe. According to his sister Paula, Adolf could not stand to be kissed by a girl or woman.[22] During the years of their friendship, Adolf and Gustl were shy and abstinent. Gustl said Adolf was the more inhibited one, becoming upset when girls made advances to him and trying very hard not to masturbate. He believed abstinence would help him overcome the desires he considered evil.

But at seventeen, Adolf saw a young woman on the street in Linz and fell in love with her. She quickly became an obsession, as he planned his future around marriage to her, giving up the idea of spending his life with his friend. According to Gustl, "Stefanie filled his thoughts so completely that everything he said, or did, or planned for the future, was centered around her."[23]

Stefanie was a year or two older than Adolf and came from from a middle-class family more prosperous than his. According to Gustl, she was elegant and refined-looking, tall and blond—the epitome of German beauty in Adolf's eyes. Day after day, Adolf returned to the spot where he had caught sight of her, and his vigil was rewarded when she sometimes passed. He stared at her and occasionally their eyes met; a couple of times she smiled at him and once threw him a flower. With a single exception, that was their only contact, but on this limited basis he constructed elaborate fantasies.

Love at a distance—fantasy love—was in the German romantic tradition and no rarity in Austria. But in that tradition it was limited to fantasy by external barriers, as when one's beloved was engaged or married to another. In Adolf's case, the barrier was internal. His inhibition had become so strong that he could not bring himself to approach Stefanie. He outlined imaginary conversations with her, but never uttered a word. He composed many love poems to her, but never showed her any. He had a fantasy that Gustl would propose to her on his behalf, but did not ask him to carry it out. Of the plots he devised to win her, one involved kidnapping her.

Gustl urged his friend to speak to Stefanie, but Adolf gave reasons for not doing so. Because Stefanie was above him socially, it would be presumptuous to speak to her. As he was in love with her and was convinced she was also in love with him, the only proper purpose in speaking to her would be to propose. But since he was unemployed and without an assured future, he had nothing to offer her. In addition there was no need to speak to her. By romantic telepathy she already knew his thoughts *and was in agreement with his wishes.*

Gustl considered the reasons to be excuses; sometimes Adolf did, too. Behind his excuses was fear:

> If I introduce myself to Stefanie and her mother, I will have to tell her at once what I am, what I have and what I want. My statement would bring our relations abruptly to an end.[24]

At most his "lacks" were a barrier to courting a woman, not to addressing one. Adolf's problem was that he felt unworthy, that "what I am" was defective. He and Stefanie were of the same class; social position was not an objective barrier. The idea that a woman is too far above a man to be approached, when untrue, is often rooted in inhibitions that go back to his mother, who is unapproachable by her position. Similarly, Adolf's regard for Stefanie as an ideal woman had no objective basis; he knew almost nothing about her. Such idealization also goes back to the image of one's mother. To have made an approach with a romantic, marital, or sexual purpose would, of course, have been improper with Klara, not Stefanie.

Adolf's most extraordinary idea was that Stefanie knew his wishes and wanted to satisfy him—a magical notion. Lovers who spend much time together do develop empathic understanding, but Adolf's relationship with Stefanie existed only in his mind; she had no basis for empathic sensing of his thoughts. Belief in romantic telepathy is rooted in infancy, when one's caretaker senses unspoken thoughts and meets unexpressed wishes. The experience is extended beyond infancy by a hovering, overprotective, indulgent caretaker who gratifies needs even before they are expressed, giving a child the experience of being understood telepathically. Stefanie showed no such understanding of Adolf, but Klara had.

Seeing that Adolf would not speak to Stefanie, Gustl suggested a note. This advice Adolf took, writing a formal letter in the romantic tradition, declaring his love. He said he was going away to enter art school and in four years, having completed his training and established himself, he would return for her. Then, if she would have him, they would marry. But he did not identify himself, sending the letter unsigned. Stefanie had no idea who her secret lover was.

Not identifying himself to Stefanie probably came from Adolf's shame, which is borne out by the strict secrecy he maintained about his interest in her. Gustl was the only one who knew, and Adolf gave Stefanie a code name to disguise her identity when he and Gustl wrote to each other—the odd name Benkieser. While the latter part of the name sounds German, the prefix *Ben* occurs only in German words that come from other languages. *Ben* is, however, a very common prefix in Semitic names. Adolf had asked Gustl to make inquiries, learning a few superficial facts about Stefanie. Her family name, Jansten, was said by biographers to be Jewish, but no basis for the statement is apparent. To Austrians, it would have sounded Danish. Adolf said a male classmate had been named Benkieser, but that does not explain choosing the name for Stefanie. Perhaps Adolf gave Stefanie a Jewish-sounding name because he associated her with forbidden desire. Years later he clearly associated Jews with forbidden desire.

Taking his promise to Stefanie seriously, Adolf pulled himself together. With Klara's consent, he withdrew his share of Alois's estate—enough to live on for a year—packed his drawings and paintings, and moved to Vienna. Brimming with confidence, he presented himself to the Academy of Fine Arts for admission and took a test consisting of impromptu sketching, which he passed. The remaining hurdle was evaluation of his portfolio, which he failed.

Rejection by the Academy was the hardest blow Adolf had suffered. He had burned his bridges in order to become an artist, and continued support from his mother was contingent on studying at the Academy. Humiliated by the rejection, at a loss about what to do, he requested an interview with the Academy's director. The result was a crushing pronouncement: Adolf had no future as an artist. He was advised to apply to the Academy's school of architecture, for he showed talent in that area.

Although architecture had become a strong interest of his, Adolf rejected the director's advice. Admission to the school of architecture required a high-school diploma, and getting one would have taken a year or more of study. Occasionally, the school waived the requirement for a candidate of exceptional promise. Whether Adolf knew these things, he seems not to have considered applying. Probably his rebellion against men in authority stood in the way of taking the advice. Instead, he set himself stubbornly against the director, deciding to work for a year on improving his portfolio and get private instruction from a teacher at the Academy. Then he would reapply as an art student.

Adolf told no one of his failure. To Klara and Gustl he indicated that he had been admitted and was pursuing studies at the Academy. Secrecy and deception became a regular practice, contributing to alienation from his family.

Perhaps sensing failure ahead, Adolf felt desperate and lonely. He persuaded Gustl to join him in Vienna to study music. The harder part was persuading Gustl's father, who saw music as impractical. Adolf won him over—a notable feat of persuasion. Having gotten his family's support, Gustl won admission to a music school in Vienna and moved into Adolf's furnished room. Though poor, the two shared the excitement of Vienna's cultural riches and, so Gustl thought, the inspiring life of students of the arts. To maintain the illusion of attending the Academy, Adolf left their room daily and lived a lie.

Adolf did work on improving his portfolio, but only fitfully, as most of his energy went into fantasy. To Gustl's amazement, Adolf found time, despite his supposed art curriculum, to write drama and opera and to study Vienna's buildings in detail and talk about redesigning the city, as he had done in Linz and would later do in Berlin. He also read about many subjects, especially Teutonic myths. The poor and other unfortunates increasingly occupied his attention, as he devised architectural and social solutions to their plight. Gustl's astonishment at how much time Adolf had for these pursuits while attending the Academy ultimately led to Adolf's angry confession about having been rejected.

Most of Adolf's money went for rent. He spent the barest minimum on basic needs, and the food he bought was hardly above a starvation level. Sometimes his landlady gave him a meal, Gustl's mother sent him a food package, and Gustl offered to treat him at a restaurant. Adolf used his money for tickets to the opera and other cultural events.

Meanwhile his life continued its downward course. Stefanie got engaged and, according to Gustl, Adolf became a woman hater as a result, experiencing her act as a betrayal. Another blow was the worsening of his mother's cancer. Following her mastectomy, she had appeared to recover, but only briefly. While Adolf was in Vienna, Klara kept news of her condition from him until it got so bad that she could not carry on. Adolf, now eighteen, came home to find her bedridden and being cared for by his aunt Johanna and his sisters, as well as by Dr. Bloch. In his effort to save his mother, Adolf came out of his dreams. He took over her care, cooking for her, cleaning, and scrubbing the floor. He comforted and nursed her. According to Paula, ". . . Adolf spoiled my mother during this last time of her life with overflowing tenderness. He was indefatigable in his care for her, wanted to comply with any desire she could possibly have and did all to demonstrate his great love for her." Bloch said, "He would watch her every movement so that he might anticipate her slightest need. His eyes, which usually gazed mournfully into the distance, would light up whenever she was relieved of her pain."[25] Apparently he saw himself allied with Bloch in a desperate struggle to save Klara. With Adolf's consent, Bloch used a corrosive drug as a last resort.

Klara had been the center of Adolf's life. Her sickness was a grim opportunity to fulfill the role for which his early experiences had prepared him—to save her. But his fight was hopeless; already feeble, Klara held on only a few weeks, dying just before Christmas. Bloch, who had seen many deaths, was especially moved by Adolf's devotion and said, "I have never seen anyone so prostrate with grief . . ."[26] Adolf was moved by Bloch's devotion, too, and pledged eternal gratitude. Many years later, when he stopped Jews from practicing medicine and then had them arrested and killed, he exempted Bloch, a Jew, from these measures.

For the rest of his life, Adolf kept a photograph of Klara with him, hanging it over his bed, taking it along on trips, looking at it daily. He also kept a sketch of her that he made as she lay dying. And he spent Christmases alone, dwelling on memories of her.

Along with losing the one he loved, as he would later realize, Adolf had lost his purpose in life. Klara had been the main person for whom he had performed, the special one who appreciated his uniqueness and, despite her doubts, encouraged his artistic dreams. She had also been the one in need of rescue, the one to whom it was worth devoting himself. He later wrote, ". . . the death of my mother put a sudden end to all of my highflown plans."[27]

Refusing an offer to move in with his half sister Angela and her family, Adolf returned to Vienna, resuming his desultory preparation to reapply to the Academy. Without his mother and without his dream of marrying Stefanie, there was little to keep him going, and his performance declined further. He did reapply, but this time failed to pass even the first hurdle.

On bringing the news to Gustl, he raged:

> The Academy, a lot of old-fashioned, fossilized *civil servants, bureaucrats*, devoid of understanding, stupid *lumps of officials*. The whole Academy ought to be blown up![28] (Italics added.)

They were like his father, with no understanding of art.

In later years he would explain his rejection by speculating that the Academy was run by Jews and claim he had sent the director a letter saying, "The Jews will pay for this."[29] By that time he would have evidence that his father had been partly Jewish. But when rejected by the Academy, he identified its faculty with the civil service and, according to Gustl:

> He spoke of the trip-wires which had been cunningly laid—I remember his very words—for the sole purpose of ruining his career.[30]

Adolf's rage on losing the lottery had been a bit paranoid. His reaction to the second rejection by the Academy was more so. He was now the victim of a concealed plot directed against him personally.

The portfolio found inadequate by the Academy has not survived, but some of Adolf's paintings and drawings have, and they show why he was rejected and advised to pursue architecture. His craft was good; the drawings and paintings of buildings and other scenes were accurate. He himself described one as "a painting executed with photographic exactitude which lends a three-dimensional effect to the architecture and decorative detail."[31] His works could have served well as illustrations, but there was no life in his art. The few human figures he did were tiny and stiff, more like figurines than people. Gustl noted, "His intention was not to express any of his own emotions but just to paint pleasant little pictures." Gustl also noted that, on impulse, Adolf made quick sketches that were fresh and alive but, by the time he finished a painting, its life had been drained by "painstaking precision."[32] This would explain Adolf's first rejection by the Academy; he passed on the basis of quick sketches, only to fail on the basis of his finished work. The originality and throbbing passion that marked Adolf's daily criticisms of life in Vienna were completely absent from his art. He copied what was in front of him, without putting anything of himself into it. His art was impersonal, objective, and sterile.

No doubt depression contributed to its flatness, but inhibition was his main handicap. He was full of rage but had stopped fighting and soon would evade the draft. He was full of desire and romantic yearnings but lived like a eunuch. Many artists have been inhibited in life and poured their passions into their work, but Adolf's art was more barren than his daily life. In childhood he had drawn caricatures of people; in middle age he would make pornographic drawings and hide them. In these he expressed his passions.

Those artists who exposed their troubled visions to public view were the ones Adolf despised, calling their work:

> . . . the degenerate, Negroid, Jewish, cosmopolitan, anti-Nordic art of mongrelized and Marxist Paris.[33]

> The degenerate art of charlatans who belong either in insane asylums or prisons . . .[34]

> Indeed, we consider most of the activities among these cultural protagonists as criminal . . .[35]

> And what do you produce? Deformed cripples and cretins, women that can only elicit revulsion, men which are nearer to animals than humans . . . And this, the horrible dilettantes in our midst dare to present as the art of our time.[36]

And he proposed sterilizing them.[37] Adolf failed to become a successful artist because of his need to suppress, hide, and disown parts of himself that disgusted him.

Over the years his rebellion and depression had narrowed the choices open to him. Some options were lost by becoming a poor student and not getting a diploma, others by disdain of jobs associated with his father—civil service and craft apprenticeship. He had given up options willingly, counting on becoming an artist, putting all his chips on one number. When the gamble failed, there was little left to try. Architecture might have been a good choice for Adolf, but the choice was foreclosed.

Adolf did not dwell long on his second rejection by the Academy, turning instead to another project, laboring on it day and night. To Gustl's question, he said, "I am working on the solution of the housing problem in Vienna . . ."[38] Adolf now included himself in the ranks of the underprivileged, whose savior he meant to become.

> He not only suffered with them, he lived for them and devoted all his thoughts to the salvation of these people from distress and poverty . . . Only by his noble and grandiose work . . . did he find again his inner equilibrium.[39]

Gustl thought the new project had brought Adolf out of despair, but he was mistaken.

Months before, as Klara was dying, she had pleaded, "Gustl, go on being a good friend to my son when I'm no longer here. He has no one else."[40] Perhaps out of modesty, Gustl did not realize how important he was to Adolf, particularly at this time. The school year had ended and Gustl left for home. Adolf had no home and no real plans—nowhere to go and nothing worth doing.

Over the summer, Adolf wrote to Gustl that he looked for projects but did nothing. Then Gustl did not come back as planned, being suddenly called up for military service, which lasted into November. When he did return to Vienna, Adolf was gone without a trace. Gustl searched long for his only friend, finding that Adolf's family had no idea where he was, learning eventually that "Adolf had disappeared into the shadowy depths" and "in this most difficult phase of his life, he no longer had a friend."[41]

A series of blows brings most people to the edge. Within a year Adolf had lost Stefanie and his mother, been rejected twice by the Academy, and then lost his last link to the world—his only friend. His depression worsened until he stopped taking care of himself. By the age of twenty, he was deep into his first breakdown.

CHAPTER 5

THE WASTELAND

For two years I had no other friend but care and need [and] eternally gnawing hunger.[1]

—Adolf Hitler, 1914

Vienna . . . is to me only the living memory of the most miserable time of my life.

Even today it can waken only depressing thoughts in my mind. The name of this Phaeacian city means five years of sorrow and misery. Five years in which I had to make my living, first as a worker, then as a painter . . .[2]

—Adolf Hitler, 1924

In legend, a prophet-to-be deprived himself of material benefits and escaped temptation by leaving his community to dwell in a wilderness. He fasted, had a mystical experience, and was transformed, returning with a vision for the community's welfare. When presenting himself as Germany's prophet, Hitler said he formed his ideas about what was wrong with society and how to transform it during his years in Vienna—ideas of eternal truth, never needing to be changed.

This was hardly true. The ideas by which he ruled Germany did begin to develop in Vienna, but they did not take form until several years after he left the city, when he had his mystical experience while hospitalized. And he did not seriously consider all his ideas to be final; he declared them eternal to impress people, to "prove" he was their prophet. Nonetheless his experience in Vienna was crucial in his development. There he hit bottom, losing many of the values and ambitions by which he had lived, needing urgently to find a new world view.

Highly cosmopolitan Vienna was, of course, no wilderness, but Adolf made it one. He fasted, deprived himself of other material benefits, and avoided temptation, coming to view the city's cultural and material riches as a wasteland. He isolated himself, at times oblivious to those around him, at other times frightened by people he perceived as alien, subhuman savages. He lived as if in a wilderness.

45

Calling Vienna a Phaeacian city was bitter irony. Adolf went there to use its resources in furthering his ambition, telling Gustl that only Vienna had what he needed to
develop his talent fully. Rebuffed by the Academy, bewildered, his spirit broken, he
would flee Vienna. By contrast, Phaeacia, in Homer's *Odyssey,* was a mythical land of
extraordinary, gracious people, "close kin to the gods." They welcomed and embraced
the stranger and freed him of trouble and toil. They honored him, bestowed lavish gifts
on him, and even treated him as a god. Then they helped him fulfill his mission.

Adolf's allusion to Phaeacia showed the persistence at thirty-five of his adolescent
wish not to have to make a living, but to be freed by grace from trouble and toil. Disillusioned in Vienna, he would seek a gracious land and a godlike people in Germany. And
not finding them there, he would try to redesign Germany, transform its people into supermen, and get them to honor him as a god.

His time of grinding poverty in Vienna was actually less than a year, but in 1914 he
stretched it to two years, and by 1924 it had grown to five. At eighteen, he had lied about
being a student at the Academy to cover his humiliation and secure permission and funds to
remain in Vienna. By the time he went into politics, he lied routinely to hide his past, to win
sympathy, and to foster the image he desired. He claimed his family was of Bavarian descent
and poor. He presented himself as hardworking to hide having spent the years from sixteen
to twenty-five largely in idleness. And he explained his poverty in Vienna as due to a lack of
jobs there and by discrimination against him, but external circumstances were not the cause.

On leaving the room he shared with Gustl, he rented another. No longer having his
friend's contribution to the rent, his expenses were higher. After a few months, he moved
to a cheaper room, and then another, and in a year was living on the street. Let us assume
Adolf ran through an inheritance from his mother. He still received an orphan's pension,
to continue until he established himself or reached the age of twenty-four. It was meager,
but he had one relative who helped with money on the rare occasion when he asked. And
if he had taken odd jobs to supplement the pension, he could have maintained a modest
standard of living, but he did not. No one has been found who could say why he gave up
living in a room, stopped drawing his pension, and went on the street.[3] We are left with
possibilities likely in his circumstances.

Formerly, Adolf had been an immaculate dandy, his clothes so impressive that Gustl
took him to be of the upper class. But now he looked the part he lived. His once-fine
clothes were gone except for a ragged, dirty suit, and by the second winter, he had no
overcoat. Reportedly, he had pawned it along with his paints, and other belongings had
been stolen. He was no longer taking care of himself in the most rudimentary ways except
for occasional visits to a soup kitchen. His mother's dying concern had proven true. To
receive his orphan's pension regularly, he had to maintain an address, and he no longer did.

He had no apparent interests, no friends or acquaintances, and no contact with relatives. The intense passion Gustl had seen was gone. Adolf had become quite passive, his
hatred turned inward, his life one of self-deprivation. Gustl had noted Adolf's suicidal thoughts over losing Stefanie. Although there is no report of his attempting

suicide in Vienna, starving himself and exposing himself to the cold were self-destructive. He was severely depressed.

The deprivation Adolf imposed on himself may have been punitive. He felt ashamed about failing in high school, failing to win admission to the Academy, and wasting the last years and much family money. He may have thought the money could have been used by Klara to consult specialists. He probably felt guilty about lying to her, not fulfilling his promises to her, and adding to her worries by not accepting the practical advice he received, knowing his pursuit of art had been a worry to her. Most likely he felt guilty about having been away during her illness. He may have thought that, but for his neglect and the worry he caused her, she might have lived, for such ideas are common in bereaved people.

Another reason for self-imposed poverty was suggested by Gustl and is supported by Adolf's beliefs during later years. He saw the middle class, like his father, as oppressive, taking advantage of the lower class. The poor of the earth were the good people. As an aspiring artist, Adolf had rejected middle-class values. But, like the people he despised, he had lived off others. Now he identified with the homeless. During the next several years, even when he could afford one, Adolf would be a man without a home of his own.

Still another reason for living marginally was to evade the draft. Adolf had passed his twentieth birthday—the draft age. When Gustl had turned twenty, Adolf had advised moving to Germany to escape the draft. People were required to register their addresses with the police. When Adolf became homeless, the authorities no longer knew where to find him.

During the second winter after Gustl was drafted, homeless and lacking warm clothes, Adolf began to seek lodging. At first he went occasionally to free shelters, which limited people to one-night stays, then to the cheapest of the flophouses, where he could remain longer. Observers described conditions in them as appalling. With his sensitivity to lack of privacy, dirt, odors, parasites, and vice, Adolf probably felt his skin crawl. He had no need to exaggerate when he later wrote:

> Even now I shudder when I think of those pitiful dens, the shelters and lodging houses, those sinister pictures of dirt and repugnant filth, and worse still.[4]

Other residents of the shelters found Adolf to be particularly woebegone and helpless. They took him in hand and taught him the rudiments of life on the bottom—where and how to beg, how to earn money by shoveling snow and carrying people's luggage at the railroad station.

Gradually, with the advice of his new acquaintances, with gifts of clothes, and with the passage of time, Adolf began to live better. A sign of emerging from depression was taking up residence in the Männerheim (Men's Home) in February 1910. This was a well-endowed institution, far above the flophouses, with adequate bathing facilities, a dining room, a kitchen for those who preferred to cook for themselves, lounges, a reading room, and a writing room. It was comparable to a modern YMCA residence, except that sleeping quarters were like barracks, lacking privacy. Adolf paid more at the Männerheim than a rented room cost, but he chose to live there until he left Vienna.

Another homeless man, Reinhold Hanisch, on learning about Adolf's artistic talent, took a strong interest in him and became his manager. He persuaded Adolf to write to his Aunt Johanna for money to buy art supplies, which she sent. He helped arrange a work place for Adolf in the Männerheim's reading room and kept after him to stick to his work, for Adolf was always ready to put his brush down and join in political discussions with residents. At first he joined in shyly, but his isolation waned, and he became sociable.

The decorative art he produced—painted postcards, posters, and illustrations used to sell picture frames (Adolf later said he did not regard them as art)—was sold to dealers by Hanisch, who split the receipts with Adolf. The partnership prospered, and Adolf became self-supporting.

He resumed going to the opera and museums and found a new interest—movies. And he began to give political harangues to fellow residents in the reading room. His main theme was liberation of those he considered oppressed Germans—people of German descent in Austria. Their cause became linked for him with the cause of the poor, and he spoke of founding a labor party to advance the struggle.

Adolf also went to cafés for binges of pastries with whipped cream, aggravating the digestive problems that had begun when he lived with Gustl. Then he had subsisted largely on bread and milk, and probably his diet was worse when he was on the street and in the poorest shelters. He evidently got medical advice about the stomach pains he now suffered and rejected it, for he wrote to an acquaintance, ". . . I'm trying now a special diet (fruit and vegetables) to cure myself, as the doctors are all idiots. I find it laughable to speak to me of a nervous complaint, when I am one of the healthiest of people."[5] This self-imposed diet may have marked the beginning of his vegetarianism.

In addition to reading newspapers available in the reading room, Adolf began to buy pamphlets and magazines of the German nationalist movement in Austria, many of which were anti-Semitic. He later wrote in *Mein Kampf* that he became an anti-Semite during his years in Vienna. Gustl reported that Adolf occasionally made anti-Semitic comments before going to Vienna and joined an anti-Semitic society there when nineteen. Gustl was more sensitive to racism than Adolf, and Adolf, already a racist, probably considered his ideas about Jews insignificant before he became a passionate anti-Semite.

Until the nineteenth century, Jews had been forbidden to live in rural Austria, which was almost the whole country. Probably Adolf had never met any before Dr. Bloch and high-school students in the city of Linz. He wrote that he had formed no clear impression of Jews nor heard of anti-Semitism before coming to Vienna.[6]

Adolf and those who knew him never reported he was harmed by a Jew. A possible exception—at least in his own mind—is the story he told of contracting syphilis from a Jewish prostitute in Vienna.[7] For many years, Adolf believed he had the disease, despite assurances to the contrary from doctors. Not counting his father, whom Adolf came to think of as being secretly Jewish, the only Jew he had meaningful contact with in adolescence was Bloch, whom Adolf admired. Rather than being harmed, he was helped by Jews. His generous landlady in Vienna, with whom his relationship was good, was a Jew.

A shelter where he stayed was financed by Jews. Some of the clothes he received when down and out came from Jews, including his overcoat, a gift from Josef Neumann, a fellow resident of the Männerheim. It was a long, dark, caftan-like coat—the type worn by Hasidic Jews. Adolf also wore a black derby and grew a long beard. As a result, he was often taken to be a Jew, and if he minded he did not say so. And Adolf had cordial relations with the Jewish dealers to whom his art objects were sold. Most accounts of him in the Männerheim mention no anti-Semitism, although one reports him saying things that offended Neumann.[8] Probably any anti-Semitism Adolf voiced then was no more than the average and was hardly noted.

Adolf wrote in *Mein Kampf* that his anti-Semitism came not from personal contacts with Jews but from scientifically established convictions that he formed in Vienna. That city, where most of Austria's Jews lived and were moderately accepted in the trades, professions, and arts as well as socially, was nonetheless a center of anti-Semitism. The literature Adolf read there has been amply surveyed.[9] Much of it was mystical, primitive, and bizarre—pseudoscientific at best. Adolf considered it "unworthy" and disreputable when he read it. Vienna's main newspapers, which ignored or opposed anti-Semitism, seemed more dignified and responsible.[10] Nonetheless he continued to read the anti-Semitic literature.

What he read would crop up in his later ideas about Jews, but hardly explains the virulent anti-Semitism he would show. A minority of Viennese found the anti-Semitic literature interesting; fewer still were persuaded by it. The key question is, what was it in Adolf that drew him to that literature?

Two parallels add to the picture. Except for his father—and the exception is an important one—Adolf is not known to have been harmed by a Catholic. He found enough of value in the Catholic school he attended to decide he would become a monk. Later, when down and out in Vienna, before living in the Männerheim, he was given refuge in a Catholic shelter and got most of his meals at Catholic soup kitchens. Nonetheless Adolf came to hate Catholicism. When in power, he would put Catholic priests in concentration camps and plan to destroy the Church.

Similarly, there is no report of Adolf having been harmed by a Czech. The best friend he ever had, Gustl, had Czech ancestry, and Adolf was treated graciously by Gustl's parents. Yet he became so anti-Czech as to plan the extermination of Czechoslovakia.

What did being Jewish, Catholic, and Czech have in common for Adolf? Religion and ethnicity are the most external features of identity, except for gender. When a child asks another, "What are you?" the usual answer is one's religion or ethnic group. For Adolf, being Jewish, Catholic, and Czech, as well as Austrian, were features of his identity—the identity he loathed. As he tried to overcome his self-hatred, he began to disown features of his identity and focus his loathing on groups he associated with those features. In adolescence, he came to hate Czechs, the middle class, and people who represented Austria to him—the royal family and the government. Later he would come to hate Jews and Catholics.

Vienna, with its cultural riches, had beckoned as the ideal place to develop his talent. Now he hated it along with the rest of Austria and decided to move to the German city of

Munich, known for its artists and Bohemian life. But he feared that a move would alert the police to his draft evasion and that he would be arrested. He apparently believed mistakenly that if he could evade the draft until he turned twenty-four, he would be free to leave. The last two years of his stay in Vienna were an anxious wait.[11]

Finally, thinking he had permanently escaped the Austrian draft, Adolf moved to Munich in May 1913. He rented a room and resumed painting and selling his work. A stranger, he had to find buyers for his decorative art on his own, and managed to do so. He also did serious painting and sold some to art dealers. And he thought again about applying to an art school.

Suddenly, in January 1914, the Austrian police tracked him to Munich. At their request, the Munich police arrested Adolf and turned him over to the Austrian government. In an effort to avoid the prosecution he now expected, Adolf sent a statement to the court in Linz that had jurisdiction over his case. To explain not registering and letting the matter slide for years, he invoked ignorance and dwelt page after page on his impoverished, desperate circumstances. Summarizing, he said:

> As far as my sin of omission in the autumn of 1909 is concerned, this was a terribly bitter time for me. I was an inexperienced young man, without any financial aid and also too proud to accept any from anyone . . . For two years I had no other friend but care and need [and] eternally gnawing hunger. I never knew the beautiful word youth. Today, even after five years . . . I have chilblain sores on my fingers, hands and feet. And yet I . . . have always preserved my name unsullied, am altogether blameless before the law, and pure before my own conscience . . .[12]

And he ended with a plea for indulgence.

Among many lies, his main one was that he had not meant to evade the draft. His basic argument was that he was a victim, not a perpetrator. His illogic was that poverty, homelessness, cold, and hunger excused his failure to register. On the contrary, joining the army would have relieved all those problems. It was a child's defense, although used by many adults: I didn't mean it; I couldn't help it; pity me and go easy on me. It foreshadowed the deception, the claim of being a victim, and the self-praise that would mark his oratory when he entered politics.

The Linz court accepted his explanation and brought no charges, simply ordering him to report for a preinduction medical exam. To Adolf's good fortune, he failed it, being found "too weak" to bear arms. Since he was in good health afterward, he may have been rejected for being thin, frail-looking, and run-down from several years of malnutrition. In any case he returned to Munich, at last truly free.

But old problems remained. Adolf, now twenty-five, was still making no progress toward getting into a school nor would he consider a regular job. As far as is known, he had no erotic or romantic involvements and no serious thoughts of settling down. Rather, from what he told friends of later years, he had begun to think conventional family life was beyond his reach. He commented about a loving couple in their home, "I have never

From: Diane Goddard

Message

Tuesday, February 15, 2000 9:22:06 AM

Subject: Big Brother

To: Pam Pinkoski

Hi Pam,

I never can find Eddie on the directory but please give him this mesage.

Eddie,

Reports from Dottie Rumpf are very positive. She tells me your have been very reliable and the little brother enjoys having you come and work with him. I appreciate the volunteering you are doing.

Diane Goddard

had such a home and I will never have one."[13] Convinced he had syphilis, he thought he would never be normal again or of any use to a woman. Whatever symptoms he thought he had are unknown. Perhaps he attributed the impotence that plagued him the rest of his life to syphilis, although it is not a symptom of the disease.

Adolf continued to follow politics avidly. He was well informed on the strains in the Austro-Hungarian Empire that led to World War I. Perhaps he foresaw the role Germany would take in encouraging military action by Austria-Hungary, or perhaps it was only his wish that Germany take a decisive role. By moving to Munich, Adolf had thrown in his lot with Germany.

Having become a nation only forty-three years before, Germany was Europe's newest power. Prosperous, a leader in education, science, philosophy, and the arts, it had a strong spirit of growth. But it also had a sense of inferiority compared to its neighbors. Austria-Hungary, Russia, France, and Great Britain had vast empires. Spain had lost most of its empire in the nineteenth century but still had colonies. Turkey's declining empire was still substantial. Even tiny Belgium, Holland, and Portugal were ahead of Germany in the scramble for colonies in underdeveloped regions. To those who saw greatness in conquest and empire, Germany was woefully behind, but it was on the move.

Adolf was one of them and believed Germany would soon start a war to expand its borders in Europe and win overseas colonies from other powers. Blocked in his own life, he believed he would find a cause and the means to take effective action—even heroic action—in Germany's rise. He waited eagerly for war.

That August, as World War I began, Adolf was eloquent in his joy:

> To me myself those hours came as a release from the vexing feelings of my youth . . . overpowered by stormy enthusiasm, I sank down to my knees and thanked Heaven from an overflowing heart . . .[14]

He had found his cause and the opportunity to break out of his inertia and the fantasy world in which he had lived for ten years. "By contrast to the events of this enormous struggle, everything past fell back into shallow nothingness." He suggested, "The overwhelming majority of the nation had already long been weary of the eternally uncertain state of affairs . . ."[15]

> A fight for freedom had broken out, than which the earth had seen no more powerful one until now . . . dealing not with Serbia's or even Austria's fate, but with the existence or nonexistence of the German nation.[16]

The uncertain state of affairs was his own. Would he break out of his inhibitions and become a real person with an impact on others, or remain trapped in the nothingness of fantasy? Germany's existence was not threatened; it was his own that was at stake.

CHAPTER 6

THE CALL

War is eternal, war is universal. There is no beginning and there is no peace. War is life . . . War is the origin of all things.[1]

—Adolf Hitler, 1932

Throughout history, wars were fought with enthusiasm or regret to advance interests—to defend a nation, to liberate it, to settle disputes, to maintain a balance of power, or to conquer. At the beginning of the twentieth century, many people still considered war a noble activity typified by self-sacrifice and heroism, in contrast to the cunning and greed associated with peace. But even among people who revered war, few saw it as desirable in itself. Hitler was one of the few, and to him war was more important than liberation, conquest, or even national survival. Under his leadership traditional thinking was reversed. People's existence and even the nation's existence were subordinated to war—a priority made clear in training given children and adults in the Third Reich:

> Every human and social activity is justified only if it helps prepare for war. The new human being is completely possessed by the thought of war. He must not, cannot think of anything else.[2]

War gave Hitler the opportunity to solve his personal problems, and he saw it as the solution to all of Germany's.

Art and architecture, although strong interests, were not going to bring him satisfaction. As blows to his self-esteem accumulated and his hate grew, he needed greatness and he felt impelled to destroy more than to create. The war was his call; it enabled him to direct his hatred outward, and he hoped it would enable him to become a hero. His combat experiences contributed to his growing belief that warfare was the most vital and noble of human activities and that its key feature was destruction. Destruction was redemptive. Such thinking was not strange to Germans, among whom the cult of death was especially popular. It was a feature of German Romanticism that made the nation receptive to his ideas when he entered politics.[3]

The development of Adolf's thinking is suggested by the heroes he took for role models. The first was a cowboy, who fought in self-defense, then Paul Kruger, the Boer who led his people's fight for independence, and Frederick the Great, known for his military success against superior forces. His final hero was Genghis Khan, known as the most destructive conqueror in history.

As the word "hero" is commonly used—an admirable person who saves the day—Adolf was not one. But common usage is incomplete and misleading about the traditional, mystical role of the hero—a role that attracted Adolf powerfully, giving him a framework for expressing his rage and offering him a new identity.

The hero of myth and history was more a destroyer than a creator. His destructiveness was accepted by his people as necessary to change the existing order, for the concept arose in a time when a community's misfortune was believed to result from the displeasure of its god. The remedy to misfortune was appeasing the god by destroying the people and practices that had given offense. That typically meant destroying the established authority and the existing order. The hero had to be an uninhibited person, a violator of taboos.

Although beliefs about the causes of misfortune became less religious and more scientific over the millennia, the idea of the hero's role persisted. Hegel, Germany's leading philosopher in the early nineteenth century, said the hero's acts, *no matter how destructive,* were the expression of a divine or historical imperative. Adolf believed it and so did Germans who accepted his message in the 1930s that Germany could be saved only through destruction.

To Adolf, something of a national misfortune had already occurred by 1914. Germany not only tolerated dangerous enemies around it (France, Britain, and Russia), but also harbored them within (foreign influences, Slavs, Social Democrats, the bourgeoisie, capitalists, pimps, and other degenerates). The war against external enemies would somehow also provide the opportunity to eliminate the internal ones. Adolf embraced his soldier's role as a mystical mission. In a letter from the front, he expressed the hope that, if he survived the war, he would return to a Germany that was "a purer place, less riddled with foreign influences"—an interesting statement since he was a foreigner himself.[4] This was a vague idea; how the purification of Germany would be achieved he did not yet know.

Germany's quick, sweeping victories brought him joy mixed with disappointment, for he feared the war would be over before he got into it. After two months of training, his regiment was sent to Belgium and into its first battle at Ypres. Compared to prior wars, World War I was extremely destructive, and the battle of Ypres was one of the bloodiest. But the losses suffered by his regiment and its failure to capture Ypres did not dismay Adolf. On the contrary, as he wrote to a friend, he was happy:

> . . . I can proudly say we fought like heroes. On the very first day we lost nearly all our officers . . . On the fourth day our regiment had been reduced from 3,600 to 611 men. For all that, we beat the English.[5]

His report of the casualties, like much that he wrote, was exaggerated; the more lost, the better. He rejoiced in the general destruction, and it made little difference to him who was killed—officers or men in the ranks; French, English, or Germans. His wish was for more:

> Heavy fire continues from 5 a.m. to 5 p.m. Our daily losses are often relatively severe . . . The strain is tremendous. Unfortunately the English have stopped attacking.[6]

Casualties were greatest in units on the attack, yet Adolf wrote about his eagerness for an order to charge, ". . . the fun is about to start," and when the order came, "At last! All of us rejoiced . . . the fun started in earnest."[7]

His officers represented the established order, and their deaths could be a step toward redemption. The decimation of his regiment also had a more personal value. To live while his comrades were killed made him special, exalted. With each battle he survived, his belief grew that he was protected by Fate, that he was being saved for a greater role to come. As he had sensed, in war he found a new life.

His four years of war service—mostly spent in France—were the best of Adolf's adult life in many ways. Participating in Germany's cause raised his spirits. He was free of pressure to get a job, of worry about career choices, and of conflict between desires and inhibitions. He had no contact with women, and the war made his destructive ideas legitimate. He was freer of psychosomatic symptoms than before and than he would ever be again. He was diligent in his duties and regular in his habits, without the procrastination and rebelliousness that had interfered with his work for fifteen years and would again afterward.

Before, Adolf had been able to mobilize his energy when his mother was dying. For many guilt-ridden people, acting in behalf of others works better than advancing their own interests. His devotion to Germany's cause was like his devotion to his dying mother and more effective, for it was a grand opportunity to express his rage. While satisfying his own wishes, he fully believed he was acting for Germany, and that helped liberate him.

After the battle of Ypres, Adolf was awarded the Iron Cross. "It was the happiest day of my life," he wrote a friend.[8] He was also promoted to *Gefreiter*. (This has been translated as corporal, but was only one step above *Gemeiner*—private—and corresponds to the United States Army rank of private, first class.) He was also given the dangerous assignment of runner (dispatch carrier), which he held for the rest of the war. Combat troops under rifle fire or bombardment could take cover, except when ordered to charge. Runners, when given dispatches, usually could not. Dispatches were crucial to the direction of armies and had to be carried without delay.

The assignment of runner may have suited Adolf because of his inhibition about killing—a lifelong inhibition that seems to have emerged during the war. In his letters home, he reveled in the slaughter of which he was a part, without mentioning that he himself inflicted harm on anyone. The enemy casualties he boasted of were inflicted by "we"—his regiment. Despite his habits of exaggeration and self-inflation, despite being in fifty battles, he took no personal credit for any killing.

Later, when leader of the Nazi Party, Adolf would order his Storm Troopers to engage in street warfare, while remaining inhibited about participating in the violence himself—an inability he would blame on his middle-class morality. Still later, he would order millions killed, while never killing with his own hand. Given this inhibition, combined with his willingness to risk death, his assignment as a runner was ideal for him.

Although extremely high casualties resulted in a shortage of leaders, Adolf was not promoted further. This was due to no lack of bravery, but to what his officers considered a deficiency in leadership qualities—an interesting irony. A further promotion would have put him in charge of others. No basis for the evaluation has survived, although his captain reportedly said, "I'll never make that hysterical fellow an officer."[9]

Probably the officers' judgment reflected Adolf's fanaticism and eccentricity. Mostly he kept to himself. During lulls between battles he took scrupulous care of his equipment and he read, sketched, and painted. Rarely did he get letters or packages from home. Among the bachelors he was exceptional in showing no interest in women or in talk about them. Members of his regiment called him a woman hater; some thought he was homosexual. As at the Männerheim, his main social interaction was in political discussions. And as the war dragged on and morale declined, fellow soldiers found his superpatriotism and ardor for the war irritating. "We all cursed him. We found him intolerable. He was a white crow among us who wouldn't go along with us when we damned the war to hell and prayed for its speedy end."[10]

Some of Adolf's fellow soldiers did admire him, however. A few later joined him in the Nazi Party.

Four years of stress with seemingly endless trench warfare, an enormous casualty rate in his regiment, which was often replenished, and being wounded twice—nothing dampened Adolf's enthusiasm for the war. It was the war's end that demoralized him. Germany's surrender—sudden, totally unexpected, and uncalled for, as he saw it—was the worst blow of his life. Neither his mother's death nor rejection by the Academy had caused as quick or severe a breakdown as did Germany's collapse.

To understand his reaction, which would later become a main point in his appeal as a politician, events leading to Germany's collapse are important. As the war began, German armies swept into Belgium, France, and Russia. Within a month they reached Paris, and the French government fled to Bordeaux. Nonetheless, the French, heavily reinforced by British armies, pushed back and then held a line that hardly moved over the next four years. In Russia a vast area was conquered, but at a heavy cost. Most of Germany's casualties were on the eastern front, and Russia's were even higher. After the Russian revolution, the new Soviet government abruptly sued for peace, giving up the lost territory and a population that doubled Germany's. Victory there freed a million German soldiers for the western front. Expecting to break the stalemate, Germany launched a major offensive that made France's situation precarious again. Then Allied forces pushed back once more, restoring the stalemate.

The war took an enormous toll. Germany had six million army casualties—nearly two million killed, more than any other nation. Blockaded by the Allies, its equipment and supplies were nearly exhausted. Public enthusiasm for the war had been replaced by massive dissatisfaction, and revolt was brewing. In July 1917, the Reichstag passed a resolution calling for an end to the war, and Germany's allies were weakening and surrendering—Bulgaria in September 1918, Turkey in October, and Austria-Hungary in November.

Germany had no fresh resources, but American troops and equipment were pouring into France. Kaiser Wilhelm II and his generals conferred about suing for peace. They decided on one last offensive, centered on the French city of Rheims, to decide the war. The Allied commander-in-chief also concluded this battle would be decisive. The offensive failed, and Wilhelm abdicated, leaving Germany's parliamentary leaders with the onus of surrendering.

At the front, Adolf knew little about political changes in Germany and was content with the progress of the war. He knew of the victory over Russia, had confidence in the superiority of the German armies, and expected France to fall also. He believed Germany was winning.

Shortly before the end, Adolf was wounded for the second time, on this occasion by mustard gas. Among the effects was temporary blindness, and he was sent to a hospital, where he recovered over the next few weeks. He was almost well when, in November, a chaplain brought the hospitalized soldiers news of the war's end. Units of the German army and navy had mutinied and coastal areas were in their hands. Local Socialist coups and revolts had resulted in autonomous governments scattered through Germany. The chancellor had resigned, a republic had been declared—the Weimar Republic—and the new government had surrendered to the Allies. As Adolf later described it, he experienced "the greatest villainy of the century" and he wept for the first time since his mother's death. The news hit him as a personal betrayal, snatching away the new life he had found. He fell immediately into a severe depression and became blind again and this time briefly mute as well.[11] His doctors called in a psychiatrist to treat him.

Adolf emerged from his despair by directing his rage outward again, but in a more paranoid way. He developed a delusional idea, shared by so many Germans similarly shocked that it would not be classified as a clinical delusion: on the verge of Germany's success, a conspiracy had sold out the country, turning victory into defeat. The brave soldiers had been betrayed. The conspirators—who besides Socialist politicians included capitalists and bankers—had tricked the kaiser and his generals and manipulated the Reichstag into surrendering. And Germany was now in the grip of the conspirators— "the November criminals" Adolf would later call them.

Adolf then extended the explanation in a way few people shared. He concluded that the conspirators were bent on destroying Germany and that they were impostors. They appeared to be Germans, but in reality were Jews. To Adolf, such an explanation needed no basis in fact; it made sense intuitively because of his own family history. His grandmother had been ruined by a secret Jew and his mother by a half-Jew who called himself a Catholic. Now secret Jews were everywhere, ruining Germany.

For the conspiracy theory to hold together, Adolf had to account for joint action by very different groups—German socialists and capitalists and the governments of France, Belgium, Great Britain, Italy, and the United States. He concluded Jews held the groups together—all of them consisted of or were directed by secret Jews. The idea would become clearer to him a few years later when his Nazi associate Alfred Rosenberg would tell him about an international Jewish conspiracy with headquarters in Moscow that controlled governments and was bent on ruling the world. Then Adolf would understand fully how different German groups could be working in concert with foreign powers to destroy Germany.

While blind, Adolf experienced a vision: a messenger from God told him his sight would be restored so that he could liberate Germany. The morning after the vision, his sight returned and his depression lifted. He then dedicated himself to a political career and to fulfilling the mission given him. Again the call had come.

In the months that followed, as the vividness of his experience faded, Adolf became less clear about what had happened. Having lost most of his religion in adolescence, miracles were not the sort of thing he believed. The vision was the result of his breakdown. Over the next few years, he told some people the story of the miracle but, by the time he wrote *Mein Kampf,* he passed over the recovery of his sight as if it were part of his physical recovery and did not mention his muteness.

The inspiration, like his earlier inspiration after seeing *Rienzi,* was short-lived, for he felt incapable of being effective: "As a nameless person I did not possess the minimum credentials to start any meaningful action . . ."[12] Presumably, by "nameless" he meant that he lacked prominence; the word may also have reflected his alienation.

Adolf's experience in the army told him war and destruction were vital, and he badly wanted another war. But with none in prospect, he returned to thoughts of art and architecture, although he did not pursue them. He waited. The Versailles Treaty limited Germany's army to one hundred thousand, and the government was discharging soldiers in large numbers. Adolf needed something to do, and the end of his wait came unexpectedly.

The army assigned Adolf to give political orientation to soldiers and to gather intelligence on revolutionary groups. Germany was in a state of chaos, with political groups sprouting throughout the country—fifty in Munich alone, where Adolf was stationed. The army, responsible for preventing anarchy, needed soldiers with political awareness and set up training classes. Adolf was made an instructor, and his political lectures went well. This was his first recognition as a speaker and, because of its special need, the army kept him on.

In September 1919, the army sent Adolf to observe and report on a local group. The German Workers Party, a tiny organization with an executive committee of six and a handful of adherents, functioned only as a discussion group, but its aim was revolution. Adolf attended a public meeting held by the Party. Moved to vehement disagreement with a statement by a member of the audience, Adolf departed from his role as observer and gave a lengthy rebuttal. Impressed, the leaders asked him to join the Party, to join its executive committee, and then to be its featured speaker. Adolf accepted, and his political career was launched.

The German Workers Party was nationalistic, socialistic, and anti-Semitic, which suited Adolf, but so also were other parties. Why did he choose this one? The answer he gave in *Mein Kampf* seems apt. Because it was new, tiny, and "not yet hardened into an 'organization,' [it] seemed to offer to the individual the chance for real personal activity."[13] The Party actually lacked effective leadership, had little ideology or structure, and had no program. Adolf was not prepared to join a well-established party and accept its ideas, its ways, and its discipline while he worked his way up to leadership. Noting how much "easier it would be to bring the [German Workers Party] into the right shape," he saw a group hungry for what he had to offer.[14] He saw the possibility of quickly becoming its leader.

As a public speaker, he was an instant sensation, for "the hate and pain that sounded in Hitler's oratory . . . its shrill pitch and brutal inflections" gave him greater power than before.[15] His breakdown had freed some of his impulses and his oratory resonated with belligerence and wildness, fitting the Party and the people it drew to meetings. And he did not have to hold back on his extreme ideas, as he did when lecturing for the army.

The Party, which had not grown since its founding the year before, suddenly came alive. It grew rapidly, expanding beyond Munich, adopting a program, and changing its name to the National Socialist German Workers Party. Informally, members called it the Nazi Party, from a contraction of *Nationalsozialistische*.

As the Party's chief speaker, Adolf was given an income. Since the Party was revolutionary, his new role put him in a position of conflict with the army. He left the army and devoted himself completely to the Party.

Members of the executive committee held various views; the Party was truly far from hardened. While Adolf's leadership was welcome, other leaders did not always agree with him. In 1921, Adolf demanded dictatorial power and, to force the issue, he resigned. Faced with the loss of their only source of growth, the others yielded. Within two weeks, he was asked to come back as *Führer*—absolute leader.

Over the next two years, the Nazi Party continued to grow, mostly in and around Munich. In 1923, Adolf judged the time ripe for taking over the state of Bavaria, of which Munich was the capital. He organized a coup in which armed Nazis marched on government buildings in Munich, but led it poorly. During the hours before the march, he was impulsive and indecisive, switching plans a few times and letting others direct it. The march was easily suppressed, and Adolf was arrested. But he was able to turn defeat into victory by using his trial to magnify himself and his "crusade" and attack Germany's "traitors." At his pretrial interrogation, he invoked his divine mission in justifying the coup—apparently the last time he spoke of his vision as real.[16] On trial, he declared that he did not recognize the authority of the court but only of God—that he was above the law. Convicted and imprisoned, he was nearly expelled from the country as an undesirable alien. While living in Germany and devoted to its cause for ten years, he had not applied for citizenship. Legally he was still an Austrian.

At thirty-five, serving a year's sentence, Adolf took stock of his life and the political situation and wrote his autobiography and manifesto. He called it *Four and One Half Years of Battle Against Lies, Stupidity and Cowardice,* but his editor changed the title to *My Battle (Mein Kampf).* Adolf elaborated his theory of a conspiracy behind Germany's surrender and a secret Jewish plot to destroy Germany and rule the world. These ideas were shared by some Germans, but his personal vision of a message from God was not, and he omitted it. Perhaps he had gotten a negative reaction to telling it and probably he had heard that psychiatrists were talking about his hallucination and psychosomatic blindness—that he was being used as an example of hysteria in lectures to medical students.[17] He became discreet about whom he told, eventually accepting the idea that his blindness had been hysterical. In a 1942 speech to army officers, he said, if what was to be seen was the nation enslaved, "In that case what can I see worth seeing?" At the end of 1944, facing defeat in World War II, he told a friend he feared going blind again as he had in 1918.[18]

Adolf had come out of his depression. His powerful position and real mission as leader of the Nazi Party greatly boosted his self-esteem. Perhaps that was enough for him, and he no longer needed to believe he had received a Joan-of-Arc-like message and mission. When he came to write *Mein Kampf,* it would have been counterproductive to explain his beliefs and crusade on the basis of a hallucination. He found a better explanation in the anti-Semitic literature he had read in Vienna and in the "research" he had done later—personal observations he now elevated to a scientific level.

Adolf's failure in leading the coup—particularly his inability to lead when violence developed—may have been in his mind, as he revised his and the Nazi Party's strategy for the future. After getting out of prison in 1924, he steered a less violent course for the Party, relying mainly on persuasion and the ballot to win power. And he absented himself from Nazi violence, delegating it to others.

At thirty-five, his formative experiences were complete, his personality set, his career launched, and his political plans made. His personal life was still a severe problem for him, but he relegated it to the background and devoted himself to politics.

CHAPTER 7

THE MAN

> You should know first of all that you will never be able to discover my thoughts and intentions until I give them out as orders . . . You will never learn what is going on in my head. As for those who boast of being privy to my thoughts—to them I lie all the more.[1]

> —Adolf Hitler, 1938

Like most German political leaders, Hitler proposed to undo the Versailles Treaty, restore Germany's dignity and power, and raise its economy. His unique and fateful offer was war, redemption, and elimination of the Jews. Although frequently repeated, the offer was not seen clearly by millions of Germans. Because of his deceptiveness and intense conflicts, Hitler contradicted himself so often that people were unsure of his intentions. They put their fate in the hands of a man known to be at least somewhat bizarre and dangerous without understanding him, inviting catastrophe. The Soviet Union was gravely harmed by Premier Joseph Stalin's paranoid destructiveness, but no country was so ruled by the personal demons of its leader as the Third Reich. Hitler's pathology disturbed the whole spectrum of German life.

Even associates did not know him well. After the end of his relationship with Gustl, no one was close to him. His foreign minister, Joachim von Ribbentrop, would later say:

> I don't think anybody ever really had a heart-to-heart talk with him as man to man. Not a single one . . . I don't think he ever really bared his heart to anyone.[2]

Instead, Hitler worked at throwing his subordinates off, keeping them guessing, as he said above to his army chief of staff. He succeeded so well in baffling people that, even after knowing the worst, von Ribbentrop would say:

> I cannot understand it. He was a vegetarian, you know.—He could not bear to eat a dead animal and he called us *Leichenfresser* [corpse eaters]. I even had to go hunting secretly because he disapproved of it. Now how could a man like that order mass murder?[3]

Hitler boasted about the killing he ordered, but also said:

> I find it insufferable when a car drives through puddles, splashing people along

the road. It is especially mean when it splashes peasants in their Sunday best! When I catch up with bicyclists, I drive at high speed only when I see that the wind has blown away the dust . . . I wouldn't want to see anyone suffering or hurt anyone . . .[4]

In the 1940s, people's mental problems were so often explained by inner conflict that the phrase became a cliché. Nonetheless, Hitler is well described as conflict-ridden. He was full of rage and wanted to become the most destructive person in history but did not tolerate seeing animals harmed (although he did occasionally thrash his dog). He watched with interest films in which men were beaten and killed but, when they showed animals being injured, he wept or covered his eyes until the scenes ended. He did not weep when his friends died but did when his canary died. For years he abstained from romantic and sexual involvement, yet was obsessed with sex. His political speeches exuded it and *Mein Kampf* contains extended digressions on sex and related topics—syphilis and prostitution—as well as being filled with veiled sexual images, especially masochistic ones.[5] These and other contradictions were a riddle his followers could not solve.

Hitler's complexion was pale and his hair dark brown. He was unhappy with his prominent nose and grew a moustache to minimize it. He used spectacles for reading, but refused to be seen in public or photographed wearing them. His shame and fear of ridicule were focused in his body. The freedom with nature and nakedness that Gustl noted was gone. Hitler advocated nudism, but hid his body, unwilling to be seen in a swim suit and cautious about being touched.

People found his blue, penetrating eyes his most expressive and arresting feature. They stood out because of the shape of his head and because he stared much of the time, out of curiosity, excitement, and aggressiveness. Curious staring is common in people who believe their lives were shaped by mysterious events—in his case probably the secret of his grandfather. His excitement partly reflected his suppressed sexuality. He enjoyed looking at women in social settings and, when chancellor, arranged to look at them naked while he remained clothed. And he had the government scrutinize the private lives of its citizens—particularly their sexual activities.

Probably the most important factor in his stare was his sense of human contact as competitive and hostile. On being asked how he would greet the Soviet ambassador, he said, "It's very simple. I look him straight in the eyes until he loses his composure."[6] He boasted that he could stare down anyone. Besides dominating people, his stare may have served to keep them from staring at him and adding to his embarrassment.

Hitler had a narrow frame and was not muscular. His height was a puzzle. Observers said he was short—a reporter on seeing him for the first time said, "short, very short, little"—and the impression stuck, although his height was average.[7] Estimates ranged from 5' 5" to 5' 9"—the latter figure confirmed by his physicians.

In adolescence, Hitler had begun to emphasize his words by studied gestures. In middle age, he added a vocabulary of aggressive words. "Brutal" was his favorite, and he used it to describe himself, the Nazi Party, and Aryans. His speeches, writing, and casual conversation were filled with powerful words—positively, absolutely, precisely, undoubtedly, certain, inevitable, and irrevocable. But at times he spoke in a syrupy way.

His body language also displayed sharp contrasts. His expression was serious, often threatening. Much of the time he carried a whip, snapping it in the air or striking it against his palm or leg. His hand and arm gestures were sometimes imperious but at other times limp-wristed, conveying both machismo and softness. His walk was sometimes a martial strut but at other times a mincing step. He was generally sentimental and easily became overwrought. During crises in the Nazi Party, he made sobbing appeals for support. But he could also be so distant about the effects of his actions as to give the impression of extreme coldness. He had tantrums over inconveniences but often took major defeats with remarkable calm.

He avoided all sports. According to an associate he was unwilling to try activities in which he could not be best.[8] Other reasons may have been his apprehension of contact and perspiring. A friend advised massage for the physical symptoms that plagued him, "But Hitler had a horror of any physical contact and the very word 'massage' upset him."[9] Perhaps for the same reason, he hated dancing and avoided it. He became especially concerned about offending with perspiration and gas, and relied on frequent bathing, changes of clothes, pills, and a largely vegetable diet to limit them.

Hitler's vegetarian ideas apparently began in adolescence with reading Richard Wagner and became stricter when he was forty-two, after the violent death of his beloved niece, Geli Raubal. The next time he was served a piece of meat, he said, "It is like eating a corpse," and ever afterward found it repulsive.[10] It seems to have reminded him of her body—not a rare reaction in people whose loved ones die violently. Meat blended into sausage was more acceptable to him.

During adolescence, he had reduced the amount he ate, perhaps with the idea that an artist should be ascetic. On entering politics, he felt a leader of the people should be ascetic. Except for binges of sweets, he continued to eat limited amounts of simple foods and to wear plain clothes. After establishing the Storm Troopers, the combat unit of the Nazi Party, he wore their plain uniform. Despite his growing prominence and means, for a time he lived simply in a poor apartment. Even when chancellor, he slept in a simple camp bed.

After leaving prison, Hitler became wealthy from his Party income, royalties from *Mein Kampf,* and lavish gifts. At first he limited his luxuries to a couple of paintings and to expensive cars, of which he acquired many along with a chauffeur, for he hardly drove. Otherwise, he continued to live plainly, until the Nazi Party became a power and he began to deal with nationally prominent Germans and foreign representatives. Then, he adopted a lavish lifestyle and ordered construction of the largest buildings in the world—monuments to his power. But during the latter part of World War II, he considered luxury inappropriate and lived again simply in bunkers.

Hitler became a supersuccessful public figure, able quickly to charm individuals and large audiences and to deal effectively with heads of state. As an orator, he bared his feelings; otherwise, he remained an extremely private person—awkward, easily embarrassed, painfully self-conscious, and basically isolated. Julius Streicher and Albert Speer, who wanted to be his friends, said he had none. Once Hitler said dogs were his only friends. In later years, his birthdays would be occasions for parties but, during his thirties, he spent birthdays and holidays alone and sad, eating sweets.

He never mastered conversation. In groups he was usually silent or lectured others, sometimes interminably. In formal settings he was stiff, with studied words and gestures. Frequently his movements were an awkward mix of embarrassment and defiance. In casual contacts with women, he flirted in the old-fashioned Viennese style—bowing, kissing their hands, and flattering them. His ideas about women were also old-fashioned— their place was in the home, bearing children, not competing with men. He said, "A woman must be a cute, cuddly, naive little thing—tender, sweet and stupid."[11] As chancellor, he discouraged women from working outside the home.

In personal relationships, he avoided women of his own age. With older ones, he played the boy, eliciting maternal responses. As he began to pursue romantic and erotic involvements in his late thirties, he favored very young women and adolescents. To impress them, he put on macho displays, snapping his whip, holding his arm up in a salute, boasting he could hold it up longer than anyone else. To impress a sixteen-year-old who strongly attracted him, he thrashed his dog. In intimate settings with women, he talked about war and torture.

Added to his problem with intimacy was his eccentricity. Nonconforming ways create social tension, and nonparticipation in conventional activities may inhibit others from enjoying them. As a result, eccentric people feel called on to manage the tension, freeing others to indulge themselves and countering suspicions about their character that deviance raises. For example, when offered a drink, nondrinkers might put others at ease by responding humorously, "No, thanks. I don't drink, but I do smoke and like sex." Hitler was unconventional and abstemious in many ways and, perhaps for this reason, devoted himself to managing social situations, becoming highly controlling. To counter suspicions of softness raised by abstention, he exaggerated his hardness and brutality.

Hitler was well aware of his eccentricity, seeing himself as a superman but also as a monster. He said he was unique, claiming to be the greatest figure of all time, but feared being embarrassed. Before committing suicide, he ordered his body burned, saying he would not let the Russians exhibit him in a freak show. The idea of being exhibited as a freak had no basis in Soviet intentions; on the contrary, Soviet leaders meant to obliterate traces of his existence to prevent future idolatry of him. His final act was the most dramatic in a lifetime struggle to control situations so that he would not be embarrassed.

Concern with their own eccentricities leads people to focus on others' deviance. The idea is that if attention can be drawn to others' peculiarities, one's own may escape notice. Hitler was extreme in drawing attention to others' peculiarities, making fun of his associates' appearance and habits and bringing the subject of Jews and their alleged deviance into most conversations.

Some friends said he was most comfortable with uneducated people of the lower class, especially those with handicaps or disadvantages. They said, because of concern about his height, he surrounded himself with short men, and he preferred homosexuals and men with physical defects. Among his closest associates were well-known homosexuals, including Ernst Röhm and Heinrich Hoffmann. He also valued homosexuals as making the best Nazis, explaining:

> My most enthusiastic followers must not be married men with wives and children. No one with family responsibilities is any good for streetfighting.[12]

And he put known homosexuals in charge of the Hitler Youth, which led to scandals.[13] Responding to questions and complaints about homosexual associates, he said their private lives were no concern of his as long as they were good Nazis.

Reversing himself when in power, he denounced homosexuals among his Storm Troopers and had many killed. Later he had many more homosexuals put in concentration camps and killed.

Some associates said he was homosexual and named his partners, but their information was based on impressions or was secondhand and has not been confirmed. He did, however, have habits considered effeminate—besides his mincing step and limp-wristed gestures, a tender way of touching his chest and cupping his hands around his face, and his easily aroused weeping. His exaggerated machismo countered the impression of these mannerisms, and most Germans thought of him as entirely heterosexual. But there is enough to suggest a kinship with homosexuals and that in destroying them he was effacing part of himself.

He also surrounded himself with sadists including Joseph Goebbels, Hermann Göring, and Streicher, and in general his Storm Troopers and SS men were sadistic. His sadism and theirs contributed to the brutalization of life in the Third Reich. Also important in its effects on Germany was Hitler's masochism, which is discussed later.

Hitler had a great many fears. He dealt with some by avoiding situations and with others by elaborate precautions and rituals. He was an insomniac with a fear of the dark. When his position afforded him the luxury, he kept people up with him almost till dawn for company. One played music for him, others watched movies with him and talked or more often listened to him. At last, feeling ready to retire, he feared harm from something unknown that might have been put in his bed. His maid, when he had one, was required each night to remake his bed as he watched. Occasionally he was in terror of ghosts. He was afraid to eat gifts of pastry from friends, thinking they might be poisoned. And until his hands became very shaky toward the end of World War II, he always shaved himself, saying he could not bear to have someone with a razor close to his throat.

Hitler was a pronounced hypochondriac. He feared he had syphilis—that it had caused his blood to be diseased and would lead to paralysis—and heart disease. The gas pains that plagued him he took as a sign of cancer. He was also troubled by symptoms he eventually accepted as psychosomatic—headaches, dizziness, eczema, and impotence.

After his failed coup of 1923, he developed tremors and paralysis in his arm and leg, which recurred at later times of high stress. Although he took his fears of grave illness seriously and at times was obsessed with them, he rarely let his doctors examine him unclothed or X-ray him.

Despite, or because of, his procrastination, Hitler had a dread of time passing. He fought time as an enemy, expecting to lose, to die before achieving his goals. He did not wear a watch, but devoted himself to beating time, as by racing when dressing, trying every day to do it faster.

Insomnia, procrastination, dread of time passing, reduced eating, bingeing on sweets, and self-loathing were manifestations of the depression that afflicted him throuhout his life but was not always apparent. More obvious was his suicidal inclination. He had considered killing himself on losing Stefanie and nearly did so after the failed coup in 1923. From his thirties on, suicide was rarely far from his mind, and his courting of military disaster was indirectly suicidal. At the heart of his fears and depression was the idea that he was unworthy to live. He lied about his origins and failures, telling some of his generals that he had been an officer in the war,[14] and denied his poor self-esteem vehemently:

> Only an insane person could say I have an inferiority complex . . . They are absolutely crazy. I have never had an inferiority complex![15]

But his self-esteem was so fragile that he hardly tolerated being corrected and rarely admitted a mistake, even when obvious. He was a balloon that needed constant pumping and was vulnerable to every pin. Once he whistled a tune and Eva Braun said he got it wrong. They argued and, to settle the point, an aide fetched and played a record of the tune, proving Eva right. Hitler still refused to acknowledge his error fully, saying, "You're right, but the composer was wrong. If he'd been as talented as me, he'd have written my version."[16]

Praise was an ever-present need, and he demanded it. A Nazi newspaper complimented him in terms we would find hard to take seriously, describing him as

> . . . the best imaginable expert in every specialized field.

> . . . the greatest German of all times.

> . . . the highest synthesis of his race . . . He embodies the universalism of Goethe, the depth of Kant, the dynamism of Hegel, the patriotism of Fichte, the genius of Frederick [the Great], the realism of Bismarck . . .[17]

He called himself "the hardest man there has ever been" and gave himself many titles. His favorite portrait of himself was as a knight in armor, carrying the banner of Germany. In time he took credit for everything:

> I overcame chaos in Germany, restored order, enormously raised production
>   in all fields of our national economy, through extraordinary exertion created
>   substitutes for many non-available raw materials, paved the way for new

> inventions, stimulated our transportation systems, and ordered mighty roads to be constructed. I had canals dug, called into existence giant factories . . .[18]

All he achieved was far from enough, and he said:

> I shall become the greatest man in history. I have to gain immortality even if the whole German nation perishes in the process.[19]

And he kept increasing his destructiveness until it won him immortality, nearly bringing on the end of Germany.

Egocentrism combined with low self-esteem resulted in his being easily insulted. After meeting two British diplomats, he complained they had treated him with deliberate insolence by wearing "tired suits." On being told his minister of war had married a former prostitute, he said, "Is there nothing I can be spared?"[20] And he conveyed his feelings of being victimized so well that many Germans echoed his words. When something adverse happened, whether or not it involved him, a common saying was, "The Führer is spared nothing."

Like others with extremely low self-esteem, Hitler was guilt-ridden. Prolonged exertion of his willpower had not rid him of forbidden desires; he had only managed to limit them. He coveted other men's wives, including those of his devoted friends Goebbels and Ernst Hanfstängl, although he did not pursue them.

His remedy to feelings of guilt and evil was to transcend them by not being a person, not having a private life. Instead, he meant to be a figure, to play a role, enhancing his performance by minimizing his private self and endowing his traits and acts with transcendental meaning. When challenged, he said, "I cannot be mistaken. What I say is historical."[21] He insisted whatever he did was an event in German history, and got his followers to accept his identification of himself with the nation. "Hitler is Germany. Germany is Hitler," said Hess over and over—a slogan echoed across the nation. Conversely, Hitler interpreted historical events as episodes in his own life. The distinction between his needs, successes, and failures and Germany's became seriously blurred. In 1932 he said, "I am now over forty, I must now rule." In 1939 he said, "I am now fifty. I would rather have the war now, than when I am fifty-five or sixty." And about World War II, he said, "I am totally convinced that this struggle does not differ one hair's breadth from the battle which I once fought out within myself."[22]

Some alienated people tend to believe that, if they play a role over and over, it may become habitual and spontaneous, and then they can become what they are playing. Hitler threw himself into the role of Germany's savior, hoping to achieve greatness. Then his guilt would be canceled; sins were excused in heroes.

He did not play his role reliably or responsibly, however. The rapidity of change under his rule gave outsiders the idea he was a hard worker, but associates noted that he wasted most of the day in escapism, ignoring government matters that required his attention. After issuing directives, he sometimes did not cooperate with subordinates who carried them out. They scheduled speeches that he failed to deliver, meetings with key people that he neglected to keep. He ignored obligations because of anxiety or to pursue flirtations. And when his string of successes turned into defeats during World War II, he did not shoulder the responsibility. Instead, he found scapegoats, ordering subordinates killed. To him the future was hazy and unreal; it would be decided by fate. Therefore, whether he performed his duties well or even at all would not be decisive.

Another factor contributing to his irresponsibility was the feeling that he had no impact. Despite intermittent efforts, Hitler had failed repeatedly at school . Then he had painted, but his serious art had gone unappreciated. His architectural efforts and early ideas for improving people's lives had also gone unappreciated. Later his paintings had been used for selling picture frames or as souvenirs—not treated as serious work. His efforts to be creative had borne no fruit, and his experience of learned helplessness had been reinforced. What he did made no difference.

Whims of the moment were as real to him as long-range consequences—including major national consequences. He spoke of the distant future—of the Reich he was build-ing so strong that it would last a thousand years; of retiring after victory, marrying Eva Braun, and living a quiet life in Linz. But the words were empty. He was deliberately reckless, inviting disaster and intending to commit suicide as an escape from it, with little care for anyone or anything that might remain.

Lack of impact had been most apparent in his constructive efforts. Perhaps he thought that by destructiveness he could force an impact. On joining the German Workers Party, he was valued for his speeches—for his skill with words and ideas. In his own eyes, such prowess was inferior to the violence in which the Party's Storm Troopers engaged. As he became a more powerful speaker—a quasi-violent speaker—he had an impact on people. But he continued to believe that physical brutality—killing—was the most important activity in which a man could engage.

Many very alienated people feel only partly alive, lacking meaningful contact or having it only through violence. Some avoid violence, choosing to be unobtrusive, ig-nored, unnoticed. Others seek violent encounters in order to feel involved and alive. As observers have noted:

> Trouble . . . makes us actively aware that we are living, and when there is little in the life we lead to hold and draw and stir us, we seek and cherish it . . .[23]

> Anger is electric, exhilarating. The angry person knows without a doubt he is alive. And the state of unaliveness, of partial aliveness, is so frequent and so frightening [that] anger feels like treasure . . . it fills the veins with purpose . . .[24]

In Vienna, Hitler had been unobtrusive, but later he sought confrontation and vio-lence. Commenting on the fact that the Nazi Party had been largely ignored in its early years, he said:

If we had been attacked at that time, nay, if one had only laughed at us, we would have been happy in both events. For the depressing thing was neither the one nor the other, but it was only the complete lack of attention we encountered at that time. This was true most of all for my person.[25]

The private life Hitler led was not only empty but also plagued by self-disgust. An apt observation was, ". . . at rest, in immobility, he belongs only to himself, belongs entirely to his own dreadfulness."[26] To get out of himself, he needed to be dramatically active—to provoke responses. Year by year, he escalated the level of violence, taking measures that could not be ignored, that had to affect people seriously.

Except for his role as leader, Hitler had little that was worthwhile and real. He was unhappy with his looks and his identity, he had no trade or profession, he had no family of his own or intimate friends, and for years he had no lover. Nor did he expect ever to have them. He had nothing but a role and, like an actor's role, it was ephemeral. It could attain substance and become a life only if carried off with spectacular success.

Meanwhile, to carry on, to pull himself out of his torpor, he sought stimulation, especially of his anger.

> . . . Hitler will almost deliberately grow heated over some small issue in conversation . . . will raise his voice and begin to gesticulate excessively, thus raising himself out of lethargic dullness . . . he will grow indignant or rapturous in the effort to fight his way out of mental shackles . . .[27]

His private life had no purpose, no significant movement, and no hope. He staked everything on playing his heroic role.

CHAPTER 8

IN POWER

I have no scruples and I will use whatever weapon I require.[1]

—Adolf Hitler, 1932

At the beginning of his rule in 1933, Hitler had individuals killed. The next year, he had a group of a thousand killed; still later, the "euthanasia" program killed tens of thousands. And during World War II, he had about thirteen million noncombatants killed. The escalating prewar slaughter, supported by heavy indoctrination, enabled Hitler to learn what the nation would accept or at least tolerate.

When he became chancellor, Hitler was in no position to exterminate Jews or wage war. He knew that he was the only high Nazi determined to eradicate the Jews and that his nation was strongly opposed to war. Hitler could not tell whether his main goals were feasible, and Germans had little idea of what was coming. And his powers were limited under the constitution and parliamentary system. The first of the following steps enabled Hitler to seize absolute power. Although they claimed that the steps were legal, Nazis boasted of them as *die Machtergreifung*—the seizure of power.

The runaway inflation of the middle 1920s spurred the Nazi Party's growth. Then control of inflation and brief prosperity led to a decline. Growth was spurred again by the Great Depression that ended the 1920s. In the 1932 Reichstag elections, the Nazi Party won the most seats. As there were thirty-two parties, winning 40 percent of the vote was an extraordinary victory—greater than any party had won during the parliamentary monarchy or the republic. Hitler was in line to be chancellor, but President Paul von Hindenburg held him in contempt, calling him "the Bohemian private, first-class" and "the Austrian private, first-class," and said he was qualified to be postmaster at best, certainly not chancellor.[2]

Hindenburg turned instead to Franz von Papen and then Kurt von Schleicher, helping them build coalitions of center and conservative parties. But von Papen and von Schleicher proved inept, failing to sustain cooperation among the parties or even to maintain enough support to govern. Meanwhile, Storm Troopers rampaged in the streets, as the threat of a Nazi or Communist revolt and a civil war grew. Other large political armies were the Stahlhelm (army veterans who often supported the Nazis), the Roter Front Kämpferbund (Communists), and the Reichsbanner (Social Democrats)—in all, millions of armed men. The national army, limited to one hundred thousand, said it would be unable to deal with a civil war.

71

Hindenburg, who had long been a force for stability, was eighty-five, and his abilities and health were fading. With anarchy at hand, he finally asked Hitler to be chancellor in January 1933. Von Papen, instrumental in persuading Hindenburg to put aside his objections to Hitler, told an associate the Nazis were terrible people but "they had the brutality to do what nobody else could have done."[3] In desperation, Hindenburg turned the country over to the main source of anarchy and violence—the main threat of civil war. But he did insist on conditions to prevent Hitler from gaining dictatorial power. One was that the Nazis hold only three of the eleven cabinet posts—two in addition to Hitler's—the others going to conservatives, including von Papen as vice-chancellor. The idea was that non-Nazis could outvote Nazis in the cabinet. The other conditions were promises by Hitler to respect the Reichstag, the integrity of the armed forces, and the powers of the president.

In return for accepting Hindenburg's conditions, Hitler won two key concessions: partial control of the press and the naming of Göring, soon to be commandant of the air force, as Prussia's minister of the interior. Since Prussia made up two thirds of Germany and included Berlin, the national capital, Göring's control and reorganization of the Prussian police would prove crucial. He later wrote:

> Out of 32 police chiefs I removed 22. Hundreds of inspectors and thousands of police sergeants followed in the course of the next month. New men . . . in every case . . . came from the great reservoir of the Storm Troops and Guards.[4]

"Guards" meant members of the SS (*Schutzstaffel,* or Protection Squad). This was originally a small group of Storm Troopers chosen to serve as Hitler's personal bodyguard. Under Heinrich Himmler's leadership, the SS grew enormously, eclipsing the rest of the Storm Troopers and taking over the concentration camps and much of Germany's police. Hitler eventually gave the SS primary responsibility for carrying out racial policy, including operating the death camps.

Göring said Communists were the enemy and:

> My measures will not be qualified by legal scruples or by bureaucracy. It is not my business to do justice. It is my business to annihilate and exterminate— that's all![5]

The Weimar Republic's libertarian constitution was unpopular and had been violated openly by prior administrations. Hitler left it in place and rendered it meaningless by a series of well-coordinated acts that unfolded with lightning speed. Despite his history of indecision and procrastination at turning points, he showed none this time, for he had made a plan in advance. The diary of Goebbels, Nazi leader of Berlin and soon appointed to the new post of minister of "public enlightenment and propaganda," indicates it was finalized the day after Hitler became chancellor:

> Imperial Palace with Hitler. We spoke about the Red terror. As yet no counter-measures. First let things burn.[6]

The fight against the "Red terror" was a cover phrase for the seizure of power, which Goebbels wrote would begin with "a masterpiece of political agitation."[7]

The Nazis stepped up their harassment of leftists, hoping to provoke violence. They threatened Communists, banned their meetings, broke them up, shut down Communist and Social Democratic presses, and arrested leading Communists and Social Democrats. A few dozen Communists were killed. Despite its history of violence, however, the Communist Party became more cautious instead. Then police raided the Party's headquarters on February 24, and Göring announced that documents found there showed the Communists were about to launch a revolt *beginning with arson against government buildings.* Göring also announced he would soon make the documents public. He did show documents to the cabinet, but they were forgeries, which he never showed again.[8] The Communist Party had quietly abandoned its headquarters a couple of weeks earlier, and the idea that it left such documents behind is implausible. Later, Communist leaders would be charged with such a plot, tried, and acquitted. The documents, had they existed, would have been crucial to the prosecution's case, but none were introduced at the trial. Nor were they ever found in government archives. Evidently, they did not exist, and Göring's announcement was intended to prepare the nation for what followed.

Three days after his announcement, arson destroyed the Reichstag building. There the police arrested Marinus van der Lubbe, a deranged Dutchman, who was half-naked. He immediately confessed to the arson, boasting of it and insisting he had done it alone, and the original police report so stated. Göring arrived at the Reichstag shortly after and, without reviewing evidence, announced van der Lubbe had acted on behalf of, and with the help of, the Communist Party.

When the fire broke out, Hitler and his friend Hoffmann were dinner guests of the Goebbels. According to Hoffmann, Hitler received a phone call and interrupted it, saying to the others, "Hanfstängl says the Reichstag building is on fire. There appears to be no doubt about it."[9] Hitler then continued the phone conversation. Ernst Hanfstängl, press secretary of the Nazi Party, was staying in the Reichstag Palace, across the street from the Reichstag, and saw the fire through a window. His version is that he spoke to Goebbels, not Hitler.[10] In either case, as Hanfstängl later said, he had no information other than what he saw from the window and was in no position to identify the source of the fire. Nonetheless, according to Hoffmann, after Hanfstängl's call, Hitler said:

> It's the Communists! We'll have a showdown over this! I must go at once. Now I've got them.[11]

Accompanied by Goebbels, Hitler rushed to the Reichstag and, without reviewing evidence, announced that the Communist Party had not only burned the Reichstag but launched a revolt. Goebbels and Göring rewrote the police report to say van der Lubbe was involved with, and acting for, the German Communist Party. Göring later said van der Lubbe had a German Communist Party membership card when arrested.[12] These statements were false. Van der Lubbe had been a member of the Dutch Communist Party but had resigned or been expelled. He had never been a member of the German Communist Party. From the information Göring received at the scene, he could not have known about van der Lubbe's Communist background. The police did not learn of it until later.[13] The inference that Nazi leaders knew about van der Lubbe before the fire was confirmed by evidence that came out later.

The revised report also said:

> The burning of the Reichstag was intended to be the signal for a bloody uprising and civil war . . . Warrants have been issued for the arrest of two leading Communist Reichstag deputies on grounds of urgent suspicion. The other deputies and functionaries of the Communist Party are being taken into protective custody.[14]

The press spread Göring's and Hitler's statements and the revised police report. At Göring's direction, the Prussian police immediately began arresting prominent Communists—several thousand, including members of the Reichstag—and Social Democrats, left-wing writers, and artists.

Foreign correspondents and historians concluded that Nazis were at least partly responsible for the fire, presenting three main arguments. Van der Lubbe said he used only minimal incendiary material, and there was technical evidence of massive arson, requiring more than what he evidently had in his possession. Experts also said the fire could not have been set by one person alone. (The expert evidence may have been biased. Introduced at van der Lubbe's trial by the prosecution, its purpose was to show that German Communists participated in the arson. The prosecution was under pressure from the Chancellery to implicate them.[15])

In addition, the Reichstag was locked to entry from the street, but access was available through the Reichstag Palace, which was Göring's residence, for he was also president of the Reichstag. This seemed relevant to those who concluded that the arson was massive, requiring a group of arsonists with much incendiary material to carry it out. Van der Lubbe had climbed the Reichstag wall to a second-floor window and broken it, enabling him to get in but limiting the incendiary material he could carry. Perhaps for that reason he had used clothes he was wearing to set the fire. In addition, van der Lubbe was not bent on destruction; he set the fire only as a political protest. Two days earlier, he had set fires in three other government buildings—small fires that did little damage.[16] In the Imperial Palace, only a windowsill was burned. He had not used incendiary material adequate for burning down buildings, but only lighters, available in many stores, used for igniting stoves and other small fires—useful only for igniting highly flammable material. He said he used the same lighters in the Reichstag, but that building, unlike the others, quickly burst into massive flame.

The final reason Nazis were believed involved was that they were the only ones who benefited from the fire, and they benefited enormously. The measures it enabled them to take swept aside the republic and constitution, giving Hitler dictatorial power.

The revised police report implied that warrants for Communists' arrests had been issued after the fire. Much later, it came out that the warrants had been issued before the fire, which was a most telling fact. And a few Nazis said Göring spoke of his complicity in the fire.[17] Rudolf Diels, chief of the Gestapo, wrote:

> Göring knew exactly how the fire was to be started [and told me] to prepare, prior to the fire, a list of people who were to be arrested immediately after it.[18]

Diels later concluded that Göring was not responsible for setting the fire, but that does not weaken his evidence about Göring's preparation for the fire.[19]

Contributing to circumstantial evidence against Hitler and his associates was their unexpected presence. On becoming chancellor, Hitler had called a new election on short notice, hoping to win a majority in the Reichstag and to entrench his rule. He aided his cause by controlling media reporting of the campaign and restricting electioneering by opponents. Hitler was a tireless campaigner; his specialty was personal appearances and speeches, traveling across Germany at a whirlwind pace. But on the day of the fire—at the height of the campaign—he had interrupted it and was in Berlin at leisure. Hitler's top campaigners, Göring and Goebbels, had also put aside the election and were in Berlin. All three were available when the fire broke out.

At his trial, van der Lubbe scoffed at the idea of accomplices, insisting he had set the fire alone. No basis for questioning his sincerity has been found. In view of his political ideas, his stated intention to oppose the Nazi government, and his personality, it is hardly likely he would knowingly have cooperated with Nazis. The possibility remains that Nazis used him without his knowledge.

Van der Lubbe had arrived in Germany a few weeks before the fire, unemployed, homeless, and friendless. He had found cheap shelter at men's hostels and free shelter in a police station. Seeking publicity and supporters for his protest, he had spoken to people he met about his intentions, and apparently Nazis heard about them.

During his trial, he maintained a determined silence when questioned, appearing to be a mute, with a notable exception. Asked by the chief judge where he had been the day before the fire, he said he had attended a Storm Trooper rally.[20] He was asked no more about it, but some people reported seeing him in the company of Nazis. A district nurse in Berlin said that a few days before the Reichstag fire, two men, one of whom she knew to be a Storm Trooper, had brought van der Lubbe to her, asking her to provide him with food and shelter. They had befriended him. Also, during his trial, the chief judge pressed him with the impossibility of his having set the fire unaided, and he responded, "Then the others must have done that."[21] Again he was not questioned further on the point.

Finally, the chain of events fitted a method of operating that the new government would use again and again—creating a pretext, usually a violent one, blaming the intended victims for it, and then destroying them.

It is clear that what followed immediately after the fire involved joint, well-coordinated actions by Nazi leaders and thousands of police. It is also clear that preparations for these actions had been made before the fire. The dramatic question is, did Nazis help set the fire? A few Nazis said they were told Goebbels recruited a team of Storm Troopers led by Karl Ernst for the arson, and one said Ernst confirmed the story. At his trial after the war, Göring admitted his preparations to arrest the Communists but denied setting the fire.[22]

A less dramatic question is, did Hitler, Göring, and Goebbels know the fire was going to be set and plan accordingly? They were looking for an incident by which to blame the Communists, institute terror, and seize dictatorial power. They found what they wanted in van der Lubbe and his arson, although it remains uncertain whether they found him before the fire.

More important than either question are the uses Hitler made of the fire. The alteration of the police report, the false statements to the public, the forged documents shown to the cabinet, the arrests—they enabled Hitler to seize power and proceed with his destructive agenda, and they are not in question. Hitler used a nonexistent Communist revolt to justify an emergency decree "until further notice," suspending constitutional rights and never restoring them. He then went before the Reichstag, requesting additional arbitrary powers to deal with the "emergency," and they were given to him.

And the nation, partly from the fear of Communism Hitler played on, accepted his actions. Von Papen said to a foreigner who was alarmed by the actions taken after the fire, "Nothing to worry about, my dear fellow; we can always outvote them in the cabinet."[23] Alfred Hugenberg, another non-Nazi cabinet member, was disturbed by the actions; nonetheless, he issued a statement supporting Hitler, saying, "Omelettes cannot be made without breaking eggs."[24] Despite their misgivings about Hitler, the cabinet members' remarks typified the outward indifference with which the destruction of the republic was accepted.

In the election a week after the fire, the Nazis increased their vote, still failing to win a majority. But using his emergency powers, Hitler proceeded to outlaw the Communist Party and later the Social Democratic Party. With Reichstag members of the two parties incarcerated, he now had his majority. The remaining parties were sufficiently intimidated by these events to disband when told to, and, by July, the Nazi Party was the only one permitted. The next year it was declared to be identical with the state. People wishing to retain government posts joined the Nazi Party. Except for Hitler's cabinet, which still had ministers chosen by Hindenburg, Nazis now held almost every managerial position in Germany's government. Having suppressed political sources of opposition, Hitler ruled on a permanent basis.

With the great influx of political prisoners, jails were inadequate, and concentration camps were established, run mainly by Storm Troopers. Officially, they were designed for preventive custody with a halfhearted idea of rehabilitating political opponents. Then the torture and killing of camp inmates began on a small scale. As rumors of the violence circulated, the government denied them publicly, blaming Jews—who numbered among the victims—for "horror propaganda." But secretly the government spread the stories in order to intimidate the public. When the nation accepted these measures, the number of camps, the torture, and the killing increased. Over the next twelve years, tens of thousands would be killed in each of the larger concentration camps—two million in all of them—as distinct from four million in the death camps established during World War II.

In Germany's chaos after World War I, the army had been a stabilizing force, more or less supporting whichever government—socialist, center, or conservative—held office. But the new Nazi government posed special problems to the army, whose leaders had strong misgivings about Hitler's war plans. When the Nazi Party had been small, the army had cooperated with Storm Troopers as a force against Communist threats and given them training and weapons. But after Hitler came to power, the Troopers swelled to nearly three million men, incorporating the Stahlhelm, and dwarfed the army. Ernst Röhm, commandant of the Storm Troopers, meant for them to become Germany's army. Hitler, too, had long meant for that to happen. Thus, the Storm Troopers were a serious rival to the army, and President Hindenburg, a former general, backed the army.

Negotiations for the two armies to merge or coexist failed, and Hitler came under heavy pressure to choose between them. After leaning in one direction and the other in 1934, he chose secretly to side with the national army. In June, he sent the Storm Troopers on furlough and had their leaders, including his friend Röhm, seized and killed. This was the first mass killing under his regime and was performed mainly by his special killing force, the SS. In reprisal, a group of Storm Troopers, calling themselves Röhm Avengers, reportedly killed about 150 SS men.[25]

Hitler officially reported that fifty Storm Troopers had been killed, then raised the number to seventy-seven. But the total, which included people other than Troopers—a fact Hitler omitted—was about one thousand. To the nation, he explained he had discovered Röhm was plotting a Storm Trooper revolt to take place the very day the arrests and killings began, which justified his instant action. But many—perhaps most—of the people killed were first taken into custody. Hitler's explanation could justify instant arrests, but not killing people in custody. *No Storm Troopers were brought to trial.*

Röhm had complained bitterly about steps favoring the army at the expense of the Troopers and talked loosely about opposing Hitler and using Troopers to force Hitler to proceed with socialist measures in the Party program. But no evidence that a revolt had been organized was ever presented except for one document, which turned out to be a forgery.[26]

The year before, the Storm Troopers had still been Hitler's favorites, and he had said of them privately, "I give my men every freedom. Do anything you like, but don't be caught at it!"[27] He had egged them on and, when criticized for their actions, had said privately:

> I abominate prudishness and moral prying . . . I won't be a spoilsport to any of my men. If I demand the utmost of them, I must also permit them to let off steam as *they* please, not as it suits a lot of elderly churchhens . . . I'm not interested in [their] private lives any more than I'll stand for any prying into my own private life.[28]

And about Röhm's homosexuality he had said:

> His private life is no concern of mine as long as the necessary discretion is maintained. In any case, I will never reproach him or take any steps on this count.[29]

After the purge, however, Hitler went before the Reichstag and said about the dead leaders of the Storm Troopers:

> . . . While the overwhelming majority in the nation is made to earn its daily bread by toilsome labor . . . [there] are still people whose sole activity consists of doing nothing . . . Because their very beings are filled with nothingness . . . these people have no living tie to the masses . . . However, they are dangerous for they are veritable germ-carriers for unrest, uncertainty, rumors, allegations, lies, suspicions, slander and fear, and thus they contribute to a gradually increasing tension . . .[30]

Hitler now pretended to be surprised and disgusted by their homosexuality, saying the Troopers "violate all laws of decency and modest behavior . . ."[31] and:

> The worst of all was that . . . there began to be formed . . . a conspiracy directed not only against the normal views of a healthy people but also against the security of the State.[32]

If his speech were true, Hitler had killed the people most like himself. His words described his own idleness, alienation, and nihilism, especially when he was an adolescent and a young man in Vienna, as well as some of his actions as chancellor. He had just begun making violations of prevailing standards of sexual decency and modesty (nude dancers, pornographic movies) a regular practice inside the Chancellery. He had launched an assault on the customs and values of Germany—on its religious, social, and personal life. He had spread unrest, lies, slanders, and fear. And he had led a conspiracy against the state and would later gravely threaten the survival of Germany.

Hitler's most telling comment about the Röhm purge was made impulsively to his secretary: "So! Now I have taken a bath, and feel clean as a new-born babe again."[33] Behind his stated motives was guilt. He had purged himself vicariously by killing those to whom he felt closest.

For years people had been alarmed by the Troopers' violence, which increased after Hitler became chancellor, and they felt safer after the Röhm purge. Hitler's manipulation of their fears was highly effective in justifying this and other destructive acts by the government. The irony in the widespread approval Hitler gained for it is that the purge was more violent and more lawless than the actions of the Troopers.

Hitler felt constrained by Hindenburg, who had for years been Germany's most popular leader. When Hindenburg objected to anti-Semitic measures, Hitler withdrew or modified them temporarily. But Hindenburg's health was declining rapidly. Saying to the vice-chancellor, "Things are going badly, Papen. See what you can do to put them right," he all but retired in May 1934, going to his estate to convalesce.[34] Hindenburg died a few months later—a year and a half after naming Hitler chancellor—and Hitler did not allow election of a new president, but simply assumed the office himself. His power was unrivaled and secure, except for opposition in the army.

The Röhm purge won Hitler the army's support, although most of its leaders continued to hold serious reservations about him. Almost all welcomed his enlargement of the army but discouraged his military ventures, from the occupation by German troops of the Rhineland in 1936 to his intended and actual invasions that followed. An opportunity for purging the officer corps came in 1938 when two ranking generals were involved in sexual scandals. Minister of War Werner von Blomberg's embarrassment came from his own action in marrying a woman with a police record for lewdness. Commander in chief Werner von Fritsch was framed by Nazis and cleared of the charge of homosexuality by an army court.[35] The causes of the scandals made no difference. Although he did not care about such matters, Hitler used the scandals to force the two out of office. He then forced out six other generals and scores of senior officers, telling the public they retired because of health problems, provoking jokes of an epidemic in the army. In addition, Hitler purged the foreign office of Minister Constantin von Neurath and other opponents of war.

The purge probably resulted from the generals' and von Neurath's negative response in 1937 when Hitler outlined his war plans to them. Von Fritsch then said, "This man is . . . running into the abyss and will drag Germany with him." He met with von Blomberg, von Neurath, and General Ludwig Beck, chief of the general staff, to formulate arguments for dissuading Hitler, which Hitler ignored.[36] As Hitler ordered preparations to invade Austria and then Czechoslovakia in 1938, Beck prepared a memo urging against the invasions. It was endorsed by the general staff and presented to Hitler.[37] He relieved Beck from his post, and Beck then resigned from the army and became the leader of a group working secretly to bring Hitler down—the group that wounded Hitler in an attempted assassination in 1944.

From Hitler's viewpoint, purging the army turned out to be a prudent move, although it did not go far enough. After the elimination of Communist and Social Democratic leaders, the army was the main source of plots against Hitler. During World War II, most of Germany's leading generals would participate at least in discussions of toppling the Nazi government and some in attempts on Hitler's life. And disobedience of Hitler's orders would come mainly from army officers.

In the six years of his rule before World War II, Hitler was more effective than his predecessors had been in dealing with hated features of the Versailles Treaty. He won more for Germany by making concessions to France, Great Britain, and Italy that his predecessors had refused to make. He could do so because he fully intended to violate the treaties he signed, and he had little concern for consequences of violating treaties because he fully intended to go to war.

Hitler's first target for conquest was Austria, and his idea was to arrange a pretext; he wanted an invasion to appear justified. One scheme he considered was to kill von Papen, who had resigned from the cabinet and become ambassador to Austria, and have it appear that Austrians had done it. Months later it was Czechoslovakia's turn and the same scheme was considered. "Czechs" were to kill the German ambassador in Prague, Ernst Eisenlohr.[38]

Neither scheme was used because both countries yielded without invasions. The Munich conference, by which Czechoslovakia fell into his hands without a shot, was seen by the world as Hitler's triumph. To him, however, it was a setback, frustrating his wishes to have his war and destroy the Czechs. He had increased his demands of Czechoslovakia again and again so they would not be met and told his generals, "It is my unshakable will that Czechoslovakia shall be wiped off the map."[39] War would have made it easier to do. After the Czechs and their allies, led by Britain's prime minister, yielded to him at Munich, he said, "That fellow Chamberlain has ruined my entry into Prague."[40] Later he would say:

> We ought to have gone to war in 1938 . . . But they gave way all along the line and, like the poltroons they are, ceded to all our demands.[41]

The "poltroons" were the prime ministers of France and Great Britain. France faltered in its treaty commitments to Czechoslovakia, and Britain, France's ally, took the lead in handing Czechoslovakia over to Hitler.

The measures Hitler took to consolidate his power and extend it outside Germany were made to look like the results of emergencies, but none of them were. Hitler spoke openly of his destructiveness, saying it was directed against enemies—Jews, Communists, Russians. The measures taken show his destructiveness was hardly limited to them. The first large group of people he had killed were not only Aryans but Nazis, including one of his best friends. No group had been closer to him. Those killings, the killing of concentration camp inmates, and the planned killings of von Papen and Eisenlohr were tactically convenient but unnecessary to achieve his goals. Associates of Hitler said the arrests after the Reichstag fire, the Röhm purge, and the anti-Semitic measures of the 1930s were experiments. They served to condition him to escalating aggression, to condition his followers and the nation for the mass destruction to come, and to find out far he could go.

From fear of Communism, Germans accepted the new regime's beatings, killings, and arrests of Communists and Social Democrats. From fear of Storm Troopers, Germans accepted the Röhm purge. By the time systematic government killing was extended to people not feared, Hitler's power was so great that opposition was ineffective.

PART II:

"THE TWISTED ROAD TO AUSCHWITZ"

In turning from a chronological account of Hitler's life, Part II is arranged by topics. Key parts of his personality are elaborated for those topics.

To become history's greatest destroyer, Hitler had to free himself from the values he was taught and from personal inhibitions. His struggle against these limitations has hardly been studied, and a new reconstruction of his efforts to turn himself into a destructive superman is presented in Chapter 9. Carrying out his program required a fanatical following. To win one, he built on his natural charisma by simulating charismatic, heroic traits (Chapter 10). To prepare for the most destructive war in history, Hitler worked to recondition the nation, transforming its education, institutions, values, and laws (Chapter 11).

What set Hitler apart from other leaders was his use of absolute power to pursue his obsession with Jews and their sexuality. His extreme ideas about Jews were accepted by many Germans because of a change in German anti-Semitism that began in the nineteenth century with the *völkisch* movement (described in Chapter 13). The combination of German history and the special meaning Jews had for Hitler and a minority of Germans was crucial to the Holocaust (Chapters 12 and 13).

Judging that open, mass killing was unacceptable to most Germans, Hitler set about eliminating Jews and part-Jews by coercing them to emigrate and by a bizarre, little-understood "eugenic" program, culminating in a secret scheme to sterilize millions of people. Behind his efforts to "purify" the race and eliminate "degenerate" sex from German life were extreme problems with intimacy in his own life. They are detailed in Chapter 14 to explain his extreme efforts to control the sexual, family, and reproductive lives of his people as discussed in Chapter 15.

Part II ends with Hitler's wartime leadership (Chapter 16). Puzzling military decisions—including some still considered blunders—are shown to be calculated risks he took to advance the extermination of Jews.

CHAPTER 9

TRANSFORMING THE SELF

Conscience is a Jewish invention. It is a blemish like circumcision.[1]

—Adolf Hitler, 1931

The heavy toll of World War I was fresh in Germans' memory, and they did not want another war. While most of them accepted exclusionary and economic measures against Jews, they opposed harming them physically. The nation was hardly prepared for war and extermination—the goals most important to Hitler. Nor was he fully prepared. Although convinced of the rightness of his goals, he was held back by conventional morals and personal inhibitions. He envied his Storm Troopers their lighthearted violence; he wore their uniform and tried to join them in combat. His efforts led to failure, however, and he concluded that he could achieve freedom of action only by eliminating the remnants of his middle-class morality. Although he advocated ruthlessness, he had not yet fully achieved it. He and the nation had to undergo transformations.

Hitler's rival in destruction, Joseph Stalin, had even more people killed (although Hitler's plan was to kill far more than Stalin did). But what happened in the Soviet Union was less of a shock, for Russia had a history of government terror and cruelty to minorities. With a gentler history, called the land of poets and thinkers, Germany was known for its enlightenment and liberalism.

World War I and its aftermath crushed Germany's prosperity and spirit, but much of Europe went through economic and political crises in the 1920s and 1930s. Conditions led to dictatorships in fourteen European countries but, except for the Soviet Union, nothing like the destructiveness that erupted in Germany. There, chaos brought to the top a leader unlike leaders of other countries—one devoted to turning its male youth into killers and plunging his nation into unending war.

In 1932, Hitler said the war he was planning "will be unbelievably bloody and grim," for its purpose would be the extinction of enemy peoples. And that war would not be enough. At its onset, he looked ahead to its end, to the peace terms he would seek afterward, and said:

> . . . we must be sure to have an opening for a new war . . . In future peace treaties we must therefore always leave open a few questions that will provide a pretext.[2]

Later he would say Germany should have a war every generation.

As an outcome of his war plans, Hitler foresaw devastation and sometimes joked about it:

> The German people survived the wars with the Romans . . . the Thirty Year War . . . the Napoleonic war . . . They survived even a World War, even the revolution—they will survive me as well![3]

In somber moods, he thought that through his leadership Germany would be destroyed totally—a possibility he mentioned repeatedly.

Hitler's most destructive acts have been explained by the stresses of war. My thesis is that World War II enabled him to order the killing of millions of people, but his intention to destroy them preceded the war. Frustration during the war contributed to his destructiveness toward Germans, but his inclination to destroy them had been shown long before, when everything was going well for him. In 1933 he had said:

> . . . if I can send the flower of the German nation into the hell of war, without the smallest pity for the spilling of precious blood, then surely I have a right to remove millions of an inferior race that breeds like vermin![4]

"Inferior race" meant Jews and Slavs. It may seem strange for leaders to speak of sending their people to death without pity, but Hitler's subordinates got used to his talk about how ruthless he could be:

> Some day, when I order war, I shall not be in a position to hesitate because of the ten million young men I shall be sending to their death.[5]

Germany's population was sixty-five million, as Hitler well knew. *Ten million would have been nearly all its young men.*

Because of the extent of Hitler's destructiveness, he was called a demonic creature. Many agreed that if anyone could be called truly evil, he should be the one. But much as we might like to, there are problems in classifying Hitler as evil. The concept of evil is flawed, rooted in the supernatural, in ideas of possession. And centuries of using the term to express disapproval of people has rendered it imprecise at best. The fact that Hitler called Jews and others evil may also serve as a caution against applying the word to him and his followers. Before the Third Reich, use of the concept of evil by the Inquisition and various governments and citizen groups in regard to heretics and "witches" resulted in millions of people being tortured and killed. In short, the sacred and secular history of the concept of evil limits its constructive use. Nonetheless, traditional concepts of evil are aids in understanding Hitler's development into a person of extreme destructiveness.

In *Politics,* Aristotle wrote that the most dangerous person was the one without attachment to home, tribe, or laws—structures that restrain destructiveness. He called an unattached person an isolated piece—a concept that fits Hitler well. He left his home at eighteen and lived in furnished rooms, shelters, apartments, and the Chancellery, none of which he regarded as a true home. The closest he came was the Berghof, his country house. Modern analogs of tribe are family and community. Hitler abandoned his family, community, and even his nation to become an alien in Germany, where for sixteen years he did not even try to become a citizen. He never established a family or roots in a community. And he did not accept Germany as it was. His commitment was to an abstract tribe—the *Volk* of Nordic Germans he dreamed of creating. As for laws, he respected none, not even those he himself enacted.

After Aristotle, a religious concept of evil came to dominate European thought. In Jewish and Christian tradition, all people are both evil and good. We are born as animals, driven by instincts and stained by Original Sin, the sources of ordinary evil. Then, we are given a bit of divinity—a conscience that enables us to rule our instincts. The combination of instinct and conscience is the hallmark of human nature. It makes for a life of self-conflict, our evil and good parts remaining opposed to each other.

Through the centuries this idea of human nature seemed adequate to explain most people's behavior but not the extraordinary evil seen in a few. Some people seemed not only more evil than the rest but also evil in a special way. And they seemed to have superhuman powers. They were understood to be people whom the Devil had possessed.

In the modern era, religious ideas about evil were less accepted, and explaining antisocial acts that went beyond ordinary bounds fell to the new medical specialty of psychiatry. To psychiatrists, it was the absence of morals that allowed some people to commit crimes freely. In the last century, the term "moral imbecile" was coined to describe them, and in this century was replaced by "psychopath" (and the equivalent terms, "sociopath" and "antisocial personality"). Psychopaths were thought to be particularly dangerous because they lacked consciences. They seemed able to violate taboos and do it lightly, untroubled by anxiety beforehand or guilt and fear of punishment afterward. They seemed not to be held back by scruples, loyalty, sentiment, or convention. In a word, they seemed free.

Later we learned that psychopaths did have consciences and experienced anxiety and other emotions. But their consciences and emotions did not stop them from committing antisocial acts. For this book, evil is defined as passionate destructiveness, justified by righteousness and expressed with little inhibition and with ruthless disregard for consequences. The question is, how does such behavior develop?

The easier part to understand is the origin of passionate destructiveness and righteousness. For Hitler, as for many other mass and serial killers, victimization in childhood was severe enough to cause hatred and a sense of worthlessness and of always being in the wrong. Desperately seeking moral superiority, such killers developed an outlook, supported by paranoid thinking, by which others were worthless and their own ideas rested on the highest authority. For some, the authority was their own special understanding of what was "really" happening around them; for others, it was the belief that they were God's agents. Hitler saw himself as combining both sources of authority.

The harder part to understand is how moral values and personal inhibitions are overcome. Hitler was taught conventional morals by his parents and teachers. In adolescence, he showed he had absorbed them by being a heavy moralizer, burdened with shame and guilt. But when it came to mass killing, his values failed to restrain him.

The explanation of why they failed begins with the way Hitler's parents conditioned him, undermining their moral teaching. His mother's indulgence was indiscriminate, and his father's punishment was indiscriminate. The lesson for Hitler was an impossible one—what he did made no difference morally; whatever he did was simultaneously good and evil. The moral precepts he was taught became ineffective guides to action.

Parts of his experience with his father helped Hitler free himself of the remnants of his moral training. He had learned to deal with Alois by exerting his will. His resolution not to cry when beaten required adopting an attitude of toughness and minimizing his sensations and emotions. The less one feels, the easier it is to hide emotions. Hitler used his will to suppress sensations and emotions aroused when confronting Alois. This was the beginning of what he later called his "iron will."

In adolescence, he used it to ignore hunger and sexual desire, while denying himself food, pleasure, and other material benefits. For long periods of time, he succeeded in not giving in to sexual and romantic impulses—even in not experiencing them.

Hitler also used his will to build up macho traits and to free his hatred. He practiced holding his arm up in the Nazi salute for hours, boasting of his ability to do it longer than anyone else. The key factors in such exercises are being determined and ignoring pain. Within a short time, one's arm begins to hurt. Later, numbness develops, helping one endure the ordeal.

The abuse Hitler suffered from his father remained the driving force of his life. Underneath the experiences he accumulated after the age of eleven was a deep sense of personal victimization, which he came to identify with Germany's victimization. And the victimization justified his hatred. After coming to power, he said privately:

> Externally I end the revolution. But internally it goes on, just as we store up our hate, and think of the day on which we shall cast off the mask, and stand revealed as those we are and eternally shall remain.[6]

He stopped implementing the socialist goals of the Nazi Party, put on a mask of peace-maker, and began to prepare for slaughter.

To develop aggressiveness, he provoked violent confrontations at Nazi meetings. And, like an athlete before a contest, he trained for verbal confrontations by practicing to work himself into a rage. Once after a pleasant lunch with his secretaries, the arrival of a foreign diplomat was announced. Hitler said, "God in heaven! Don't let him in yet—I'm still in a good humour." In front of his staff he worked himself into a rage and then went to meet the man. After shouting at the diplomat for ten minutes, he returned in a sweat and said happily, "He thinks I'm *furious*."[7] In time Hitler could transform himself easily, even in front of the person he was trying to intimidate.

Hitler saw confrontations as tests of willpower. While he argued at length with foreign diplomats, he believed his success with them came not from the content of his arguments, but from intimidating them by staring them down, shouting, threatening, and his willingness to go to the brink—by playing on his madness. Until 1938, he went to the brink tentatively, prepared to pull back if his opponents were resolute. Eventually, however, he became eager for war and willing to carry threats out no matter how great the risk, which increased his effectiveness in dealing with diplomats and heads of state.

Hitler's relationships with his parents gave him little opportunity to develop life skills. Mastering relationships with parents is the foundation for developing intimate relationships with others and for dealing with life. Hitler learned to relate only in simple ways with his parents. His handicap in intimate relationships does not bear directly on his moral behavior, but it does bear indirectly. Selfishness, willfulness, and destructiveness are restrained by caring relationships. Beyond the immediate effects of what we do are long-range effects in building, sustaining, or spoiling important relationships—considerations that restrain us most in actions involving loved ones but also in actions outside the relationships.

Hitler's relationships were deliberately superficial. He cared about people in his adult life only to a limited extent, and he made clear to them that their feelings and values were not to limit his political actions. Those he cared about were replaceable. With the single exception of his disastrous relationship with Geli Raubal, no one was particularly close or important to him. Few mattered enough to have a restraining effect on his destructiveness.

Destructiveness is ordinarily inhibited by anticipation of consequences. For them to weigh against the temptation to act on impulse, one must have a sense of one's future as real and valuable. To young children, the future rests on the actions of their parents. Since Alois's and Klara's attitudes toward him were fixed, he was in a poor position to learn how his actions affected his future or even to develop a sense of one. Living for the present because the future seems unreal or nonexistent is common in very alienated people. The sense of continuity in relationships and of an investment in one's home and job gives one a stake in preserving what one has. Without them, there is little to lose. Therefore, to satisfy an impulse, to gain something immediate, the boldest risks seem worth taking— even the risk of death. Hitler had lived his life much that way.

Another effect of fixed parental attitudes is fatalism, which can serve to justify harmful acts. The underlying idea is that what one does makes no difference because the future is already determined. Hitler often justified destruction by invoking Germany's destiny, declaring only history could judge his acts. He did not know Germany's destiny, but he did not need to know. If its destiny were to rule the world, any act that advanced its rule was justified. If its destiny were to perish, whatever harm he caused would make no difference. And to rule or to perish were the only outcomes worth considering. He exaggerated his grandiose, paranoid thinking and minimized practical, reality-bound considerations, becoming increasingly reckless, inviting disaster, and intending to commit suicide as an escape from it, with little care for anyone or anything that might remain. In short, Hitler chose to live in ways that supported his pathology and weakened restraints on bizarre behavior.

The main way Hitler freed his destructiveness was by widening the split in his personality, which had begun in his childhood. Having a highly punitive parent fosters dissociation. Parts of the self are identified as evil, and a common adaptation is to deny and disown them. He rejected as evil his Austrian, Czech, and reputedly Jewish parts of his identity, and tried to develop and free a primeval Teutonic spirit he thought lay buried under the values civilization had imposed. He believed Germans had lost their heritage of nobility and conquering power—the power of their heathen ancestors. They were living in a trance, unable to free themselves or even solve their economic and social problems, needing desperately to open their eyes, recognize the true nature of their blood, throw off their Judeo-Christian and middle-class yokes, and engage in unrestrained destructiveness.

Like Shakespeare's Hamlet, whose mission of revenge was also blocked, Hitler concluded that conscience was what made him a coward. It crippled him as it crippled others; his guilt was so oppressive that he could find no peace. Freeing himself and others was a first step toward greatness:

> Only when the time comes when the race is no longer overshadowed by the consciousness of its own guilt then will it find internal peace.[8]

> I am freeing men from . . . the dirty and degrading modification of . . . conscience and morality.[9]

Thus, his need to stand up to his father, his grand ambition, his ineffectiveness, and his self-hatred all brought Hitler to try deliberately to split off his conscience and free his destructiveness—to become a raging madman. To accomplish this, he adopted a new set of values that he associated with heathen Germans of the distant past and tried to model himself on their chief god Wotan in appearance, bearing, and action.

Wotan was the god of war and death and was typically pictured riding in a storm at the head of a raging army of the dead.[10] Hitler presented himself as the world's greatest warlord, and the rituals he introduced at Party rallies, in which the names of fallen Nazis were intoned and bloodstained, tattered flags were kissed, may have come from copying Wotan. In addition, he arranged for wounded soldiers to lead Nazi parades.

One can embrace a set of values intellectually, but making them a part of oneself is harder. Alienated people try to change themselves by pretense, by acting a role they wish to adopt. The logic is that by pretending over and over, the desired behavior will become habitual and then, they hope, spontaneous and natural. "Fake it till you make it!" This is what Hitler did, relying on his talent for mimicry.

In adolescence, he had begun striking poses to impress people. After World War I, his stage became the speaker's platform at Nazi meetings. He replaced his nondescript hair style and handlebar moustache with the hanging forelock and brush moustache for which he became famous. According to a biographer, he copied them from a painting of Wotan with such a hair style and moustache.[11] The painting, *The Wild Chase*, is of the genre depicting Wotan as a figure of terror in a frenzy of action.

The name Wotan comes from the word *wüten* (raging), and the god is a stranger and wanderer as well as a berserk warrior. His assistants are a pack of killer wolves. Hitler's choice of the name Wolf for himself may have been influenced by the connection with Wotan. He said, "That was my code name in the years of struggle." During World War II, he called one of his command posts the Wolf's Lair, another the Wolf's Gorge, and still another the Werewolf. He called young members of the Hitler Youth "wolf cubs" and the SS "my pack of wolves." And late in the war he established a guerrilla force to operate behind enemy lines, which he also called the Werewolf. Then he used it to kill and terrorize Germans he saw as unpatriotic. Its slogan was, "Hate is our prayer, revenge is our battle cry."[12]

Hitler began wearing a military uniform to fit the warrior image. His friend Hoffmann, a photographer, helped by taking pictures of Hitler so he could study the effects of his costume, posture, and gestures. He spent much time in front of the mirror, perfecting his body language. And before delivering speeches, he rehearsed ideas and phrases for hours, working himself up. Then he presented himself to the public as a berserk warrior with forceful, imperious body language and a message of heathen, uninhibited, ruthless power to redeem Germany.

A Nazi wrote, "The immoral course . . . gives the effect of strength and daring . . ."[13] The effect of Hitler's speeches was powerful. People became excited, fainted, had mystical experiences, applauded and cheered Hitler loudly, and became devoted to him. Reward for behavior is a powerful conditioner, and the effect of his speeches brought him intense gratification.

Even negative reactions to his belligerence gratified him, as when he said of conservatives in the cabinet:

> They regard me as an uneducated barbarian. Yes, we are barbarians! We want to be barbarians! It is an honorable title. *We* shall rejuvenate the world! This world is near its end. It is our mission to cause unrest.[14]

Hitler's freedom to be destructive was aided by his growing grandiosity, which came originally from being adored and spoiled by his mother but, even more important, from being treated as worthless by his father. As Alfred Adler pointed out long ago, feelings of inferiority are the main source of striving for superiority and for believing that one is superior. The lower one feels, the more desperate the need for superiority. Hitler presented himself as superhuman and got many followers to believe it. The Party's and then the public's acceptance of him as a destructive superman supported his growing belief that he was above people and beyond the law.

Setting himself beyond conscience, custom, and law was exciting but still did not rid him of guilt. Some people say they have succeeded in eliminating morality when making decisions by acting simply on the basis of consequences. Very few, however, are comfortable without a sense of being right morally, and neither was Hitler. For all his boasts about having no scruples and his efforts to undo his moral training, his concern about being right survived and his guilt grew. After the purge of Röhm and the Storm Troopers in 1934, his insomnia was worse and his minimal sleep interrupted by crying spells. A ringing in his ears developed that would last the rest of his life, and his fear of being poisoned increased.

To deal with his guilt, Hitler kept justifying his actions and finding scapegoats. As he was about to die, he reviewed and justified his main actions again and in the most implausible ways:

> It is untrue that I . . . wanted war in 1939. It was wanted and provoked exclusively by those international politicians who either came of Jewish stock, or worked for Jewish interests. After all my offers of disarmament, posterity cannot place the responsibility for this war on me . . .[15]

He also said:

> I have always been absolutely fair in my dealings with the Jews. On the eve of the war, I gave them one final warning.[16]

This referred to his oft-quoted speech of 1939, made after he had decided to start World War II:

> . . . if international finance Jewry inside and outside Europe should succeed once more in plunging our peoples into a world war, the outcome will . . . be . . . the destruction of the Jewish race in Europe![17]

Since he was the one who started the war and decided the Jews' destruction, the "warning" was a threat. If the Jews did not leave, they would be killed, and the responsibility would be theirs.

Hitler's efforts to find a substitute for Jewish and Christian values were superficial. While familiar with Teutonic myths, he apparently had not studied the ancient culture and did not know its values and taboos. His idea of heathen ways was based on what he saw as animal instinct, and it was an oversimplified view of animal instinct—little more than the expression of his inhibited impulses. In 1933 he declared:

> We must be ruthless. *We must regain our clear conscience* as to ruthlessness . . . Only thus shall we purge our people of their softness . . .[18] (Italics added.)

His goal in training Germany's boys embodied what he himself wanted to be:

> My theory of education is harsh. All weakness must be hammered out. The youth who grow up in my [academies] will terrify the world. I want a youth that is violent, masterful, intrepid, cruel . . . They must endure pain. There must be nothing weak and tender about them. The magnificent, free predator . . . Thus will I wipe out the thousands of years of human domestication. Thus will I see before me the noble raw material of nature.[19]

To become a free predator himself, he needed a value system that permitted violence and cruelty and more—a moral sense that approved destructiveness. He made a virtue of violence and ruthlessness and elevated himself to a position beyond all laws, quoting Raskolnikov in *Crime and Punishment:*

> Extraordinary men have the right to commit any crime and to transgress the law in any way, just because they are extraordinary.[20]

This idea is common in serial and other mass killers—in people who kill not for material benefit but for the value they find in killing. Nietzsche had noted an important truth: in maturing we can see that the morality we were taught is arbitrary—that it was forced on us and is false in some respects. Nonetheless it limits us. If we are clever enough to see that and an alternative way of acting, we can become independent of conventional morality and of law. People who feel inferior and unable to act find freedom and grandeur in such thinking.

In Hitler's eyes, the more laws he broke, the more extraordinary he became. And the more extraordinary he became, the more right he had to commit crimes. *If, as he claimed, he was unique, then he was bound by no laws.* Like Nietzsche, Hitler boasted of having transcended good and evil.

He espoused violence and ruthlessness over and over. The idea was simple: shrinking from violence showed moral weakness, while willingness to destroy showed moral strength. And repeated acts of destruction increased one's moral fiber.

To justify such behavior, he forced moral decisions into stark opposites in which the only alternative to killing was still worse. He insisted that the nation must choose between him and Communism, and he proceeded to kill Communists. He insisted that he must destroy the Jews or they would destroy Germany. Calling such reasoning "the either-or," he used it to persuade others and himself.

Still his guilt continued to grow. Like addicts, what made him feel better for the moment pulled him down in the long run. The accumulation of acts by which he transcended his conscience and raised his mood made him increasingly desperate. "Hitler hated and destroyed not because of a lack, but because of an excess of . . . guilt . . . he vainly tried to escape the pain of guilt by committing more crimes."[21]

People who try to transcend good and evil have hardly been studied in person. Absorbed in their charisma and paranoia as well as in feverish activities to escape themselves, they do not consider themselves in need of help nor do they consult psychotherapists. Hitler did, however, leave a wealth of speeches, writings, and recorded conversations. By studying them, Henry Murray concluded:

> *Having once started on a career of brutality, he can only quiet the pain of a bad conscience by going on with even greater ruthlessness to achieve successes, and so to demonstrate to himself and others that God approves of him and his methods.*[22]

According to Murray, every venture in destructiveness was a gamble. Every success meant Fortune favored Hitler because he was good, bringing momentary relief and exhilaration. Every failure meant Fortune rejected him because he was evil, increasing his guilt. In this vein, Hitler said:

> There are two possibilities for me: To win through with all my plans, or to fail. If I win, I shall be one of the greatest men in history. If I fail, I shall be condemned, despised, and damned.[23]

His exhilaration in destructiveness and his dependence on it made him impatient for war. Disregarding calculations, including his own, that Germany would be best prepared militarily in 1943, he spoke more and more of his eagerness to start a war. He tried in 1938, but his opponents yielded without fighting. The next year, brushing aside warnings of his military and diplomatic staffs, he sent his armies into Poland, and the invasion was only the visible tip of the slaughter he ordered there. Destruction itself became his goal, driving him on long after all hope of victory was gone. Like addicts who require larger and larger doses, he got caught in a spiral of destruction, until he brought Germany down.

CHAPTER 10

EXHIBITING CHARISMA

His words were like a scourge. When he spoke of Germany's disgrace, I felt ready to spring on any enemy. His appeal to German manhood was like a call to arms, the gospel he preached a sacred truth . . . I felt sure that no one who had heard Hitler that afternoon could doubt that he was the man of destiny . . .[1]

—Kurt Lüdecke, 1937

B esides freeing and hardening himself, Hitler needed to inspire the nation for destruction. Perhaps two million Germans participated in killing innocent people, while tens of millions were bystanders who did not try to stop it. The great majority followed him even to their own destruction. That one person—a madman—had an extremely destructive agenda and carried it out when he had the opportunity is understandable. We can use his deviancy to distance ourselves from him and what he did. More disturbing is the fact that he was aided by ordinary people, most of whom accepted him and stood by him until he committed suicide.

Early measures against Communists, Social Democrats, and Jews aroused little protest except among the victims. As political and racial measures became increasingly severe and violent, they were deplored by many individuals, and some group protests were organized, notably by church leaders. Sterilizing and killing people considered unfit also aroused opposition, particularly from the churches. During the war many people hid Jews, risking their own lives and sometimes losing them. Networks were organized to provide Jews with false papers and smuggle them out of Germany. Groups worked to topple the Nazi regime and made attempts on Hitler's life. But altogether they were a small minority.

Many writers tried to explain what happened by invoking German character—an explanation permitting non-Germans to believe a holocaust could not happen in their own countries. German character was also used by defense attorneys at the Nuremberg trials:

> . . . Germans were brought up in a way which caused them to presume as a matter of course that state measures were lawful and legal and to feel that it was improper to question them.[2]

Obedience was said to be a German trait.

Concern with the willing obedience of Germans in harming innocent people later prompted psychological research in the United States. The finding was that ordinary

Americans were also reared to obey; they followed instructions to harm innocent people. And the minority who refused did so politely. They neither protested what was being done, nor tried to stop others from doing it, nor reported perpetrators to the police.[3] Obedience and conformity are found in many countries.

Another explanation was the threat of heavy punishment, including death, for disobeying. Hitler demanded blind obedience and created a coercive atmosphere. The terror of his regime made it hard for subordinates to know what was safe. When fear is aroused, people react with limited judgment. Charisma is awesome, as are vengefulness, ruthlessness, and recklessness. Children are reared to fear the consequences of disobedience, and early fears, even when seemingly overcome with maturity, are aroused by an awesome person. Even though he had been a hero of air combat in World War I, Göring confided he became frightened every time he was in Hitler's presence. Probably he spoke for many. And Hitler did threaten people with death for disobedience. Subordinates at various levels believed they might be killed even for asking to be relieved of a given duty or transferred to a different job.

That was what they thought, but exhaustive research found their belief unwarranted. People who disobeyed Hitler to his face usually got no more than an angry scolding. And those who disobeyed at a distance—for example, generals in the eastern campaign who disregarded or even countermanded his orders to have their troops shoot Soviet Jews and commissars—escaped even that. Summarizing the findings, Eberhard Jäckel said:

> Not one case is known in which a person's life was in danger or in which a person suffered serious consequences by refusing to participate in a crime, such as the murder of unarmed people.[4]

Particularly instructive was the experience of a police battalion sent to Poland in 1942. Among groups that carried out extermination, the battalion was exceptional in not having special training for it. On receiving orders to slaughter Jews, the commandant was deeply troubled. He complained (but not to his superiors); he drank and wept. On the eve of the killing, he told his lieutenants about the orders. One refused to carry them out and requested reassignment, which the commandant granted. The next day, the commandant announced the assignment to his battalion, adding that any of the men who did not feel up to it would be excused. Of the 500, a dozen requested to be excused and were. Most of the men became disturbed when they started shooting Jews. Some then asked to be excused and others deliberately missed their targets. Still others evaded the killing by lingering over other tasks or hiding during the shooting. But the great majority persevered, becoming increasingly disturbed. To help them carry out the assignment, they were given much alcohol, and many completed the first day's killing while drunk. Some who balked were spoken to harshly, but there was no insistence that individuals carry out the orders; coercion or fear of grave consequences were unnecessary in getting the majority to comply. Four hundred—80 percent—persevered in their assignment, shooting thirty-eight thousand Jews in a year and a half.[5]

Years afterward, those who refused or evaded the assignment were questioned. They did not explain their noncompliance on moral grounds, but said they were too weak to do the killing—too weak to tolerate the disgust aroused.[6]

Hitler's influence over people came from his inadequacy. His desperate sense of ineffectiveness made him try to dominate everyone. His difficulty with his own sexuality made him try to regulate the nation's. His failure to manage his own life made him try to create a new world order. He is a prime example of Goethe's observation, "He who knows not how to rule his inner self would gladly rule his fellow men according to his own arrogant conceit."

Many of his followers were obviously superior to Hitler in that they held jobs and had families and social lives. Some were better educated and clearer thinkers, yet they adored him and submitted to him as if they were his inferiors. Hans Frank, a lawyer, said Hitler was a superman. General Wilhelm Keitel considered Hitler his superior in military knowledge and gave him the name Gröfaz, which stood for *Grösster Feldherr aller Zeiten*—Greatest Warlord of All Time. Himmler, a college graduate, said Hitler was a leader so exceptional as to be found in a nation only once in two thousand or five thousand years and called him "the greatest genius who ever lived." After the invasion of France, General Eduard Wagner said:

> And wherein lies the secret of this victory? In the enormous dynamism of the *Führer* . . . without his will it would never have come to pass.[7]

Later Goebbels wrote in his diary, ". . . the Fuehrer alone saved the Eastern Front this winter."[8]

Wagner's words of awe followed a smashing victory, but Goebbels's followed the first defeats—defeats owing to Hitler's interference in his generals' direction of the campaign in the Soviet Union. The adoration of Hitler's followers was supported by his successes but did not depend on them. It persisted after the failure of the 1923 coup and it persisted in 1944 and 1945 when Germany was being destroyed. It was an emotional response to him, not one based in reality.

A traveling companion noted that people lined the road to greet Hitler with a "facial expression of an almost biblical devotion . . . as if in ecstasy and almost bewitched. It was like mass intoxication."[9] His power was strongest in his speeches. Many who went to listen with skepticism or even opposition were converted. A new follower said he saw a halo around Hitler's head.[10]

Among those mesmerized were Germany's most educated. The philosopher Martin Heidegger viewed Hitler with mystical awe as guided by destiny, saying, "The *Führer* himself and he alone is the German reality, present and future, and its law." Despite Hitler's book-burning anti-intellectualism, Heidegger saw him as leading Germany to new intellectual heights.

As these reactions show, Hitler had succeeded in assuming the hero's role, and his power rested on the function of charismatic leaders from ancient times to the present. By objective measures like logical presentation, marshaling of facts, and command of language, other Nazis were better orators than Hitler, but he was the one who moved people deeply. His power was not as much in the content of his message as in his character and his hysterical style of speaking. His bizarreness turned some people against him, but for most it contributed to his appeal. The religious tradition of charisma and recent social research go a long way in explaining his success.

Charisma means "divine gifts." Gods were said to bestow the gifts on men for them to become leaders and ministers to their people. The main and most dramatic gifts were prophecy, speaking in tongues, and healing.

The gift of prophecy brought a leader superhuman wisdom. By knowing the future, he could know what to do, even if he lacked expertise about his community's predicament. Hitler thought he received the gift during his vision in 1918, enabling him to know he would be Germany's savior. He told people this prophecy and foretold grander events. He foresaw the biological evolution of Germans into supermen. He foresaw the rise of Germany from its abject position to rule the world for a thousand years. These and other prophecies were uttered with absolute assurance, as if they rested on superhuman knowledge. "It cannot be otherwise," he would say, declaring that every one of his earlier predictions had come true. Thus he "proved" to his followers that he had prophetic vision, and many believed he did.

Speaking in tongues is the utterance of incomprehensible sounds by which charismatic leaders were thought to communicate with God. During his speeches, Hitler often became very excited, losing control of his voice. The words he then tried to utter came out as incomprehensible sounds. While not taken to be charismatic, Hitler's hysteria and inability to continue speaking probably heightened the dramatic power of his speeches.

> . . . his capacity for surrendering himself to, and becoming possessed by, the unconscious. The . . . wild state . . . the hysterical transports . . . fanatical excitement, the oratorical intoxication of the demagogue, the orgiastic frenzy . . . are forms in which the state of being possessed by the unconscious is deliberately cultivated . . .[11]

In the Christian tradition, leaders healed sick individuals, while in the older Greek tradition, it was the nation they healed. Hitler did not try to treat individuals, but propaganda in the Third Reich presented him as "the great physician of his people," and a doctor published an article entitled "Adolf Hitler as the Physician of the German People" in a medical newsletter for the public. When the war began, propaganda said Hitler healed wounded German soldiers.[12] His grander claim was that he was healing the entire nation. Over and over he said Germany's problems were the result of sickness—microbes, maggots, infection, and diseased blood—by all of which he meant Jews. Over and over he said his fight against Jews was the same as Pasteur's and Koch's fight against microbes—that he and they provided cures to the world.

Other supernatural charismatic gifts are having faith so powerful as to move mountains, having the power of exorcism, and being immune to mortal dangers. Hitler's faith in himself was grandiose. He believed he could overcome all obstacles and defeat armies vastly superior in manpower and equipment to his own. What he believed was important because he conveyed it to his followers, inspiring their belief.

Exorcism as the symbolic function of Hitler's actions against Jews is taken up later. Some of his followers took seriously the idea that Jews were satanical, that they possessed Germany, and that Hitler was exorcising the nation.

Hitler's belief that he was immune to danger began during his brushes with death in many battles during World War I. He told the nation he was divinely protected against death, and his survival of assassination attempts reinforced the belief.

By Christian tradition, charismatic leaders also had ordinary gifts: teaching, governing, and serving. Teaching gifts included knowledge, wisdom, and skills in lecturing and oratory. Hitler had an extraordinary memory, recalling details from his cursory reading on many subjects, which he used to bolster the impression of being an expert in all fields. And he performed tricks. When visiting a regiment, he memorized soldiers' names and showed he knew more of them than the regiment's officers. Hitler thought of himself as wise and boasted of his wisdom. And his followers believed that he was wise, even when his personal life and rule of Germany showed striking lack of wisdom.

Hitler believed he had extraordinary gifts for simplifying complex matters and for governing. In fact, he oversimplified issues and was a poor administrator. Nonetheless, his simplifying added to people's impression of him as an effective leader. Other contributing factors were his stubbornness, boldness, willingness to take risks, and ruthlessness. While not listed in descriptions of Christian charisma, they are common in history's charismatic leaders.

Serving gifts are helping and mercy. Hitler did try to help people. He gave his subordinates advice, gifts, jobs, and wealth. He promoted them, sometimes at a dizzying rate, giving young men positions of high authority and power. He also tried hard to help the nation. Mercy he considered a weakness which he strove to overcome in himself.

In short, Hitler had many traits of traditional charisma—traits that have inspired awe, faith, and obedience over thousands of years. During those years, people have become less religious and religions have become more modern, but the response to charismatic leaders remains strong. Some charismatic traits came naturally to Hitler, others he cultivated, and still others were illusions he created for his followers. Changing himself to fit the image of a charismatic leader and devoting his life to the role contributed heavily to his success. His effectiveness is explained further by modern studies of charismatic leadership.

According to Jay Conger, who summarized recent studies, charismatic leaders mesmerize their followers. With extraordinary energy, they draw people into a sense of urgency about a project or mission, often eliciting a level of performance the followers did not know they possessed. They make things happen. There are three basic parts to a charismatic leader's appeal. He (and occasionally she) offers a strategic vision, offers himself as a special agent of change, thereby encouraging followers to have faith in him, and empowers them.[13]

The vision consists of an authoritative, persuasive evaluation of the present situation as unacceptable and a new program as the best alternative. Germans already considered their situation after World War I highly unsatisfactory. Hitler intensified their dissatisfaction by telling them their government consisted of impostors (Jews posing as Aryans) and traitors (Aryans serving as agents of Jews) and was deliberately leading them to destruction and slavery. He worked to persuade them that their situation was intolerable and moved them to act.

A charismatic leader's vision is deviant, calling for sweeping changes of the established order. But it is most powerful when also traditional, when it identifies the leader and the movement with the founding myth of the culture and with sacred heroes.

> In times of change and danger when there is a quicksand of fear under men's reasoning, a sense of continuity with generations gone before can stretch like a lifeline across the scary present.[14]

Hitler presented his "New Order" as a return to ancient ways and values. It was not a genuine revival, but tying it to tradition worked; many Germans thought it was a revival. According to Thomas Mann, "Intellectuals did not consider [Nazism] as a low, modern fad, or as a cultural degradation. Instead they welcomed it as the rebirth of mystic powers of life and of the soul of the people."[15] Hitler also identified himself with Jesus, promising to take away his people's guilt, to rid them of corrupt Judaism, and to die for them. Thus he combined his vision for Germany with powerful traditions.

Offering oneself as a special agent of change depends on stating or proving that one is uniquely qualified, unconventional, creative, fanatically devoted to the cause and to one's followers, and willing to take risks. Hitler offered all of these. The overall qualification he claimed was being chosen by Providence and German destiny to rescue the nation. This "proved" he was uniquely qualified.

Willingness to take risks is necessary in opposing an establishment, and Hitler was very willing. Hardly having a personal life, he was available to devote his energies and commit himself fully to a cause, with little to balance his intense, suppressed passions once he channeled them. He was built to be a fanatic and fitted the hero's mold:

> There he stands . . . not only bearing the magic tool of death but a magic tool of death [himself], his commitment total. He is a fanatic of dedication . . . desperate and therefore vulnerable . . . totally at risk and therefore brave . . . Most of all, he is someone wholly given over to passion. But his passion is death.[16]

A historian emphasized that no one had adequately explained how a man of "such insecurity and personal weakness" could inspire a nation with confidence.[17] Turning the puzzle over gives part of the answer. The extremity of his insecurity and ineffectiveness drove Hitler to present himself as a superman.

Hitler's insistence that he was always right—that he had learned everything by the time he was a young man and had not needed to change a single idea—was part of his charismatic strategy. He regretted parts of *Mein Kampf* and even regretted having written it. But although it went through many editions, he did not allow substantive changes. He regretted some articles of the Party program adopted in 1920 but rebuffed proposals by Nazi leaders to change them, saying the program was "unalterable." The reason was that he believed the masses wanted faith more than truth—faith above all. And faith in himself and the Party depended on the impression that they represented destiny and divine will and that their statements were eternal. He wrote:

> A Führer who is forced to depart from the platform of his general world view . . . because he has recognized it to be false . . . must, at the very least, forego the public exercise of any further political activities. Because he was once mistaken in his basic beliefs, it is possible that this could happen a second time.[18]

He tried to prove he had never made a mistake. Changing the program, changing *Mein Kampf*, changing his ideas, admitting error—any of these, he thought, would jeopardize people's faith in him.

Behind political reasons for making his ideas and actions "unalterable" was his need to play his role convincingly. More than anyone, he knew how ephemeral his identity was, how false, rehearsed, and artificial his role playing. To be convincing, Hitler needed to make the details of his role dramatic. He suppressed his doubts and dramatized everything, as if even his least important words had eternal validity.

Empowerment, as used here, means helping people use unused abilities. Explaining the success of his oratory, Hitler said:

> . . . I always talk as if the fate of the nation were bound up in their decision, as if they are in a position to give an example for many to follow. Certainly it means appealing to their vanity and ambition, but once I have got them to that point, the rest is easy.

> Every individual, whether rich or poor, has in his inner being a feeling of unfulfillment. Life is full of disappointments, which people cannot master. Slumbering somewhere is the readiness to risk some final sacrifice, some adventure, in order to give a new shape to their lives . . . The humbler people are, the greater the craving to identify themselves with a cause bigger than themselves . . .[19]

Charismatic leaders lift conventional barriers and personal inhibitions to action. The result is a release of energy and a feeling of importance and effectiveness.

An observer said Nazi leaders "felt themselves supermen who had sprung fully armed from the head of Hitler, possessed of a statesmanship that came, not from knowledge and experience, but from intuition and inspiration."[20]

The architect Albert Speer said:

> . . . he communicated to me a strength that raised me far above the limits of my
> potentialities . . . Sometimes it seems to me as though I . . . owed to him all the
> surges of vitality, dynamism and imagination that gave me the sense that I was
> soaring up above the ground on which everyone else was condemned to stand.[21]

> In Hitler's presence, we felt we were the lords of the imaginary world that we
> had created.[22]

In short, Hitler fitted the modern profile of a charismatic leader even better than the
traditional one. The amount of charisma a leader has is measured by the number of
charismatic traits he shows and the intensity with which he shows them. By Conger's
criteria, Hitler had maximum charisma; his traits and behaviors do explain his enormous
impact on his followers and the nation.

The power of charismatic leaders also comes from the needs of people to whom they
appeal, and the needs help explain the response elicited by leaders. Looking back over
his collaboration with Hitler, Baldur von Schirach, leader of the Hitler Youth, said:

> He was not—as many consider him today—the demonic beast who, favored by
> special circumstances of the times, seized power. He was, if we are to be com-
> pletely honest, our Hitler, the man we wanted, and the man we ourselves made
> the master of our destiny through our boundless adulation.[23]

In essence, the conditions that call for a charismatic hero today are the same as always—loss of confidence in ordinary leaders, chaos with uncertainty about what to do,
and despair. They prevailed in Germany, creating a need for a savior. Alfred Rosenberg,
an early Nazi, wrote:

> In our time, which is confused to the point of insanity, the individual does not
> know any more whether he is standing on his head or his feet. He . . . watches
> the machinery of the world absolutely fall to pieces, and finally beholds public
> deformity, dissociation, chaos.[24]

A lower-ranking Nazi wrote:

> The general confusion became greater and greater. No man knew where he
> stood.[25]

Many people experienced the situation as intolerable and felt unable to carry on.
Some picked up the saying, "Better an ending by terror than terror without end."[26]
Ironically, the man Germans chose to end the chaos did so by imposing unending
terror.

Hitler did end the chaos that preceded his rule, giving the nation a framework by
which to operate. Despite its contradictions and despite the harm that resulted, they
valued his "New Order" for telling them who they were and what they should do.

Because they felt they were a valued part of the norm he established—and therefore normal—they perceived him as a normal person. From early times up to Charles Manson and Jim Jones, the most paranoid charismatic leaders have been perceived as normal by their followers for that reason.

Many charismatic leaders attract hate-filled people. Among Hitler's leading associates, Goebbels, Göring, Reinhard Heydrich, Röhm, Rosenberg, and Streicher were extreme in their urge to destroy. They were drawn to Hitler because he gave them the opportunity to express it. He turned their deviance into the norm.

Charismatic leaders also appeal strongly to people who seek relief from responsibility, guilt, and blame. People like Goebbels and Göring need relief because they are obsessed with forbidden urges. But most people carry more responsibility than is comfortable, readily feel guilty, and appreciate someone who offers relief. Hitler was a rare gift to people burdened with guilt. He sanctioned their vices, transforming them into virtues. He said, ". . . I unconditionally assume responsibility for everything that happens in the movement," removing the burden of their acts from them as long as they were doing his bidding.[27] In effect, he said: "What's wrong is not your fault; it's the fault of the Jews. You are good. And if you follow me, you will get what you want and deserve." He suggested that being Aryan and making sacrifices entitled them to the forbidden.

Charismatic leaders are masters of an illusory type of intense sincerity. Hitler boasted he was the greatest of liars—a boast he fulfilled—yet he came across as sincere. An observer said:

> Not only did he say what seemed most advantageous to say at the time; he actually believed it; such liars are always the most convincing.[28]

Passionate oratory, combining underlying sincerity with false words—as opposed to honesty—is what gives words "the ring of truth." Nietzsche explained charismatic leaders' combination of illusion and sincerity:

> In all great deceivers, a remarkable process is at work to which they owe their power. In the very act of deception with all its preparations—the dreadful voice, the expression, the gestures—they are overcome by their belief in themselves, and it is this belief which then speaks so persuasively, so miracle-like to the audience.[29]

Even foreign leaders, whose job it was to deal with others' deceit and practice it themselves, were impressed with Hitler's sincerity. After their meeting at Berchtesgaden over Hitler's demands of Czechoslovakia, Britain's prime minister Neville Chamberlain said to his colleagues, ". . . in spite of the hardness and ruthlessness I thought I saw in his face, I got the impression that here was a man who could be relied upon when he had given his word."[30]

Hitler's word was that he wanted the Sudetenland, the part of Czechoslovakia where ethnic Germans lived, and nothing more. In a follow-up meeting at Godesberg, Hitler increased his demands. Chamberlain was shocked; the new demands meant Hitler had broken his word. Hitler then flattered Chamberlain, saying, "You know, you're the only man I've ever made a concession to." (They were the same words he had said several months earlier to the Austrian chancellor in the negotiations that preceded annexation of Austria.) Chamberlain returned to England and told his cabinet he thought he had "established some degree of personal influence over Herr Hitler . . ."[31] Reportedly, he saw himself as the only one who knew how to deal with Hitler. Then he went to the famous meeting at Munich and agreed to Germany's acquisition of the Sudetenland, based on Hitler's assurance to take no more. When Hitler subsequently took more of Czechoslovakia, Chamberlain complained that Hitler had made a fool of him.

Chamberlain's desire to avert war contributed to his victimization. Before Munich, he read a book exposing Hitler's deceptiveness, reportedly saying he did not believe a word of it. He read another about Hitler's determination to go to war and wrote in his diary, ". . . if I accepted the author's conclusions, I should despair, but I don't and won't . . ."[32] Regardless of his evaluation of those books, Chamberlain was or should have been familiar with *Mein Kampf*, in which Hitler had boasted of his deceptiveness and described his plans for conquest—plans he was now carrying out. Chamberlain's victimization also testifies to Hitler's skill in offering people what they wanted and convincing them they could have it. For Hitler's followers, the problem created by his lying was worse. He gave them a life to lead, a future in which to have faith. To stop believing him, they had to give up the world he made for them.

Hitler's speeches contained many careless misstatements and deliberate lies, but also a core of passionate sincerity. He fully believed he was a victim entitled to revenge and that Germany was, too. For him these were burning truths—the basis of his life and the essence of his message. He did not care whether the details were true or false.

Followers also did not care. In a lecture on Jews to a college class, a Nazi said: "Read the *Protocols of the Elders of Zion*. They say that it is a forgery. What difference does it make? The idea behind it is not forged."[33]

Like many charismatic leaders, Hitler relied on symbols. Metaphors and myths are more evocative than concrete, factual words and lend themselves to loose, vague arguments. His arguments were especially loose and vague, as he blurred the distinction between symbol and reality. "Hitler, more than any other twentieth-century leader, focused on the irrational through myths and symbols . . ."[34]

Hitler's oratory was a combination of belligerence, romanticism, and eroticism new in German politics. Of these, the belligerence was most obvious. His speeches were mainly about Germany's victimization and the people responsible for it. Since the sense of being victimized was widespread, Hitler's references to "the infamy of Versailles" and "the Jewish world conspiracy" and his calls for revenge got the most applause. The calls and his rhetoric of violence energized audiences. When people who consider themselves victims decide to fight, they often become euphoric. Still another source of excitement was the permission Hitler gave people to do what was forbidden, especially to figures of authority. Standing up to figures of authority violates a prime taboo and liberates people.

Many fathers used violence on their sons. The extreme brutality Hitler suffered at the hands of his father exceeded the experience of most boys but resembled it. His fight to stand up to his father and to liberate himself by opposing established authority touched their needs. Noting this, Erik Erikson said, "It frequently happens in history that *an extreme personal experience fits a universal latent conflict so well that a crisis lifts it to a representative position.*"[35] At times the bizarre vision of a would-be ruler fits the predicament of a nation. Then the candidate's ideas—no matter how unfounded or implausible—seem true, powerful, and even the only solution to the nation's problems. Hitler's thesis that Jews were behind Germany's misfortunes provided a simple explanation for everything that was wrong. And to the extent that it was based on secrets revealed only to him, it could not be disproved.

In his speeches, Hitler scolded those he held responsible and threatened them with death, as in these excerpts from the early 1920s:

> There will be no peace in the land until a body is hanging from every lamp post.[36]

> On one point there should be no doubt: we will not let the Jews slit our gullets and not defend ourselves.[37]

> Let us be inhumane! But if we save Germany, then we will have accomplished the world's greatest deed. Let us do injustice! But if we save Germany, then we will have eliminated the world's greatest injustice. Let us be immoral! But if our folk is saved, then we will have opened the way for morality again![38]

His words were accompanied by an angry frown, hysterical tone, and vehement gestures. As Lüdecke said, Hitler was indeed a scourge. He fixed members of the audience with a penetrating stare. His harsh voice was also described as penetrating. He pointed at people in the audience vigorously, jabbed at them with his finger, shook his fist, and sometimes pounded with it. He addressed anger to enemies as if they were present, even when his audience consisted only of followers. He exhibited anger to members of the audience, threatening them with disaster unless they supported him. To those who hesitated, he ominously insisted they had to choose between him and Communism or between victory and annihilation; there was no middle ground. He rose to his toes with excitement, he screamed at the audience. When interrupted with applause or cheers, he often scowled, eager to continue, to maintain the intensity. And sometimes he staged "spontaneous" violence at meetings.

Hitler also appealed to Germans' romantic streak, offering to bring back the imaginary past, the time of the heroic gods and godlike people of German mythology. His promises to relieve people of the burdens of reason and responsibility and restore them to a paradise in which their needs would be guaranteed touched the core of Romanticism. He offered gratification of old yearnings and a return to a child's concept of Eden. He evoked Romanticism's various forms—myths, adventures in war and love, extravagant fancy, and sentimentality. Germans dissatisfied with eighteenth-century Rationalism, which they found cold and burdensome, yearned for the past. Visionary thinking is often a return in a situation of high stress to more primitive modes of thought. Hitler's offer fitted the trend back to Romanticism in the late 1800s and early 1900s.

Romanticism stresses nostalgia over modernism, idealism over reason, subjectivity and mysticism over objectivity, intuition and revelation over evidence, symbolism and obscurantism over literalness and clarity, and nationalism and racism over internationalism and universality.[39] Hitler and the Nazi Party were clearly in the Romantic tradition. In addition, Hitler had a tragic look, which he played up by offering to die for the people. It appealed to men as well as women. The anti-Nazi George Orwell wrote:

> The fact is that there is something deeply appealing about him . . . It is a pathetic, dog-like face, the face of a man suffering under intolerable wrongs . . . He is the martyr, the victim, Prometheus chained to the rock, the self-sacrificing hero who fights against impossible odds . . .[40]

From its beginning, the Nazi Party had an idea of appealing to people's gender needs. To men it offered satisfaction of macho needs not only by participating in violence and in the rise of Germany to world dominance but also in reversing the liberation of women and restoring them to a traditional position of subservience. "The National Socialist movement is in its nature a masculine movement," said Goebbels, adding that the "directing and shaping" of public life "must be claimed by men" by eliminating women from it.[41]

Before finding Hitler, the Party leaders had been seeking a figurehead who would be particularly attractive to women. One had said, "He must be a bachelor, then we'll get the women." When they found Hitler, they used him particularly to win members, votes, and contributions from women.

Besides meeting these expectations, Hitler affected women in a dramatic, unforeseen way. "Women by the thousands abased themselves at Hitler's feet, they tried to kiss his boots and some of them succeeded, even to the point of swallowing the gravel on which he had trod . . ." Others saved the gravel as souvenirs. Some begged to bathe in the tub he had used when in prison. Thousands of single and married ones wrote letters offering to be his lovers and to have children by him. A teenager who came home pregnant from a labor camp and was confronted by a distressed mother said, "I am proud to be able to give HIM (Hitler) a baby. I hope it will be a boy to die for HIM." She added, "I am one of the Fuehrer's brides . . ."[42] As nuns were recognized to be Jesus's brides, so unwed mothers were given recognition as Hitler's brides. Unlike nuns, Hitler's brides had pregnancies and live children to cherish.

During his speeches, some women became highly excited and fainted. After noting this effect, he deliberately had women seated in the front rows to enhance it. And the excitement and fainting of women in front stimulated women and men behind them.

The sexual part of Hitler's oratory is hardest to specify. Many observers got the impression that his behavior when orating was erotic, and he confirmed it by telling Hanfstängl, "The crowd is a woman and has sexual appeal, after a speech I feel as if I had a sexual release." He told two of his physicians that at the climaxes of his speeches he had orgasms. One advised him to do nothing about it, for eliminating his sexual arousal would reduce the power of his oratory.[43]

Love is aroused by many behaviors that are not necessarily loving and that do not lead to wholesome relationships. It is aroused especially by the sense that someone understands our unspoken needs and will satisfy them. Hitler's sensitivity to others' needs and his offer to satisfy unspoken needs gave people the impression that he understood them and loved them. He was passionate and gave the utmost during speeches, becoming drenched with sweat. He also stared at people and "his eyes seemed to bore into each one . . . giving each a sense of personal contact."[44] Being stared at is exciting; it arouses fear and desire—a combination that makes for awe. Even in large audiences, people got the impression that he was looking at them individually and that he cared for them individually.

During the years of his most effective oratory, Hitler loved only one person intensely, Geli Raubal. Except briefly with her, his tender emotions had little outlet. Probably during peaks of emotion he experienced while orating, besides sexual arousal, Hitler's loving feelings were also aroused and conveyed to the audience, adding to propaganda that portrayed him as loving the people.

Little has been written about people's love for Hitler, perhaps because the idea that he was lovable is repugnant. But millions adored Hitler, killed for him, and died for him. Without taking the love he aroused into account, explanations of Hitler's influence are incomplete. Göring said Nazis' regard for Hitler came from "the close inner bond between Hitler and his men," believing the bond was mutual. He said he would be loyal to Hitler until death, just as Hitler would be loyal to him. He was right about himself and other Nazis, who remained loyal even after Hitler betrayed them. Some who were killed on Hitler's orders cried "Heil Hitler!" before dying. But Göring was wrong about Hitler. Like other charismatic leaders, Hitler impressed his followers as devoted to them but was too narcissistic and hate-filled to be truly devoted. As in the Röhm purge, during crises he killed his followers.

CHAPTER 11

TRANSFORMING THE NATION

In the course of years we want to insure that a gun feels just as natural in the hands of a German boy as a pen.[1]

—An administrator of the Hitler Youth

When Jewish blood spurts from the knife,
Then everything is fine.[2]

—From a song of the Hitler Youth

Hitler had hardened himself for the coming slaughter. The nation, which did not share his craving for war and extermination, also needed hardening. Using totalitarian control of German institutions and his charisma, Hitler began conditioning the nation in hate and uninhibited destructiveness. From his first speeches for the Nazi Party until his death, one theme remained constant. The nation's troubles were caused by oppression by enemies whose purpose was to annihilate Germany. The only way to prevent annihilation was to fight them and annihilate them. The fight was war, requiring what war required—zeal, ruthlessness, and sacrifice. In war, extreme acts were not only permissible but also noble. The Nazi Party endorsed the views of a military scientist who wrote in 1932:

> War is not only a factor of extermination but a principle of regeneration. It alone enables the human soul to reveal all its riches and all its force. Biology will stamp the next war as an extermination fight of entire nations . . .[3]

Germany's struggle went beyond ordinary war. In history, war was rarely total and enmity was temporary. Italy, Germany's enemy in World War I, would be its main ally in World War II. Hitler's basic sense of war, however, came not from history but from his relationship with his father—his permanent enemy who had almost ended Hitler's existence, who even after death remained his oppressor.

Hitler couched his rhetoric in primitive, Darwinian slogans about animals and their biological nature. To him the struggle of a species to survive meant constant war with another species until one of them was extinct. (Survival struggles of most species have no resemblance to genocidal warfare. Some species kill members of another species at hand, but they have no instinct to eradicate the species.) He believed Aryans were more than a national group—they were a genetically determined race, a species superior to others. And Germany's enemies—Jews and Slavs—were enemies by nature and evil by nature. They could not change, and the only sensible strategy was to eradicate them. A Nazi publication said:

> The war of the future will be total war . . . total war means the complete and final disappearance of the vanquished . . .[4]

Hitler's wearing of a military uniform in many settings contributed to his image as a leader in a war. He declared the war to come as the most important in history—so vital that life in the Third Reich must be subordinated to it. A Nazi military scientist wrote:

> . . . in the future every German will be judged first and last, once and for all by the place he fills in the scheme of national defense. Whoever fails in this capacity forfeits his claim to be a citizen.[5]

Everyone and everything could be sacrificed in war and in preparing for it.

The spirit of war was brought into daily life by military trappings and activities—soldierly organization, uniforms, martial music, marching, drills, and the frequent sight of thousands in impressive military formations—pageantry that gilds aggression. A leader of the Storm Troopers said:

> The sight of a large number of men, disciplined and co-ordinated both mentally and physically, with a patent or potential will to fight to the limit, makes the greatest impression on every German; the language of the message which it carries to the heart is more convincing and more compelling than any writing, speech or logic.[6]

Military saluting became part of everyday life, along with *"Heil Hitler!"* As more and more settings and occasions were militarized, children were required to salute about 100 times a day. And the government substituted military words and phrases for nonmilitary ones. For example, job procurement was called "labor battle"; a worker was called "a soldier of labor"; and production was called "production battle."[7]

The militarization of civilian life made the public into members of a romanticized army. Throughout history, heroism in answering the call to be a soldier has impressed people more than heroism in refusing, even when refusing was more difficult or more dangerous. And to children, the romantic appeal of being offered adult roles as soldiers in Germany's mission to dominate the world was especially powerful.

Hitler imposed his military outlook on the Nazi Party and then the government. He made the Party dictatorial by introducing the Führer Principle. Decisions were his alone, and he demanded "blind obedience." As chancellor he applied the principle to the nation. In passing orders down to those who carried them out, Hitler introduced the concept of the Führer Order. People questioned some orders, but questioning could be stopped by telling them they were being given a Führer Order. It meant that no matter how low the position of the person passing the order, the authority behind it was Hitler. No matter what commandment, law, program, or policy it violated, the order had to be obeyed. As long as people were carrying out such orders, what they did was automatically right and protected against punishment. Individual judgment and conscience were irrelevant.

Preparation for killing began in childhood with simulated warfare. In athletics for twelve-year-old boys, the javelin and discus were replaced by the hand grenade. Camouflage, rifle training, and war games became part of the curriculum for girls, too, even though Hitler had no intention for them to become soldiers.[8]

Gregor Ziemer, an educator who studied the Nazi school system, called the part for boys "education for death," meaning they were trained both to become killers and to give their lives readily. A slogan of the Hitler Youth, "We were born to die for Germany," was put above the entrances to their camps.[9] (And the sign "We were born to die" was placed at army training centers.) At fourteen boys were told:

> You may all have to die for Hitler before you are twenty. But is that not a wonderful privilege? What greater and more glorious mission can a German boy have than to die for the savior of Germany? And now raise your right hands and repeat after me the oath that will indeed make you Hitler soldiers, ready to lay down your lives for him.[10]

Songs of the Hitler Youth carried the double message, as in:

> Triumphant we will beat the French,
> And die brave heroes.[11]

School books dwelt on suffering, sacrifice, war, and death.[12]

Observing a war game of Hitler Youth, Ziemer noted:

> . . . one of the prisoners . . . was brought into headquarters . . . His hands were tied behind him so firmly that the wrists were swollen. He was gagged with strips of adhesive. His eyes were pasted shut. He was kicked along and called names.[13]

Ziemer protested the boy's suffering, and was told contemptuously by the leader that boys had to get used to suffering.

Education emphasized that as Aryans, as members of the master race, as gods emerging from their fetters, they were not limited by ordinary restraints. On the contrary, they were entitled to the fulfillment of their desires. Violating moral and legal codes was not only their right but also their duty in fulfilling their destiny. Boys were told over and over that their superiority required them to do what was unjust by ordinary standards. To be unscrupulous in performing duties was necessary in the national interest. This was urged most on those selected to be the best of all—boys accepted into an elite order of the Hitler Youth:

> The members of our Order must be willing to obey even when it is unjust for them to do so. That is the greatest test.[14]

Disregarding morals was what would make them superior to other boys. Von Schirach told them:

> Before other races, which are decadent or even completely degenerate, we must reach that state of the perfect and complete human animal—the Superman! . . . *it is imperative that no one and nothing be allowed to stand in our way* . . . You must be faithful in heart to the mission with which our Führer has entrusted you—by blind obedience of the discipline imposed on you, and obedience to the orders given you, *no matter what they may be*.[15] (Italics added.)

Just because Germans were neither a decadent nor degenerate race, just because they were approaching perfection, they had the right and duty to act unscrupulously—to be criminals.

Hitler believed indifference—like that of an animal to the suffering of its opponent—was critical in elevating the new German to be the "beast of prey" that would rule the earth. According to one analyst, the words found most in *Mein Kampf* are "harsh," "brutal," and "merciless." Hitler advocated "brute force" and "barbaric ruthlessness" against all opponents.[16] He urged subordinates to develop indifference to the suffering caused by his programs—indifference based on hatred of the victims.

Most of Hitler's subordinates were not indifferent. While visiting an SS death squad, Himmler witnessed the shooting of a hundred prisoners. At the first rifle volley, he staggered, almost fell, and cried out in anguish, but he stuck out the killing to the end. While visiting a death camp, he vomited and, on another occasion, fainted. Adolf Eichmann, an administrator of the Holocaust, was also sickened when he visited death camps.[17] But like other leaders, they told their subordinates they were indifferent to the suffering and death. Frank, who became administrator of part of Poland and responsible for the killing there, was often upset by it. Nonetheless he told subordinates:

> . . . for all I care, mincemeat can be made of the Poles and Ukrainians and all the others who run around here—it does not matter what happens . . .[18]

In carrying out Hitler's orders, when able to control themselves, they pretended indifference.

The most extensive training was for the SS. Recruits were required to observe and participate as assistants while others beat, tortured, and killed prisoners. Those who did not faint were rewarded. And they were subjected to insults, humiliations, and violence. Some SS men were given dogs to rear as their own and then ordered to strangle them. Others were given infants to use for target practice. Still others were forced to kill Jewish babies in front of the babies' mothers.[19] Voicing scruples and flinching when witnessing or performing such acts were called softness, unmanliness, weakness, and cowardice before the enemy. Signs of revulsion at what occurred or of compassion for victims were punished as unsoldierly and undutiful. The statement in his file that a member of the SS performed his duties with "personal ruthlessness" was good for advancement.[20] A recruit wrote in his diary:

> It's as though our instructors wish to draw a crude line across our past lives, to brutalize us, to prove to us that in the SS everything is different.[21]

The training was supported by indoctrination to regard victims as having no worth and therefore not meriting even minimal consideration. An SS indoctrination pamphlet, *The Subhuman,* said:

> . . . just as light and shadow are eternal enemies—so the greatest enemy of man, the master of the earth, is man himself.

> The subhuman man—that creation of nature appearing wholly identical in all biological respects, with hands, feet, and a species of brain, with eyes and a mouth, is in reality something quite different, a dreadful creation, a mere first draft of a human being with facial features resembling those of human beings— but mentally and spiritually inferior to any animal. The inner life of one of these people is a hideous chaos of wild and uninhibited passions: a nameless will to destroy, desire in its most primitive form, the most manifest vileness.[22]

The pamphlet went on to say that the true man created everything—tools, ideas, cul- ture—that raised him above animals.

> In this way he became akin to God!

> But the subhuman man . . . hated the work of the other man. He raged against him, secretly as a thief, openly as a blasphemer—and a murderer . . . The sub- human creature never kept the peace; he never gave the others any rest. For he needed twilight and chaos.

Few SS recruits may have realized that the pamphlet described Hitler and what mem- bers of the SS were meant to become rather than the Jews, Gypsies, and Slavs to whom it referred.

The most extreme training in cruelty and ruthlessness was given to candidates for the Death Head Division of the SS—the elite of the elite in the eyes of Theodor Eicke, their commandant. They were the men trained for work in concentration camps and later in death camps and were a specially selected group. Ninety-three percent of them were single, compared to 57 percent in other SS divisions, and they were more ideological than other SS members. Eicke put the greatest pressure on them to renounce their religions, causing parents to disown some. Noting the estrangement from their families, Eicke wrote, "We must make sure that the [Division] is a home for them," and he invited them to spend their vacations in his house, becoming known as Papa Eicke.[23] They were closer to each other than men in other SS units, using the familiar form of address not only with each other but also with their officers. Probably these conditions made them more receptive to the training. For killing they received medals, and Hitler and Himmler made a point of praising those who performed the most destructive acts.

To maintain secrecy about extermination, citations accompanying medals were misleading: ". . . for the conferment of [medals] to SS members who participated in the executions, under 'reasons' enter 'completion of vital war assignments.' The word 'execution' should under no circumstances be mentioned."[24]

Despite all their special training, the tasks of mutilating and killing innocent civilians, mostly women and children, and dismembering their corpses proved too much for many in the SS. Mutilation was part of medical experiments performed on camp inmates. Also, Jews' body parts were systematically removed for special study by Nazi anthropologists and gold fillings for their intrinsic value. And, some commandants had skin and body parts removed to make lamp shades and other objects. Himmler said, "It was the most dreadful assignment and most awful commission that an organization could ever receive: the commission to solve the Jewish question," for it required "superhuman acts of inhumanity."[25] Death camp administrators had a heavy morale problem. Some requested transfers to the front, risking death to get out of their extermination assignments. To limit the number of men who knew about the extermination, their requests were denied. And to raise their morale, Himmler stressed the idea that doing the most repugnant tasks made them the best of men:

> Among ourselves it should be mentioned quite frankly—but we will never speak of it publicly—that just as we did not hesitate on June 30, 1934, to do the duty we were ordered, to stand comrades up against the wall and shoot them, so we have never spoken about . . . cleaning out the Jews, the extermination of the Jewish race. Most of *you* must know what it means when 100 corpses are lying side by side, or 500 or 1,000. To have stuck it out and at the same time . . . to have remained decent fellows, that is what has made us hard. This is a page of glory in our history which has never been written and is never to be written.[26]

The shooting of comrades referred to the Röhm purge. Himmler also told them:

> Do not lose your courage, for future generations will thank you for overcoming your Christian weakness and finishing this good but dreadful work.[27]

For his subordinates, Hitler arranged an abbreviated form of the SS training. New administrators were also made to observe and assist while others harmed and killed people. Colleagues of Hitler said that, besides getting subordinates accustomed and calloused to destruction, the experiences were designed to bind them to him as accomplices in crime. One wrote:

> Demands have actually been made of individuals in order to have a future hold over them . . . to make the élite a following . . . from which every member's escape is cut off, because he has been incriminated.[28]

Hitler put them in the position of being subject to prosecution if he did not protect them. He ordered photographic and film records made of SS men torturing victims, and the purpose may have been to have them know that evidence of their crimes was on file. Robert Waite put the idea aptly:

> . . . in order to enforce absolute loyalty and obedience, organizers of terror societies force a prospective member, as part of his initiation rite, to commit an act which directly and flagrantly violates his most important personal taboos. Such an atrocity, by cutting the initiate off from society and from his previous value system, ties him irrevocably to the new organization because it is the only group which sponsors and approves the outrage he has perpetrated.[29]

This idea seems to have been in Hitler's mind when he said about his followers:

> We must compromise these people so that they have to march with us.[30]

A paltry way of making forbidden acts more acceptable was referring to them by euphemisms, which became standard government practice. Hjalmar Schacht, minister of finance under Hitler, said that "every piece of injustice was tricked out with its deceptive formal caption. The result was that when [oppressive] decrees were published most people had no idea at all of their real significance or of the sinister intent behind them."[31] Suspending constitutional protection of Germans and their property was called "protection of the German people." The assumption of dictatorial power was called "An Act for Relieving the Distress of Nation and Reich." Stealing from Jews, as when SS or Gestapo men arrested them at home and took whatever property they fancied, was called "voluntary surrender" and "transfer to Aryan possession." Jews and people with partial Jewish ancestry were eliminated from the government by the "Law for the Restoration of the Professional Civil Service." Jewish children were denied an education under the "Law Against the Overcrowding of German Schools." Abolishing political parties was called "strengthening the solidarity of the people." Invading and occupying a country was called "protecting" it (Denmark and Norway) and "insuring its neutrality" (Belgium and Holland). Looting art and other property in occupied countries was also called "protecting" it. Razing a city or town to the ground was called "pacifying" it. Incarceration in concentration camps, often with death as the likely result, was called "change of residence," "preventive detention," "protective detention," and "re-education into the discipline of work." A proposed measure in 1939 to kill mental hospital patients was to be called "The Law for the Granting of Last Aid" or "The Law for Granting of Special Help." Killing under the misleading "euthanasia" program was called "mercy killing" and "final medical assistance" and done under the auspices of the Community Foundation for Institutional Care. Deliberately working incurable patients to death was called "forced-labor therapy." Places where concentration camp inmates too sick to continue working were sent to die were called "convalescent camps." Places where Jews were sent to die by starvation and freezing were called "retirement villages." Death camps were called "health resorts" and "charitable foundations for institutional care." The extermination program was called "negative population policy," "disinfection," "deportation," "evacuation," "relocation," "resettlement," "forced labor," "housecleaning," "special treatment," and "the final solution." Facilities for killing German children were called "infant homes," "specialist children's wards," and "infant concentration camps." Children of slave laborers were taken from their parents and sent to be starved to death in "care centers" for foreign children. When "special treatment" became a notorious term, Himmler ordered that it not be used any longer in documents, but replaced by "transit," which became the main euphemism for extermination.[32] Gas chambers in the death camps were disguised as shower rooms to mislead the victims more than anyone else. Nonetheless, the concept of disinfection and the labeling of death chambers as showers were used and are still used by people to deny that extermination took place.

Another use of language may not have been deliberate. Analyzing Nazi documents, Lucy Dawidowicz found unusually heavy use of indirect, vague, and passive phrasing like "prompt Aryanization is to be sought." An effect was to minimize individual responsibility, as if things happened because of inevitable, impersonal forces.[33] Orders often left unsaid who would take action, what the action would be, and who the victims would be.

Responsibility was also undermined by restricting information. Hitler ordered that officials receive only the minimum needed to perform assigned duties. And they grew afraid to ask for more, to consult each other, and to share their reservations. As a result, people focused their attention on what they themselves did and thought they were not implicated if they did not take part directly in killing. For example, people involved in arresting Jews and shipping them to death camps, including those who knew the Jews would be killed there, considered themselves innocent because they did not do the killing. Speer concluded, "The whole structure of the system was aimed at preventing conflicts of conscience from even arising."[34]

Secrecy and misdirection had been marks of the Nazi regime from its first days. Theresienstadt was made a model concentration camp so that it could be shown to representatives of the International Red Cross and foreign diplomats, to convince them the camp program was benign. During the war, secrecy and misdirection reached an extreme, as programs less acceptable to the nation were established. Jews sent to Auschwitz were made to write postcards for mailing after their deaths, to mislead people at home into thinking they were alive. In a mixup, an Aryan woman and her two small sons went with a group of Jews to the death camp at Treblinka. Realizing the mistake, she showed the commandant papers identifying her as the wife of an army officer, but he was suspicious. She even pulled down her boys' pants to show they were uncircumcised. Finally the commandant was convinced. After consultation, he had the three of them sent to the gas chamber along with the Jews to preserve the secrecy of the extermination program.[35]

No matter how impulsive, bizarre, destructive, or lawless his actions were, Hitler rationalized them as legitimate. And he offered one broad justification for whatever he did—he was expressing the will of the German race. In the myth he created, Hitler was the incarnation of the race's historic mission, from which his supernatural powers came. In turn, he fused the activities of the people, the Party, and the state in fulfilling the race's destiny by emitting a mystical energy—*Führergewalt*—leadership power.[36] The race's will—like Providence, destiny, and history—was an abstraction, and only Hitler was in a position to know what it was in a specific situation. He said it was manifested in an instinctive sense of what was right—a sense that had nothing to do with traditional religious, ethical, or legal codes, a sense that was superior to those codes. He called it "the sound judgment of the German people" and presented it as the governing principle of the Third Reich.

The people were not permitted to express their judgment. Their "sound judgment" was also an abstraction. Hitler said the Nazi Party spoke for the people, and he controlled what the Party said. In practice, the people's judgment meant his own judgment.

To lend an air of legitimacy to his programs, Hitler used Germany's legal system, bending it to his will. His authority was imposed on prosecutors by Göring, who told them, ". . . the law and the will of the Fuehrer are one."[37] Hitler declared himself to be the highest judge of the nation with the right to have whomever he chose killed or protected.[38] Frank, who was also commissioner of justice and president of the Academy of German Law, urged judges to adopt a single, simple legal principle:

> In any matter of consequence, think of the Führer. Ask yourselves: How would the Führer decide in my place? Act accordingly and you will find yourselves on a far higher plane. You will feel fortified by this thought and invested with an altogether new moral authority.[39]

He told the Academy, "Love for the Führer has become a legal concept."[40]

Judges were tempted with extraordinary power. As long as they were doing Hitler's bidding, their discretion was unlimited. A high judge declared:

> Not until the National Socialist State arrived, did the judge achieve the position that is his due. Now the judge is completely independent, no longer the slave of paragraphs in law books . . . he is absolute king, for he carries the heaviest responsibility of all—that of being responsible to no one.[41]

Hitler's reshaping of justice was a prime example of his subversion of German institutions. Ideally, a system of justice is embodied in a constitution and laws, traditions, and forms, which are designed to guide and restrain individual judgment. It is a result of evolution, incorporating countless experiences, distilling them into precedents and principles. And the judiciary is protected against interference from other branches of government and the private sector, which tends to make it the most stable and conservative of the branches—a bulwark against illegal change and especially against an outbreak of tyranny. All this Hitler attempted to sweep aside with one stroke.

Göring proclaimed, "Right is that which serves the German people."[42] He accompanied the slogan by reiterated declarations that his main goal was exterminating enemies of the state—Communists. And under cover of fighting Communists, he proceeded against non-Communists. Werner Best, chief of the Gestapo's legal division, persuaded the Academy of German Law to adopt as its guiding principle the slogan "Right is that which serves the State" to justify arbitrary, oppressive practices of the police. He said, "As long as the police carries out the will of the leadership, it is acting legally."[43] Himmler, whose SS took control of much of Germany's police, declared, "It makes no difference to me whether the letter of the law says I can or cannot do something," and "the police . . . can act only according to the orders of the leadership and not according to the laws."[44] The Prussian Supreme Court ruled that whatever the police did served the general purpose of resisting Communist threats, *no matter against whom police actions were directed.*[45] The authority to act outside the law, accorded here to the regular police, the Security Police, and the Gestapo, was then extended to Storm Troopers and members of the SS.

A judge protested the "euthanasia" program to the minister of justice, proposing to file charges against the program's administrators. The minister, who himself had called the program "murder by assembly line," showed the judge a copy of Hitler's secret authorization for the killing, but the judge responded, "Injustice cannot be turned into justice by formally correct . . . legislation." The minister told him that a judge who "does not recognize the will of the Führer as the source of law . . . cannot be a judge anymore." The judge retired.[46]

Nietzsche had advocated control of the law by a superior group, itself above the law, using it for its own benefit at the expense of inferiors. Hitler was exceptional in openly doing so. In this vein, Rosenberg suggested a new purpose of justice:

> Punishment is . . . simply the separating out of alien types and deviant nature.[47]

The minister of justice wrote to Hitler's secretary Martin Bormann:

> With a view to liberating the body of the German nation from Poles, Russians, Jews, and Gypsies . . . I intend to hand over the criminal prosecution of Poles, Russians, Jews, and Gypsies to the . . . SS. My assumption here is that the justice authorities can contribute only in small measure to the extermination of members of these peoples . . .[48]

But Hitler insisted that the justice system participate in the extermination.

Bizarre as this use of law may sound, it was accepted by Nazi law professors. One said criminal trials were to become "an evaluation and segregation of types."[49] And in fact the courts became an instrument for purging Germany's population.

The principle that "the law and the will of the Fuehrer are one" was vague. Judges who meant to comply did not know how Hitler would decide each case. To help them and to coerce judges reluctant to comply, a program of directives, hints, and threats was instituted. Judges received circulars about how to administer Nazi justice. Nazi publications criticized and vilified judges for decisions considered unsatisfactory and attacked the judiciary as a whole. Hitler repeatedly did the same, saying judges were "remote from life" and sticklers to the dead letter of the law, without links to the race. He did not hide his contempt for them. In private Hitler threatened to cut the judiciary by 90 percent and even to do away with the legal system. Lawyers too were vilified. An associate said ". . . he hated no profession as much as the law."[50] The legal system stood for the rules against which he was in rebellion.

When trying cases, prosecutors suggested to judges what verdicts and sentences the Chancellery expected. And members of the police or SS often sat in court as observers and hinted to judges about whether their conduct of cases was likely to lead to punishment.

Laws and the constitution no longer meant what they said, for they had to be reinterpreted in the light of Hitler's will. Even with the directives they received, no judge, prosecutor, lawyer, or police official could be sure what a law meant in general or how it should be applied in a specific case, unless advised by the Chancellery. Their uncertainty weakened prevailing moral and ethical rules as well as legal ones. Right and wrong were less clear than before. Nazi law professors noted that Nazi justice made it harder—in fact, impossible—for people to know whether their acts were illegal or what the consequences might be. One found the uncertainty desirable as it increased the pressure on people to conform![51]

Three trends, however, were clear. First, the new system usually protected Nazis who committed acts for which the rest of the nation was punished. In clearing the streets of Nuremberg for the annual Nazi Party rally, Storm Troopers picked up a Communist, took him to their guardhouse, and beat him to death. They were arrested and charged, but Hitler's representative intervened, urging:

> If . . . the trial . . . were to be conducted, it would prove impossible—even if the trial itself were held in closed session—to prevent the public at large from finding out what occurred. That would severely damage and undermine the reputations of the [Storm Troopers], the Party, the police, and the National Socialist State in general.
>
> However, the damage to the German Reich would be even greater if—as is bound to happen—other nations were to learn of these events . . .
>
> Because the deed did not result from an ignoble motive but instead was designed to achieve a highly patriotic goal and served to promote the National Socialist State, the cancellation of the proceedings . . . does not appear incompatible with the orderly practice of criminal law.[52]

The prosecutor dropped the charges.

Another Storm Trooper was prosecuted on charges resulting from an automobile accident. The Court of Appeals reversed his conviction since "every action performed by [a Trooper] . . . in the course of his duties occurs under the aegis of the National Socialist Party . . ." Therefore, such acts were political, and courts had no jurisdiction over them.[53] Eventually, Nazis were made immune to prosecution except by Party courts.

On coming to power, Storm Troopers carried out a pogrom against Jews in scattered parts of the nation. It was the first in Germany in a long time and aroused protest by non-Jews. In November 1938, perhaps judging five years of anti-Semitic indoctrination to be enough, Hitler ordered another throughout the nation. Disguised as a spontaneous act by the people, the violence was carried out mostly by Storm Troopers in civilian clothes. The Troopers destroyed Germany's 200 temples, over 7,000 Jewish stores, and 170 homes. Glass from temples and stores littering the streets gave the pogrom the name *Kristallnacht*—night of broken glass. In addition Jews were assaulted, raped, and killed.

Kristallnacht outraged many Germans, and prosecutors launched investigations and brought charges against Storm Troopers for beating, raping, and killing Jews. The Nazi Party intervened, claiming jurisdiction over the accused. Walter Buch, chief judge of the Party, reviewed some of the cases. Most involved killing, shooting, or otherwise injuring people, and Buch asked Hitler to quash proceedings in regular court against the men accused. Buch punished most of them with reprimands and warnings for exceeding orders.

The basis Buch gave for his decisions was extenuating circumstances. He found the orders given the Troopers to perpetrate *Kristallnacht* so unclear they might have thought shooting and killing were authorized. In addition the Troopers believed their acts provided a service to the Führer and the Party. Buch's strangest extenuation was, "The men had moreover to conquer the heaviest inhibitions to carry out the order."[54]

The second trend in Nazi justice was to increase convictions and sentences for non-Nazis. The increase was due partly to Nazis using the system as an instrument of revenge for political, business, and personal injuries. But mostly it came from Hitler's severity, which kept increasing. With little regard to old laws still on the books or even laws enacted by the Third Reich, judges were urged to construe any act of which Nazis disapproved as a crime and to apply severe penalties. And if an act was not punishable by any law, they were to apply the law that came closest to prohibiting the act and to stretch the law as needed. The Ministry of Justice planned a comprehensive revision of the penal code, but it was easier to reject established principles of law than to develop a new system. In addition, Hitler did not want to be bound by new laws. The revision was postponed and never done. But in 1935 a temporary administrative ruling said courts were to convict and punish for any act that violated the principles of the intended revision or violated "popular feelings."

The third trend was to replace specific prohibitions with vague values. Dishonor, disloyalty, violation of duty, and treason—all broadly defined—became the basic, serious crimes. This development appealed to people frustrated by a sense that the nation had long been degenerating while criminals were going free on legal technicalities. But the vagueness of the new laws, decrees, and policies opened them to arbitrary application. For example, an ordinary theft could be defined as disloyalty to Hitler or the *Volk*.

In addition, the political and ethnic identity of accused people decided whether they were acquitted or convicted and, if convicted, the severity of the punishment. Even though Hitler declared over and over that he was creating a classless society, Nazi justice and other institutions dealt with people according to classes into which they were put. Consequently, a theft committed by one person could be excused completely but, when committed by another, could result in the death penalty. The minister of justice wrote:

> National Socialism replaces the concept of formal illegality with the concept of material illegality . . . Hence, the law renounces its claim to be the sole source for determining what is legal and illegal.[55]

"Material illegality" meant an act was committed by a person of low value in the nation or for a purpose not approved by Nazis. The same act, when committed by a valued person or to further a valued purpose, was not a crime. By deliberate policy, at times stated openly, some people literally got away with murder, while others were executed for minor offenses or no offense against the law.

Despite its cultist basis, Nazi justice did not relieve judges of the obligation to justify their verdicts and sentences and couch them in terms of specific laws. When evidence of a serious crime was lacking, judges filled the gap by imputing character defects and criminal motives to defendants and declaring them dangerous to the nation. The result was injudicious rhetoric and tortured logic. For example, a local official banned all activities of Catholic youth groups. Catholic youths met nonetheless, engaging in outings and sports. They were brought to trial and found innocent. The State Supreme Court overturned their acquittal, finding them guilty on the grounds that:

> . . . this kind of emphasis on [religious] divisions carries within it by nature the seeds of a subversion of the German people, and every such subversion represents a potential furtherance of Communist aims and support of its goals.

The Court explained:

> Such a public display of personal opinion or belief can all too easily become an encouragement to Communists, Communist sympathizers, or persons currently of unsettled political allegiance, who would then develop and spread the opinion that the National Socialist state did not have the people behind it.[56]

Another example involved one of Hitler's first decrees, prohibiting criticism of the government in public—only in public. But the Supreme Court upheld convictions for private criticism as well on the grounds that it could be considered public if the possibility existed that it might be repeated in public by the hearer. And the Court stressed that such a possibility could never be excluded.[57] The Court held in effect that "private" meant "public," and people were executed for private remarks.

Cases of race and sex involving Jewish defendants became notorious for contrived justifications. A Jewish man was convicted of a glance at an adolescent girl on the grounds that:

> The behavior . . . had a clearly erotic basis and could only have had the purpose of effecting an approach to the girl . . . the accused clearly assumed that he could succeed in his attempt to approach her . . . Even if the defendant pursued no further intentions with regard to the witness, his outward behavior at least could not be interpreted otherwise.[58]

The court had no evidence of the defendant's assumptions or intentions.

Nazi racial justice is best illustrated in a case against a non-Jew, Jan Lopata. A slave laborer from Poland, he was working on a German farm when his employer accused him of touching her genitals. Let us assume her accusation was true and his denial false. In Germany cases are ordinarily heard and verdicts rendered by judges—single judges in minor cases, panels of judges in major cases. Finding Lopata guilty of personal assault, his judge added:

> The manner in which the accused committed this act of insult to the honor of his employer shows an enormous degree of insolence and shamelessness which can be found only among persons belonging to the Polish people.[59]

Lopata was sentenced to prison for two years.

The prosecutor appealed Lopata's sentence as too lenient, and the Supreme Court agreed:

> . . . *the possibility exists* that the defendant knowingly took advantage of the wartime conditions when committing the crime inasmuch as he was aided by the lack of other labor and a thereby conditioned insufficient supervision and watching, or inasmuch as he presumed that because of the labor shortage no charges would be preferred against him lest not to lose a hand.[60] (Italics added.)

The Supreme Court had no evidence of Lopata's thoughts. Its speculations about what he had in mind when he touched the woman raised the level of his offense to a capital crime by invoking a principle Hitler had introduced during the war. Offenses that were otherwise minor, but in some way exploited wartime conditions, should be punished as major crimes. For example, a small theft committed under cover of darkness caused by a blackout could be punished by death. The principle was vague and could be applied to almost any case.

The Supreme Court sent Lopata's case back to be retried before a special court—a panel of three judges headed by the chief justice of Nuremberg. This court also found Lopata guilty. He did not know German law or even the German language and hardly understood the proceedings. Brushing that aside, the court found that he *knowingly* violated the "prohibition to have sexual intercourse with a German . . ."[61] This referred to the Nuremberg Law—The Law for the Protection of German Blood and German Honor— which prohibited intercourse between Jews and Aryans. After the occupation of Poland, the law had been extended to intercourse between Polish men and Aryan women.

The court concluded Lopata violated this law because he was "a definitely degenerate personality," which was proven by "his belonging to the Polish subhuman race."[62]

The remaining gap—that the law prohibited intercourse while Lopata had only touched the woman—was covered by stating without evidence that, in touching her, "the attack of the defendant is directed against the purity of the German blood."[63] Lopata was sentenced to death and executed.

Initially, Lopata's act—or at least testimony that he had committed one—was the basis of the charge against him and of his conviction. In the end, his conviction and death sentence were based on a motive imputed to him without evidence. And both times the key fact was his being a Pole.

As the Lopata case shows, people's intents or presumed intents became more important than acts they committed. Character or presumed character also became more important. People were punished for what they were or were thought to be, not necessarily for what they did. The new system of justice embodied the presumption that Jews, Poles, and others were criminal personalities by nature. They could be prosecuted or incarcerated without prosecution whether or not they violated a law. They were scapegoats, and the courts—having turned from judging violations of law to getting rid of people considered undesirable—were an instrument of scapegoating. Occasionally this approach was spelled out:

> A person taking an object not belonging to him is not therefore necessarily a burglar—only the nature of his personality can make him such.[64]

Stealing by Nazis was condoned on the grounds that they were patriots. Stealing from Jews was especially condoned on the grounds that it meant restoring to Aryans what had presumably been stolen from them. This followed from Hitler's belief that Jews created or earned nothing. Therefore, whatever they possessed must have been stolen.

Some judges balked at punishing acts that violated no law or alleged acts for which evidence was lacking. Resisting coercion, they acquitted defendants. Nonetheless, the administration had the defendants punished. On acquittal, they were simply arrested by the Gestapo or other police and put in concentration camps, where some were killed.

A great many people who served the sentences prescribed by Hitler's laws and guidelines were punished further. In 1942, the Ministry of Justice gave the SS authority to correct "overly lenient" sentences of the courts.[65] But even before that, after serving prison sentences, people were quietly picked up by the SS or the Gestapo and put in concentration camps, where they served indeterminate sentences or were killed. During the war, this practice increased. The minister of justice said, ". . . congenital criminal inclinations are easily aroused in wartime . . . and the release of prisoners constitutes a danger to the folk community."[66]

Before the war, some judges who found defendants innocent proceeded to convict them and impose light sentences to protect them against arrest by the Gestapo, incarceration in camps, and death. And during the war, judges imposed unduly long prison sentences, expected to last through the war, to protect those convicted against being sent to concentration camps and to their deaths.[67]

Hitler's regime was basically criminal, and a great many people were drawn into complicity. Officers of the justice system—police, prosecutors, and judges, aided by clerks and lawyers—became criminals by involvement in the system's operation. Many people participated by spying on others and denouncing them. Actions against Jews alone involved people who kept records, inventoried and audited businesses, and issued documents. From boycott to expropriation, professionals and business people participated passively or actively in the elimination of Jewish competitors, acquiring their clientele and assets. Ordinary citizens acquired homes, jobs, and property they often knew were taken from Jews. One said, "I was given Herr Mayer's apartment, and I was supposed to throw him out."[68] Extermination involved medical and paramedical workers and about a million transportation workers over the years. And actions against Jews were only a fraction of the government's lawlessness. Industrialists and farmers used slave labor, paying little or no salaries. Insofar as slave labor was used deliberately to work ill-fed groups to death, industrialists and farmers became accomplices in murder. In all, as accessories and beneficiaries of crimes, many millions of Germans became accomplices. For twelve years, they became the actors of Hitler's dream of freeing himself and becoming a ruthless predator.

CHAPTER 12

PURGING THE BLOOD

> . . . my first and foremost task will be the annihilation of the Jews . . . until all Germany has been completely cleansed . . .[1]
>
> —Adolf Hitler, 1922

While living in Vienna, Hitler had meant to found a political party to liberate the Germans of Austria, to improve the lot of the poor, and to establish social justice. By the time he became chancellor of Germany, his main goal was eliminating the Jews. Meanwhile, he developed a new understanding of what was wrong with himself—a change that paralleled the change in what he thought was wrong with society.

In his early twenties, Hitler came to believe he had caught syphilis from a Jewish prostitute and to fear that it would prevent him from marrying or leading a normal life. The disease—its name probably came from *synphilein* (from a kiss)—was known to be transmitted sexually. Lay people considered it a blood disease—a belief supported by the blood test for it. At the turn of the century, lay people also believed that blood ruled life—that it controlled the body and its functions as well as heredity. The idea of having syphilis may have marked the origin of the belief Hitler would carry through life that his blood was poisoned.

Seeking treatment for syphilis in his thirties, he was told he did not have it. But his belief had become fixed, and he insisted he was syphilitic and persuaded some of his physicians to remove his "diseased" blood with leeches. And he saved samples of his blood, staring at them to find the "taint." After repeated bleeding without relief, Hitler turned from believing he had acquired syphilis sexually to believing he had inherited diseased blood from his father and, therefore, could never be free of it. His grandfather's pollution of his grandmother and his father's pollution of his mother were what Hitler saw as the causes of his hopeless condition.

Hitler's delusion about being controlled by Jewish blood became the basis of his rule of Germany. He projected his self-perception onto the nation, seeing it as controlled by Jews in the government and in other key institutions, and seeing its people as infected by Jewish blood.

Nations as anti-Semitic as Germany and even more anti-Semitic ones did not perpetrate the Holocaust. The Nazi Party came to power with a strong anti-Semitic program but not a deadly one. Most Nazis refused to believe what they heard about Jews being exterminated and, when they accepted the facts, were horrified. The anti-Semitism of Germans and even the more virulent anti-Semitism of Nazis do not explain the Holocaust.

Hitler was the only leader in Germany known to advocate extermination of Jews, and he believed he was the only Nazi leader determined to carry it out. High-ranking Nazis who participated in the Holocaust—Bormann, Frank, Heydrich, Himmler, and Rosenberg—did so as followers of Hitler's orders. Even those Nazis who enthusiastically advocated ridding Germany of Jews balked when it came to extermination. Frank and Göring opposed extermination. The prominent Nazis most like Hitler in hatred of Jews and in ruthlessness and fanaticism undeterred by consequences were Streicher and Goebbels. Streicher had fallen from power and was not involved in the Holocaust, and the intentions of Goebbels, who was involved largely as Hitler's propagandist, are hard to establish. His main record, his voluminous diary, discreetly omits extermination except for a hint that he was shocked at the extent of it. Hitler may have been right in thinking he himself was the only one who would order the Holocaust.

Hitler's description of his first perception of Jews as evil indicates it came to him as a revelation. He wrote that during childhood he had known a couple of Jewish children, but had formed no special impression of them. His realization of how different Jews were occurred when he was living in Vienna—a reaction to the appearance of one man, a reaction of shock:

> . . . I suddenly ran into an apparition in a long caftan with black curls.[2]

Hitler was fascinated. "I observed the man furtively and cautiously . . . I stared at this strange face and scrutinized one feature after the other . . ."

Hitler did not explain his shock beyond mentioning the man's appearance. While his description suggests that the man was Hasidic, Hitler thought he was a rabbi.[3] He noted that the man looked rather different from the average Aryan, and that fact opened his eyes to the evil nature of Jews. He also noted that the man looked rather different from the average Jew. "In Linz they certainly did not look like that."[4] The Jew to whom he had been closest, Dr. Bloch, had looked like the average Aryan. Hitler said his reaction to the appearance of the Viennese man—to his features and clothes, not to anything the man was doing—was the beginning of his aversion to Jews and it remained at the heart of his animosity. In later years, he identified the Jews he hated most as Hasidic ones who had emigrated to Germany from Poland and retained their distinctive appearance.

Hasidic men dressed in dark clothes from their hats down to their boots or heavy shoes and had long beards. Probably Hitler had never seen them before; they were not found in rural Austria or perhaps in the small city of Linz. But Vienna abounded with people from many parts of the Empire with their distinctive hairstyles and clothes—people unlike those he had seen before. The fact that Hitler did not have such a reaction on first seeing people of other groups supports his statement that the appearance of this man—not Jewish men generally and not Jewish women—was a shock with a unique meaning.

The traits he went on to impute to Jews suggest what the meaning was. In them he saw uncontrolled lust, especially for Aryan girls and women, the employment of Aryan women in prostitution rings, and other materialistic vices. These traits had nothing to do with Hasidic men who, as members of a fundamentalist, exclusive sect, particularly avoided involvement with Aryan girls and women. But the traits did fit Hitler's father, a man of uncontrolled lust who had employed and seduced Aryan girls and was materialistic.

Hitler seems not to have connected the man with his father consciously, but men with long beards commonly evoke images of severe paternal authority. And Hitler's idea that the man was a rabbi suggests he saw him as a figure of authority. The formal look of Hasidic men, suggesting severity, may also have reminded Hitler of Alois. In addition, Hasidic men wear much the same clothes—a virtual uniform—almost everywhere. Alois had worn his uniform both on and off the job, and Hitler probably associated his father with formal attire as well as severity. In addition, Hitler spoke over and over of his need to "resist" Jews. Since they had done nothing to him, the need probably came from being oppressed by his father.

Earlier Hitler had not noted Jews in Vienna, although they made up nine percent of its population. But once he saw the man, he could not stop seeing him. "Wherever I went, I now saw Jews . . ."[5]

In recounting his experience, Hitler seems to have been describing a recognition—a realization as if for the first time of something based on the past. He wrote, "Later I often grew sick from the smell of these caftan-wearers."[6] Before his revelation, he had not perceived an odor on Jews. Such an alteration of consciousness is the mark of an inner change, a reorganization of prior experience. As a result, things acquire new meanings. In paranoid people, the reorganization comes with a sense of having been duped in the past and now seeing what is really going on. Hitler wrote:

> For me the time of the greatest mental upheaval that I ever went through had come.

> From a feeble cosmopolitan I had become a fanatical anti-Semite.[7]

"Cosmopolitan" was what he considered his father.[8]

The inner changes marked a further rejection of the part of his identity that linked him to his father. Actually, he did not become a fanatical anti-Semite then. Only by steps leading to a further revelation when he suffered his second breakdown in 1918 did he become a fanatic. But his encounter with the "apparition" was an important step.

Hitler's father was part of him, as all parents become parts of their children. Those who hate their parents are upset by similarities to them, which they tend to deny. Hitler denied any similarity to his father, even though he thought the essence of his father—

demonic Jewish blood—was an evil force controlling him, filling his veins with lust, allowing him no peace.

Exceptional as Hitler was in his drive to exterminate Jews, extreme as his beliefs about them were, the mental process that shaped his ideas—projection—is a common one. He said Jews posed as democrats and socialists, exploiting the people's need for social justice in order to seize power. Then, "The democratic people's Jew becomes the blood-Jew and tyrant over other peoples. In a few years he tries to exterminate the national intelligentsia, by robbing peoples of their national intellectual leadership [and] makes them ripe for the slave's lot of permanent subjugation."[9] But he was describing himself, not Jews. While seeking office, he insisted he was a socialist and his speeches and writings stressed the need for social justice. On coming to power, he made himself a tyrant and his "blood" program the cornerstone of the Third Reich. He put some intellectuals in concentration camps, frightened others into fleeing Germany, and subjugated the nation.

As he planned to kill Jews, Hitler said they meant to destroy Germany. Later, as he extended the Holocaust to all of Europe's Jews, including infants, he said Jews meant to kill every single German. He believed this was what Jews meant to do—a belief most bizarre in imputing murderous intent to infants. But for adult Jews also, it had no basis in fact, not even in mistaken fact. *Hitler made no effort to discover the intentions of Jews he killed.* The destructive wish he saw in them existed in his own mind; it mirrored his own intentions.

Hitler had been yearning and planning for another war since the end of World War I. When he started World War II, the public was against it, his generals were against it, leading Nazis were against it, and his ally Italy was against it. The decision for war was entirely his own. Nonetheless, after invading Poland he told leading Nazis privately, "I know [the Jews] are guilty of starting this war—they alone and nobody else."[10] And at the war's end, as he was about to commit suicide, Hitler repeated the accusation as his dying statement. He seems to have believed it. Throughout his career, he failed to see that his own wishes and actions were what he imputed to Jews.

In *Mein Kampf* Hitler presented a detailed analysis of the political use of lies, including:

> . . . the masses . . . will more easily fall victim to a great lie than to a small one . . . such an untruth will not at all enter their heads . . . therefore, just for this reason, some part of the most impudent lie will remain and stick.[11]

He added that the people best at lying were Jews. Meanwhile he boasted of his own skill as a liar, and his government became infamous for its use of the "great lie."

Freud defined projection as an unconscious process; when projecting an intention onto others, people were unaware of having it themselves. On the contrary, they earnestly denied having any such intention. Projection was an effort to rid themselves of undesirable traits, like saying, "It's not I who is evil; it's they." That is true of many, but some people recognize in themselves what they project onto others. Hitler, Heydrich, and Streicher were aware of their own destructive impulses, but that did not hinder them from imputing destructiveness to Jews. In December 1941, Hitler said, "Many Jews have not been conscious of the destructive character of their existence . . ."[12] By then, he had been boasting for years of his own destructive character and had already killed over a million innocent civilians. He was well aware of his destructiveness.

For some people, projection is enough. They feel only limited animosity toward the targets of their projection and are content to vilify them or suggest that they be made to suffer, without needing to act on their ideas. But Hitler's self-loathing was extreme and he was troubled by more than a trait of his, by more than a few traits. The evil that haunted him seemed to be the core of his being. Projecting his traits onto Jews was hardly enough. He was driven to get rid of Jews—to obliterate the hated images of himself. That set him apart from most anti-Semites.

Among the first traits Hitler imputed to Jews, based on his impressions of them in Vienna, were dirtiness and smelliness. The connection with himself is unmistakable. In Vienna he was reported to have been extraordinarily dirty, even for a homeless person. Earlier he had been scrupulously clean and neat, and in later years he was again, bathing and changing his clothes more than once a day. The extreme concern with cleanliness that lasted the rest of his life reflected unending worry about offending by his body odor and by passing gas. This is not to say that he was smelly, but that he thought he was.

Such concern about odors usually comes from shame about one's body. That this was true for Hitler is supported by his refusal to let people see him unclothed or lightly clothed and his avoidance of being touched. Reportedly, as an adult, he often did not let his physicians examine his genitals.

A possible defect of which he might have been ashamed was suggested in an autopsy of a body thought to be Hitler's, which found only one testicle.[13] The identity of the body was disputed, and it was cremated after the autopsy. The inference some have made that Hitler was born with only one testicle cannot be evaluated on the basis of the autopsy alone. Doctors who treated Hitler said he was normal in this and other anatomical respects.

Since no body defect has been established, Hitler's shame about his odors and body may have been a displacement of other shame. Hiding one's body and obsessive concern about being dirty or smelly usually reflect sexual guilt. To many children of Hitler's time, sexual thoughts and acts were "dirty." Those who grew up sexually inhibited often continued to regard sex as unclean. It fits that, along with perceiving Jews as dirty and smelly, Hitler saw them as sexually unclean.

Guilt about his own sexuality—depraved sexuality by his culture's values—was at the core of Hitler's sense of what was wrong with himself, and he saw it all around him.

> Our entire public life today resembles a hothouse of sexual performances and stimulants . . . Public life must be freed from the suffocating perfume of our modern eroticism . . .[14]

He had to eliminate sexual depravity to save future generations, for children "are the grievous misery resulting from the progressive infection of our sexual life; in the diseases of the children, the vices of the parents are manifested."[15] The statements parallel his understanding of his own history—his paternal grandfather's and his father's sexual vices resulting in Hitler's own disease. His suppressed desires were what he saw as the depravity of Jewish males, and his most revealing projection was:

> The black-haired Jewboy lies in wait for hours, satanic joy in his face, for the unsuspecting girl . . .[16]

The words recount what happened when he became obsessed with Stefanie. He himself was a black-haired boy. (His hair was brown, but so dark that people called it black.) He lay in wait hour after hour, day after day, for the unsuspecting Stefanie.

Hitler's gravest accusation was that Jews carried toxic blood—blood poisoned by its genetic roots and by syphilis. Their blood was the cause of the evil in them—their sexuality and criminality. And the gravest danger was that Jewish males were driven to mate with Aryan females, polluting them with their blood. As noted, this was his perception of himself.

Without realizing the contradiction, he saw Jews as a remarkably pure race because of mating only with each other—"thousands of years of incest" he called it. Often he mixed the ideas together, blaming Jews for the "incestuous poisoning of the blood" of Aryans.[17] Racists before him had called sex or marriage between Jews and Aryans *Rassenschande* (racial disgrace or pollution). Hitler also used the word *Rassenschande* for such relationships, but sometimes he called them *Blutschande* (incest).[18] Since Jews were not ordinarily close blood relatives of Aryans, sex between them would not ordinarily be incestuous. Hitler's inappropriate use of *Blutschande* for intimate relationships between Jews and Aryans did, however, make sense in his own family. He had heard his father was of mixed parentage (*Rassenschande*) and his father and mother were cousins (*Blutschande*). The mating between his father and mother seemingly combined the two types of disgrace. Presumably he had heard the stories as a child before he could understand what they meant, before he could distinguish one concept from the other.

Hitler said of Jewish men, "These black racial parasites systematically rape our naive, young, blonde girls and thereby ruin something that can no more be replaced in this world," adding that Jews were pimps, perverts, and effeminate spreaders of homosexuality.[19] During middle age, he was particularly attracted to blonde, adolescent girls and, as chancellor, he arranged through various programs for them to be used sexually, raped, and made pregnant. One program involved centers where members of the SS could go for intercourse with them—centers that became known as brothels. In effect, Germany's ruler was a pimp for the SS. In addition, he had mannerisms considered effeminate, and he fostered homosexuality among the Storm Troopers and the Hitler Youth.

Another major indictment was that Jews were parasites; wherever they settled, they lived off the host country, contributing nothing:

> The Jew has never founded any civilization, although he has destroyed hundreds. He possesses nothing of his own creation . . . Everything he has stolen.[20]

Jews were criminals, avoiding honest work and lacking creativity. No advance in civilization or culture, in science or art, came from them. On the contrary, they sapped the lifeblood of the peoples they lived among. Hitler went so far as to say Jews did no work.

Again he was describing himself. Since adolescence, he had disdained ordinary work. On dropping out of school, he was supported by his mother. During his years in Vienna, he lived on his inheritance, on a government pension for orphans, on charity, and by begging. During World War I, he was, of course, provided for by the government. And afterward, he was supported by the Nazi Party.

While he accused Jews of evading military service, he had been a draft dodger. As Nazi leader, he ordered people beaten. As chancellor, he used his power to have political opponents and others killed. This sampling shows his antisocial pattern well before he embarked on mass-scale kidnapping, beating, torture, mutilation, and killing. In short, he himself was the criminal parasite.

Additional parallels between Hitler and what he saw in Jews will be noted briefly. He said, "The Jew is the incarnation of egoism."[21] He himself claimed to have been chosen by God to save Germany and lead it to a thousand years of greatness and to be the only person who could do it. He saw himself at the center of events, taking credit for every national accomplishment.

He accused Jews of corrupting Germany morally, particularly of undermining its family structure. He himself worked to undermine conscience and religion and deliberately subverted Germany's legal system. And, while fostering marriage in some ways, he deliberately prevented it in others and encouraged infidelity and unwed pregnancy (Chapter 15).

He accused Jews of corrupt business practices and of stealing Germany's wealth. On becoming chancellor, he used his power to evade the large income taxes he owed from the sale of *Mein Kampf*, which he required many Germans to buy, and to be paid a royalty for every postage stamp on which his portrait appeared, amassing wealth at the nation's expense. He also encouraged his followers to use their positions to enrich themselves. When criticized for this by his conservative allies, he said, ". . . would they prefer me to let my [Storm Troopers] loose to loot in the streets? I could still do this."[22] His regime was very corrupt.

He said Jews used people's hunger and misery to achieve their ends, that Jews deliberately starved peoples. As chancellor, he deliberately starved millions of people—Jews, Poles, Russians, and even Aryans—to achieve his ends.

Hitler's most prophetic accusation was:

> One can only understand the Jews when one realizes their final purpose: to master the world and then destroy it . . . while they pretend to raise mankind up, actually they contrive to drive mankind to despair, insanity and destruction. If they are not stopped they will destroy us.[23]

Then he set out to conquer the world and destroy and enslave much of its population. During the last two years of World War II, he spoke increasingly of destroying Germany totally. And if his subordinates had carried out orders he gave before the end, Germany would have been destroyed.

This partial list of evils Hitler imputed to Jews shows how utterly unworthy to live he judged them to be. They were beyond any possibility of redemption because their depraved nature—like his—was in the blood. While he saw the same evils in himself, he did not recognize that his self-perception was what he imputed to Jews. Nor did he see that he also projected his self-perception onto most Aryans, whom he would later judge unworthy to live. He said, "All of us are suffering from the ailment of mixed, corrupted blood. How can we purify ourselves and make atonement?"[24]

Before turning toward total destruction of Germany, Hitler thought removing Jews from the nation might suffice to purify it. Although he retained rather few of his childhood religious beliefs, he did perceive Jews as supernatural, particularly in the sense of possessing and controlling Aryans. He said, ". . . no one need be surprised if among our people the personification of the Devil as the symbol of all evil assumes the living shape of the Jews." He declared that Jews seized control of nations and destroyed them, thereby ensuring their own destruction. "With the death of the victim, this people's vampire will also die . . .[25] And his remedy for their "poisoning of the soul" of Germany was a biological version of religious remedies against possession.

Possessed people were considered incapable of overcoming their evil because the Devil had entered and taken control of the core of their being—their souls. Nor could they be helped by ordinary means. The cure was exorcism. By incantation, the Devil was commanded to leave the sufferer's body. If that failed, the sufferer was tortured to compel the Devil to leave. If that too failed, no cure was possible; the sufferer—the host of the Devil—had to be destroyed.

When he became chancellor, Hitler suggested Jews leave Germany, urged it, and threatened them with grave consequences if they stayed. Then he had Jews put in concentration camps, where they were beaten and tortured and some were killed. Partly this was done to frighten Jews into leaving. Finally, he had those who remained killed and ordered Germany destroyed. The sequence of telling Jews to leave, using torture to force them out, and finally trying to destroy them along with Germany, parallels the steps of exorcism.

Hitler thought what had ruined him was mixed breeding—the most destructive process on earth:

> *The sin against the blood and the race is the hereditary sin of this world and the end of any race that yields to it.*[26] (Emphasis in original.)

> The lost purity of the blood alone destroys inner happiness forever, sinks mankind down eternally, and the effects can never be removed from the body and the spirit.[27]

He gave up trying to purify himself, apparently convinced his evil blood could be eliminated only if he died without having children. Because he believed most Germans were similarly poisoned, they also might have to die without passing on their blood. He wrote:

> *Whoever is not bodily and spiritually healthy and worthy, may not pass on his affliction in the body of his children.*[28] (Emphasis in original.)

He had said in 1920:

> . . . it's a problem of whether our nation can ever recover its health, whether the Jewish spirit can ever really be eradicated. *Don't be misled into thinking you can fight a disease without killing the carrier . . .*[29] (Italics added.)

As a last resort, destroying Germany (the victim and carrier) might be the only way to eliminate the Jews. A less extreme way of killing the carrier was to kill or at least sterilize every German with a quantum of Jewish blood. For even if one part-Jew remained, because of the genetic dominance of Jewish blood, as Hitler saw it, he or she could become the progenitor of a resurgent Jewish population.

CHAPTER 13

SCAPEGOATING

I know perfectly well, just as well as these tremendously clever intellectuals, that in the scientific sense there is no such thing as race. But . . . I as a politician need a conception which enables the order which has hitherto existed . . . to be abolished and an entirely new and anti-historic order enforced and given an intellectual basis.

[If there were no Jew] We should have then to invent him. It is essential to have a tangible enemy . . .[1]

—Adolf Hitler, 1934

As the quotation shows, Hitler's use of Jews as scapegoats was deliberate. He needed scapegoats, and he believed Germany needed them, once saying, "Experience teaches us that after every catastrophe a scapegoat is found."[2] Nonetheless his hatred of Jews was sincere, and his passion contributed to partial acceptance of the idea that they were an evil to be eliminated. While most Germans did not fully believe what he said about Jews, they did believe his words contained a kernel of truth. That belief, combined with the well-established practice of scapegoating, made Germany receptive to his message, as other European countries had long been receptive to such messages. Two additional factors made Germany especially receptive. The catastrophic consequences of World War I had fostered extraordinary despair, and German anti-Semitism had taken a new turn in the nineteenth century. The path to the gas chambers was prepared by a combination of ancient practices and modern developments.

In ancient Israel, a goat was chosen from within a community. The sins of the people were laid symbolically on it and it was driven into the wilderness. The ritual purge redeemed the community and was the origin of the word scapegoat—literally an escape goat. Which goat was used made no difference. Simply by being chosen and having sins laid on it, a goat became the right one.

The Israeli practice of sacrifice served the same purpose. An animal (usually a lamb) or person (usually a small child) was killed to appease God, whose anger was thought to have been aroused by a human, adult sin. The innocent creature sacrificed belonged to the individual or community making the sacrifice, which was cleansed by the ritual. The main difference was, the scapegoat was driven out while the sacrifice was killed. Similarly, in pre-Christian Greece and nearby cultures, an affliction was explained by the presence in a community of people who offended its god. By killing the offenders, people believed they restored their good standing with the god and were relieved of their affliction. All the practices were similar in redeeming a community by removing creatures from it.

Originally, scagegoating was a deliberate act in that people believed they were guilty and the goat, lamb, or child they used was innocent. But as the practice of scapegoating expanded, the basic idea became unconscious. Communities denied their own follies and vices and projected them onto a chosen group of scapegoats. The human goats used came to be considered genuinely evil, which made it easy to justify harming them and facilitated indiscriminate, mass destructiveness.

As the ritual meaning of scapegoating and sacrifice was forgotten, larger and larger groups in a community were identified as offending its god. A duty of religious and temporal leaders became detecting offenders—who might try to hide their evil nature—and disposing of them.

Unlike ancient scapegoaters, Nazis did not identify Jews they drove out and killed as their own; they insisted Jews were aliens. Nonetheless there is ample evidence that not only Hitler but other key Nazis also felt a crucial kinship with Jews.

After thousands of years of scapegoating in Europe, Germany needed no new training, but it got a painful lesson. The nations that fought World War I were willing participants; some were enthusiastic about the war. But at its end, the guilt for the war was laid mainly on one nation. Germans were vilified and became the scapegoats, paying for the foolish, destructive acts of both sides in the extremely costly war. Pieces of German territory were taken by France, Belgium, Denmark, Lithuania, Poland, and Czechoslovakia, and Germans were barred from the Olympic Games of 1920 and 1924. A more bitter insult may have been unintended. When France left an African occupation force in the Rhineland, many German men found this particularly degrading, and developed the paranoid belief that the Blacks were raping German women. Most harmful were the reparations imposed on Germans, which crippled their economy. In addition, under pressure in 1923 from the United States to pay its war debt, France solved the problem by stripping Germany's industrial Ruhr valley, which further damaged its economy. Inflation accelerated wildly. Restaurant prices rose while customers were eating. Life savings were wiped out, as bankers wrote to depositors that once-large accounts were no longer substantial enough for banks to carry. Many a depositor received a postage stamp—the value to which an account designed for retirement or children's education had shrunk. People on fixed incomes were destitute and demoralization was widespread. Unable to end the oppression, humiliation, and chaos, Germans were ready to find a scapegoat.

By tradition, Jews were established scapegoats in Europe. In the ninth century, Norman pirates captured Bordeaux, and the community put the blame on its Jews. Then,

Moors captured Barcelona, and the community put the blame on its Jews. In the eleventh century, Caliph Hakim destroyed the Holy Sepulchre in Jerusalem, and the community of Orleans put the blame on its Jews. The First Crusade stirred intense zeal and resulted in beating, killing, and expelling many more Jews than the earlier events, as they were blamed for Moslems being in possession of Jerusalem. Crying "Hep, hep, hep!" crusaders killed thousands of Jews in France and Germany. ("Hep" is thought to have stood for *Hierosolyma est perdita—*Jerusalem is lost.) And in the fourteenth century, the Black Death (the bubonic plague) aroused still more scapegoating. Because it was catastrophic— killing one third of the population—and its cause unknown, people turned to mystical explanations. The pope declared it a pestilence sent by God to punish Christians for an unknown sin. Then their sin was identified as tolerating Jews, the rejectors of Jesus. The reasoning was the same as in early times: God was offended by the presence of evil people (Jews) and could be appeased by killing or driving them out. Another explanation of the plague was that Jews—already believed to be poisoners of rivers, wells, and fountains—had caused the epidemic as agents of Satan. Blame was fixed and sacrifice was demanded, resulting in a slaughter of German Jews.[3]

Hitler presented himself to his followers and the public as an expert in detecting evil people who disguised their nature by simulating good intentions and deeds. He said, "The Jews may deceive the world . . . but they cannot deceive me."[4] Over and over he declared that the calamity gripping the nation could be ended only by disposing of Germany's Jews. He was skilled at rationalizing his scapegoating but, under all his racial theories and proofs, it still meant victimizing people he sometimes knew were innocent. Occasionally this was obvious, as in 1942 when Heydrich, then the German governor of part of Czechoslovakia, was assassinated near the village of Lidice. Unable to find the assassins, Hitler ordered Lidice burned and its men killed, which was done without regard to religion. Unsatisfied, he then ordered an additional forty thousand Czechs killed, again without regard to religion. Heydrich's deputy objected, arguing that it would result in a Czech uprising. Hitler rescinded the order and instead had seven thousand Jews killed. Similarly, when the British bombed Cologne, he had 250 Jews of Berlin killed.[5]

Many of Hitler's ideas and much impetus for Nazism came from the nineteenth-century *völkisch* movement, which combined nationalism with the belief that the German *Volk* was descended from a genetically unique, noble race. The idea went back to the Roman historian Tacitus. Not having visited Germany, he knew little about its people. According to some scholars, he deliberately idealized them in his book *Germania* to provide a role model of a simple, free, brave people for his fellow Romans, whom he saw as degenerate and servile.[6] Tacitus described ancient Germans as tall, blond, and blue-eyed and added an idea that would dominate *völkisch* racism:

> . . . the peoples of Germany have never contaminated themselves by intermarriage with foreigners but remain of pure blood, distinct and unlike any other nation.[7]

Rediscovered by German nationalists, his book was taken to be literal history, and the idea of racial purity became the basis of the *völkisch* claim to racial superiority. To *völkisch* theorists, the key difference between Aryans and Jews was not in their religions but in their blood. This was a mystical idea and referred to nothing objectively detectable. Nonetheless, racists took the theory of the blood literally as scientific fact.

According to their belief, Aryan blood was superior to alien blood and German soil was superior to foreign soil. And the full greatness of the German *Volk*—biological and moral—came from the special connection between Aryan blood and Germany's soil. The soil and its products nurtured Aryans better than non-Aryans. And Aryans nurtured the soil in a unique way; when they died, their blood enriched the soil by passing into it. By contrast, Jewish and other alien blood polluted the soil by passing into it and then polluted Aryans who lived on the soil.

The Aryan blood-soil combination was the life force and the basis of the soul. "Blood and soil" became a rallying cry of the *völkisch* movement, which described aliens as not only lacking a connection with nature but also as having no souls. They were destroyers of life, eternal enemies of Aryans. Mystical ideas about nature were believed to be keys to life. Ultimate wisdom came from the intuitive application of ideas about the plant and animal worlds to human affairs.

The *völkisch* movement emphasized positive values—the nobility of peasants, the power of nature, the creativity of the life force, the goodness of the soul, and the superiority of Germans as a race. But behind its idealism, the movement was a reaction against Germany's fragmentation and inferior status compared to nations around it. Behind the idea in *völkisch* treatises that Aryans were destined to rule the world was the awareness that Germans had for centuries been victims of invaders from the east, north, and west. Behind the animosity directed at foreigners was the sense that being an ordinary German was not good enough.

Feelings of inferiority and spoiled identity were evident in the movement's leaders. Guido von List countered his low self-esteem by claiming to be superhuman—a prophet endowed with psychic powers—calling himself a magician. Georg von Liebenfels, as he later named himself, was born Adolf Josef Lanz. Among other names he took was the somewhat French Lancz de Liebenfels; he also claimed nobility by adding *von* and *de* and the title Baron. He also gave himself a degree, calling himself Dr. Jörg Lanz. The third of the leading *völkisch* theorists, Paul Bötticher, also added a *de* in taking the French name Paul de Lagarde.[8]

As a Nazi leader explained *völkisch* theory, the peoples of the world fell into three groups. The best group was the peasants—the workers and creators—unique in caring for the soil and possessing true culture. ("Culture" and the German *Kultur* come from a Latin word for farming.) Out of their determination to be connected with and to harness the powerful forces of nature, they were the explorers and inventors of the world. During World War II, they were making a last stand to preserve themselves, their land, culture, and everything their ancestors had created against destruction by an alliance of the other two groups.[9]

The evil groups were the nomads and merchants. The nomads exploited the soil without caring for it until it was used up, ruined. Then they wandered off to find fresh soil. And wherever they went, they attacked and robbed the peasants. Considering work a curse, they had no culture except what they took from indigenous peoples. The merchants, men of the city, were originally wandering seafarers. Much like the nomads in lacking culture and valuing only money, they also exploited the industry and creativity of peasants.

Völkisch theorists believed they were explaining Germany's misfortunes by applying the study of peoples and nations, but as historians they were dabblers who missed parts of history that underlay their mystical ideas, especially those about Germany's seafaring mercantilism and urbanization. Germany's Teutonic ancestors lacked the rootedness and racial bondedness imputed to them. They wandered over much of Europe and divided into a multitude of estranged tribes. And when they did join to make nations, Teutonic ethnicity was unimportant to them. The Burgundians, Franks, and western Goths joined with Gauls—a Celtic people—to make France. The Lombards moved south and joined with Italians. The Jutes became part of Denmark; the Angles, of England; the Flemings, of Belgium. A few tribes became Holland. And descendants of these tribes hardly thought of themselves as Teutons or Germans. Those who stayed in what is now Germany—mainly the eastern Goths, Saxons, and Vandals—remained isolated longer than the others.

Medieval northern Germany had begun to change from an agricultural society into one of merchants and urban people. The First Reich was in so grave a decline by the thirteenth century that it could not protect its international traders from pirates. Many German coastal and river towns, having become independent as the Reich grew weak, formed leagues that provided navies to protect their merchants' shipping. With this assistance, the merchants achieved great prosperity, and the towns grew rapidly. The largest was the Hanseatic League, which admitted member towns in Poland, the Baltic states, and Scandinavia that had settlements of German merchants. Thus, the league transcended national borders, bringing foreign contacts to north Germany, in contrast to the provincial south.

The league monopolized trade in various commodities, increasing suspicion among country people of sharp practices by town merchants. Suspicion, as well as actual exploitation, contributed to traditional animosity toward the towns and imputing evil to town merchants. And the growing wealth of traders, seemingly at the expense of "honest peasants," added to rural people's resentment, especially during hard times when peasants lost their land and homes. Furthermore, the merchants became the main source of the *burgher* (middle-class) culture that would come to dominate Germany—the source of its intellectuals and artists and of the modernism, internationalism, and materialism that provincial Germans experienced as alien and evil.

German urbanization and industrialization were extremely rapid. By the twentieth century, Germany had as many industrial cities as the rest of Europe combined. Most

Alois Hitler in his forties, wearing his uniform, with his official hat on the table.

Klara Hitler, about thirty years old.

Adolf Hitler at sixteen, sketched by a fellow high school student; Hitler's signature when he was seventeen, eighteen, twenty-four, and twenty-five years old. His style at seventeen is the most grandiose, with the A and d together looking like a W. Later he used the name Wolf.

St. Michael's Church in Vienna. This watercolor, done by Hitler in his youth, shows his precision in painting buildings and his stiffness in painting people.

Hitler (right) in World War I.
He was still rather slender and appeared average in height.

The Wild Chase *by Franz von Stuck depicts the god Wotan as a berserker. Hitler was said to have copied his mustache, hair style, and oratorical style from the painting. (Painting in Municipal Gallery in the Lenbach House, Munich; used by permission.)*

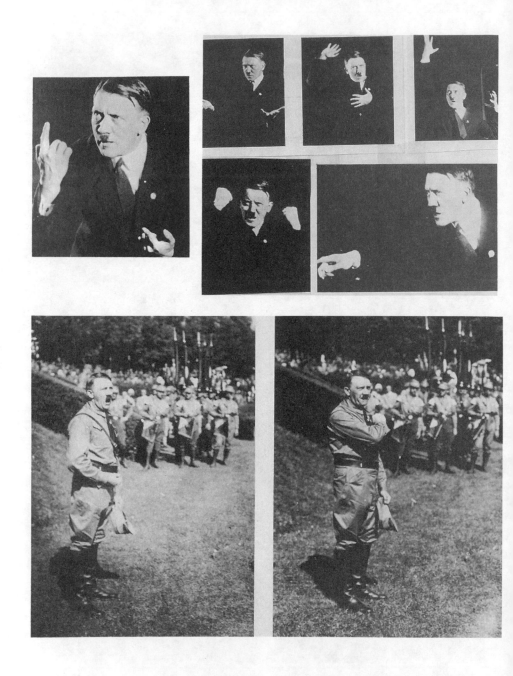

From Top: *Hitler used these photos, taken by his friend Hoffmann, to practice the postures and gestures he used during his oratory; Hitler in Storm Trooper uniform addressing his Troopers in the berserk style. He was about forty-five at this time, and his added weight contributed to the impression of him as short.*

Hitler and his "sweetheart." Distributed in the millions, the picture was used to prove Hitler's love of children and their love of him. It was withdrawn when an associate identified the child as partly Jewish. (Photo by Hoffmann.)

*Medusa by Franz von Stuck. On seeing the painting, Hitler exclaimed,
"They are the eyes of my mother."*

Sensuality *by Franz von Stuck is an example of the type of erotic painting that Hitler acquired.*

"A Jew attacks a girl!"
A drawing from Der Stürmer of the type said to fascinate Hitler.

Gas chamber disguised as a shower room in the Bernburg hospital. Bernburg was one of six mental hospitals used to kill sick and mentally and physically handicapped people. (Photo by Bernburg Memorial Building for Victims of National Socialist "Euthanasia." Used by permission.)

Germans lived in towns and cities, while those in rural areas retained their hostility to city life and all it represented.

Meanwhile, as Jews had spread through Europe, many had become traders. Those in the import business were aided by connections with family and friends in countries they had left. They became so well-known as traders that people used the word Jew to identify merchants. But the growth of medieval merchant guilds, which had Christian affiliations and excluded Jews, drove them into marginal commerce—door-to-door selling and peddling used goods. By the sixteenth century, some guilds began admitting Jews, and by the nineteenth century, a substantial minority of established German merchants was Jewish.

Awareness of merchant Jews probably contributed to animosity toward Jews but does not account for the *völkisch* idea that nineteenth-century German merchants as a class were descendants of Jewish merchants from antiquity or for the idea that Jews dominated German trade and were the oppressors of peasants. It was resentment of their own merchant class, intelligentsia, and artists, along with traditional resentment of the town, that *völkisch* Germans focused on Jews. The evils associated with mercantilism, urban life, Jewishness, and foreign influences were combined in the concept of rootlessness— a basic evil in their theory. The sense of being oppressed and corrupted by its own merchant class was redefined as Germany's "Jewish problem." And the idea caught on; millions of Germans, including minimally anti-Semitic ones and even defenders of Jews, talked about the "Jewish problem" and how to solve it.

As religions became less effective in providing hope to despairing people during the nineteenth and twentieth centuries, the promise by *völkisch* writers of connecting individuals with the mystical forces of nature and merging them into a superior *Volk* was an inspiration. In a time when anti-Semitism was declining, people who did not believe in the "blood and soil" nonetheless tolerated as respectable and sometimes believed bizarre stories about "rootless Jews" and what they were doing to Aryans. By the twentieth century, fears of foreigners and Jews came to a head in the idea of a mysterious, international conspiracy bent on ruling the world and destroying Germany. The idea was promoted in a document, *The Protocols of the Elders of Zion*, that purported to be the minutes of a meeting by the conspirators. *The Protocols*, forged in Russia by copying a French political satire unrelated to Jews, was taken to be genuine by many Germans.

Mystical *Völkisch* ideas appealed most to romantic Germans. Rejection of Rationalism and resurgence of Romanticism were especially strong in Germany. The main promoter of *völkisch* ideas at the beginning of the twentieth century called them "the New Romanticism."[10] Germans were especially impressed by fantastic ideas if presented in a scholarly style with ponderous implications, and *völkisch* treatises were in this style. In addition, nationalism was popular and moderate racism was considered respectable. As a result, even people who rejected *völkisch* ideas did not necessarily consider them bizarre or nonsensical.

Völkisch novels pictured Jews as pouring out of the cities, stealing peasants' wealth and land, severing their bonds with nature, and corrupting them. Ideas about Jews polluting German soil may already have had a symbolic sexual element. Later ideas about Jews polluting Aryans had a clearly sexual theme, which came to an extreme in a *völkisch* novel *The Sin Against the Blood* by Artur Dinter. Published in 1918, its plot was as follows.

Hermann and Johanna, pure Aryans, marry and have a baby, who they are horrified to discover is visibly Jewish. Johanna then confesses that ten years earlier she had been seduced by a Jew. Hermann still does not understand how their baby can be a Jew until he discovers a "law" of horsebreeding: if a pure mare mates once with an inferior stallion, her blood is forever polluted. Never again, no matter with what superior stallion she mates, can she bear a pure foal. Realizing the Jew has ruined Johanna, Hermann seeks him out and kills him. Returning home, he finds Johanna has killed their baby and committed suicide.

Their deaths were an apt resolution of the plot for, to the *völkisch* mind, a Jew, a "hybrid" baby, and a "polluted" woman were abominations. Dinter concluded with a warning to the reader:

> Now consider the damage which year in, year out, is inflicted upon the German race by Jewish youths who every year seduce thousands upon thousands of German maidens![11]

The Sin Against the Blood was a best-seller and especially popular with Nazis in the 1920s. Streicher, the Nazi leader whose ideas about Jews, sex, and reproduction were most like Hitler's, adopted Dinter's biology in *Der Stürmer*, an official Nazi newspaper:

> For those in the know, these are established facts: 1, The seed of a man of another race is a 'foreign protein'. During copulation, the seed is, in part or in whole, absorbed by the woman's fertile body and thus passes into the blood. A single act of intercourse between a Jew and an Aryan woman is sufficient to pollute her forever. She can never again give birth to pure-blooded Aryan children, even if she marries an Aryan. Their children will be [hybrids] . . .[12]

Streicher added:

> Now we know why the Jew uses every artifice of seduction in order to ravish German girls at as early an age as possible; why the Jewish doctor rapes his female patients while they are under anaesthesia . . . He wants the German girl and the German woman to absorb the alien sperm of the Jew. She is never again to bear German children![13]

Der Stürmer carried so many fabricated items on this theme that it could truly state, "A regular classic is the story of the German girl, raped by a Jew, who produced a horribly deformed child."[14]

To Hitler, Dinter's biology had the most personal meaning, providing an explanation of his own tragedy. Whether the phantom Jew had impregnated Hitler's grandmother made no difference. Simply by having had intercourse with her once, the Jew had polluted Maria forever. Even if Alois had been fathered by an Aryan, he was a "hybrid Jew," and so was Hitler. And to him, as to Streicher, a "hybrid Jew" was the worst abomination, more evil than any other person or any animal.

Believed by key Nazis, these ideas lay behind plans of the Third Reich to castrate Jews so that they could not "pollute" Aryan women and to kill "hybrid" babies. A superstition about animal breeding was accepted as an ultimate truth about human mating; it became a basis for the Nuremberg Laws and the Holocaust.

Hitler and others also held Jews responsible for "polluting" German women indirectly. He wrote:

> Jews were and are the ones who bring Blacks to the Rhine, always with the same ulterior motive and clear purpose, by the inevitable bastardization that takes place thereby to destroy the White Race which they hate . . .[15]

When anti-Semitism was a matter of religion, Jews were blamed for something they did—adhering to their beliefs and rejecting Jesus—and they could be saved by conversion. But according to *völkisch* and Nazi theory, they were rootless polluters by nature, and salvation was impossible. Regardless of what individual Jews did, getting rid of them all was justified. In a 1937 speech to the Reichstag, Hitler said:

> Perhaps for the first time in the history of man, a nation has realized that of all the tasks laid upon our shoulders the most sacred and the most inspiring is the preservation of the pure blood given us by God.[16]

"Preservation" was a euphemism for the blood purge he had in mind.

The Nazi Medical Association searched in the laboratory for differences in the blood of Aryans and Jews, for:

> . . . then neither deception, nor baptism, nor name change, nor citizenship, and not even nasal surgery could help. One cannot change one's blood.[17]

The association's failure to find differences made administration of racial programs difficult but did not shake racist beliefs. Some racists thought blood differences had been proved scientifically, but most found all the evidence they needed in what seemed obvious to them—Jews simply did not look or act like Aryans.

Hitler believed the ability to recognize one's own race and reject alien races was instinctive, as an animal distinguishes between its own species and others, especially in choosing a mate. Aryans should be able to identify Jews and reject them as sexual and marital partners, but Jewish tricks and corruption of German culture made identification difficult:

> There were times when there was no danger of a Jewish bastardization of the people . . . Racial instinct protected the people; the odor of that race deterred Gentiles from marrying Jews. At present, in these days of perfume, where any dandy can assume the same odor as anyone else, the feeling for these finer distinctions between peoples is being lost. The Jew counts on that.[18]

Hitler claimed he had regained his instinct, boasting of his accuracy in identifying Jews, even though he was often wrong. For example, a picture of him with a little girl companion was distributed throughout Germany to enhance his image as a lover of children and beloved by them. It was withdrawn when an associate identified the child as partly Jewish. Behind Hitler's boasts about how good he was at detecting Jews was his fear that he would fail to recognize them. He confided to a Nazi associate, "Ever since I have got to know them . . . I have been unable to meet a man in the street without wondering whether he was a Jew or not."[19]

Jews' position in Germany made them an easy target. Centuries of being barred from owning land, holding certain jobs, and having civil rights left them at a disadvantage after the bars were lifted. And the last group to gain full citizenship remains most vulnerable to losing it. Jews were clearly vulnerable, as were Gypsies, Blacks, homosexuals, and mental patients, and vulnerability was a factor in the scapegoating of these groups.

A frequently given reason for animosity toward Jews is that they were "over-represented" in banking, trade, the professions, the press, and the arts compared to their proportion in Germany's population, which understandably led to resentment. Hitler stretched reason so far as to say Jews were "over-represented" in all vocations.

Groups are drawn to occupations for various reasons. In the United States, Chinese have been concentrated in laundries, Greeks in restaurants, Italians in construction, and Blacks in sports. Such concentrations may have reflected ethnic traits or preferences, but they also reflected patterns of exclusion, of which the minority was the victim more than the perpetrator. This was true in Germany. In addition to any preferences that drew Jews to banking, trade, the professions, the press, and the arts, their concentration in these fields reflected past patterns of exclusion. For example, Jews had long been barred from the professions. When allowed into medicine—the first profession opened to them— Jews flocked into it. Explaining German anti-Semitism by a high proportion of Jews in certain fields smacks of blaming the victim.

The image of the Jewish banker and the older one of the evil Jewish moneylender were most obviously the result of past exclusion. Usury—lending money at interest— had been discouraged among ancient Israelis. The Christian church took a stronger position, enforcing a ban vigorously. ("Usury" became a pejorative word, meaning charging excessive interest, but lending at low interest was equally forbidden.) As a result, European commercial centers, dependent on loans, invited Jews to settle and provide lending services—often with the support of church officials—while barring them from other occupations. Where the need was urgent, Jews were welcomed with special privileges and even provided with money to help them get started as lenders.[20] There is no question that this history contributed to the development of Jewish-owned banks. Meanwhile, the ban on usury subsided. By the twentieth century, most German banks were not Jewish.

The allegation of Jews being "over-represented" in certain fields was related to two more serious accusations: that Jews refused to serve in the army and that they controlled key institutions. These were untrue. Jews had been excluded from the army until fairly recently and from high positions in the officer corps until very recently. Nonetheless, in World War I, Jews had been "over-represented" in the German army and its casualties.[21]

Most racists made statements about Jews controlling institutions without real evidence. In *Mein Kampf* Hitler described the research behind his conclusion that the press and other key sectors of Germany were controlled by Jews. He had examined lists of the owners, managers, and staffs of newspapers and other organizations and identified family names that were Jewish. He gave an example of four Jewish names he found over and over in key positions: Adler, Austerlitz, David, and Ellenbogen. Hitler's method led him to amazing findings. He said that when he came to power Jews held 62 percent of government positions.[22] Jews were in fact underrepresented in the government as a result of past exclusion, holding two-tenths of one percent of government jobs. The fact that Jews constituted less than one percent of the population made many of the statements about them impossible.

A survey before Hitler came to power found 16 percent of lawyers to be Jews, 10 percent of physicians, 5 percent of journalists and other writers, 4 percent of accountants, 3 percent of university teachers, artists, and entertainers, and 2 percent of bankers. The largest concentration of Jews was in commerce and sales, and the only field they dominated was department-store chains.[23] There were two large Jewish-owned newspaper chains, but most German newspapers belonged to Alfred Hugenberg, a Christian member of Hitler's cabinet. Nonetheless, Hitler found Jews everywhere he looked, and millions of Germans believed Jews dominated the professions, the media, trade, and banking.

In some countries Jews had ancient Jewish family names (for example, Cohen and Levy), but in Germany most bore names indistinguishable from Christians. David is a Jewish name; the other three are not. Jews were named Adler, Austerlitz, and Ellenbogen, but most people with those names were not Jewish. By Hitler's method, used by other racists also, identifying Jews in key institutions was as likely to be wrong as right. And when they did not recognize names as Jewish, racists speculated about Jewish origins. For example, Himmler suggested a Nazi leader named Conn had Jewish ancestry because his name was probably derived from Cohen.[24] The point is not about how many Jews there were in the press or the government, but about how eager Hitler and other racists were to find Jews in control of Germany's institutions.

In the common view, animosity toward Jews came from their being different. Difference—deviation from a norm—lends itself to suspicion and scapegoating, and killing has long been based on religious differences. The Holocaust was an outgrowth of thinking in which differences between groups are accepted as a valid basis for imputing evil to people and killing them.

Jews were considered different in appearance and character as well as in religion. The religious difference between Jews and other Germans was a fact but, considering the religions of the world, Jews and Christians were more similar than different. And after the Reformation, Catholics and Protestants had done more to destroy each other than to destroy Jews, especially in Germany. Difference in itself is too vague a concept to be of much use in explaining the extermination of the Jews. If it were the main cause of hatred, the people most visibly different—Blacks and Asians—would have been most hated in Germany. To some racists they were, but not to Hitler and his associates responsible for the Holocaust.

An answer to "Why the Jews?" that goes against traditional thinking has been ignored. According to the historian Gordon Craig, Aryans hated Jews not because they were different but because they were kin:

> The family resemblance between the two peoples is striking and is evident in their industry and frugality, their perseverance, their strong religious sense, the importance they place on family, and their common respect for the printed word . . . their intellectual pretensions, refusing to restrict themselves to pragmatic and utilitarian goals, but sharing the Faustian ambition to find the secrets of the universe and to solve the riddle of man's relationship to God . . .[25]

Craig considered these positive traits and found a kinship in negative ones also: feverish pursuit of business, obsessive pushing of a good idea until it becomes oppressive, belief in absolutes, arrogance, tactlessness, oversensitivity, and—perhaps most important—self-contempt.

Such a survey of ethnic traits is impressionistic. Even if accurate, there is no basis for deciding which traits are important in comparing one group to another. Craig's impression seems apt and psychologically it is very interesting. If we assume that he is correct—that Aryans and Jews were alike—how does that explain the destruction of Jews?

Craig suggested that Aryans felt oppressed by conscience and reacted to Jews as symbols of conscience. By killing Jews, they were trying to rid themselves of the oppression. The old idea that anti-Semites perceived male Jews—particularly bearded ones—as oppressive authority figures seems to have fitted many Germans. Hitler especially felt crippled by conscience, which he saw as the part of him that came from his father—the Jewish part. As will be seen, other leading Nazis involved in the Holocaust also had a troubled affinity with Jews.

In explaining the Holocaust, Craig used Edgar Allan Poe's story *William Wilson*, of the genre in which the protagonist is haunted by his double. Wilson ends by killing his double. The theme of the double is rooted in German culture, and a double is called a *Doppelgänger* in many parts of the world. The German word and fiction from which it came suggested a man's double walked in his place or took his place—the upstart-pretender ousted the true self. (It was men who had doubles.) Hitler had a similar idea about Aryans being ousted by Jews:

> . . . an asocial, inferior section of the nation is gradually moving up to a higher social class. This is a great danger to the German people . . . an alien people takes possession of their language . . . The true German is merely a tolerated stranger in his own nation.[26]

A particularly galling idea was that upstart Jews got the women who rightfully belonged to Aryans. Hitler said:

> Again and again Jews slid into the upper families, and these got their women from them. The result was that in a short time precisely the ruling class of the nation had become completely alien to its own folk.[27]

A Nazi leader said:

> The Jew has stolen woman as a wife from us . . . We, the young generations, have to march off and slay the dragon, in order that we may win back the holiest thing in the world: the wife who is both servant and slave.[28]

To racists, awareness that Jews held good jobs turned into the idea that Jewish men were taking jobs away from Aryan men. Awareness of affairs and marriages between Jews and Aryans turned into the idea that Jewish men were taking women away from Aryan men. Hitler and others were obsessed with the idea that Jewish men stole Aryan girls and women.

The affinity Nazi leaders felt for Jews was not always apparent. The question here is whether Nazi racists perceived Jews—consciously or unconsciously—to be their doubles and consciences. Usually, they said the opposite, insisting no people was as different from Aryans as Jews, not even Japanese and Africans. But the vehemence of the statements suggests they were protesting too much. Nazis proclaimed themselves to be the conscience of the world, saying it unreflectively, as if not realizing they were taking a position long held by Jews. Hitler and some Nazi leaders, however, were obsessed by the affinity. He said:

> Just as the Jews became the all-embracing world power they are today only in their dispersal, so shall we today, as the true chosen people of God, become in our dispersal the omnipresent power . . .[29]

Usually, he insisted that Aryans and Jews were utterly different, but he sometimes emphasized a kinship:

> The two are as widely separated as man and beast . . . Has it not struck you how the Jew is the exact opposite of the German in every single respect, and yet is as closely akin to him as a blood brother? . . . two groups so closely allied and yet so utterly dissimilar.[30]

Streicher also openly linked himself to Jews, once explaining awkwardly, "I have studied [Jews] so long that I have adopted myself to their characteristics." And Adolf Eichmann read Zionist literature and claimed to be a convert to Zionism. He also told people falsely he had been born in Palestine.[31]

Most Nazi leaders were short and dark-haired. They failed to meet the physical standards set for inclusion in the race of supermen they were building. Instead they resembled the hated stereotype of the Jews against whom they campaigned. By their own criterion they were inferior, and Jews personified the identity of which they were ashamed. The most anti-Semitic of them were uncomfortable in the presence of Jews, for Jews reminded them of their own shame.

The *völkisch* movement ran counter to the emancipation of Jews and their integration in German life. Unification of Germany in 1871 fostered a wave of nationalism that carried Jews along. They identified with the culture and made major contributions to it. "No one took German culture more seriously than did Jews."[32] With these changes and with Jews converting to Christianity in increasing numbers, separation between Jews and Aryans was shrinking. Jews had come a long way from the ghetto, and a quarter of them were marrying Christians. But according to Craig, Jews "inflamed the hostility of their partners the more they came to resemble them."[33]

More accurately, most Aryans increasingly accepted Jews and more of them married Jews. Christianity had become well established in Europe and lost much of its missionary zeal. Jews' rejection of Jesus was no longer a major issue. But the *völkisch* movement was at odds with the times. As Germany became a power and enjoyed an outpouring of cultural and scientific accomplishments, *völkisch* Germans grew more frustrated and angry. And the more Jews became assimilated, the more threatened *völkisch* Germans felt.

After Hitler, the most virulent anti-Semites were Streicher, Heydrich, and Rosenberg. And like him, they were haunted by stories of Jewish ancestry. Julius Streicher, Nazi leader of the Nuremberg region, was the most rabid. While the source of allegations about him is unknown, the name Julius, which was considered Jewish, may have contributed. (Under the Nazi regime, Julius was officially declared to be a Jewish name.) Streicher reportedly said, "You have to have a good dose of Jewish blood in your veins to hate that race properly."[34] He read the Talmud and had a subscription to the *Israelitisches Wochenblatt* (Israeli Weekly), explaining that studying Jewish documents gave him proof of the evil of Jews. Before his execution by the postwar Nuremberg tribunal, he asked his captors to let him go to Palestine to become an Israeli.

Streicher led his followers in an annual heathen ceremony on what he called The Holy German Mountain. He symbolically laid their sins of the past year on trees, which were then burned, redeeming Streicher's followers.[35] The ritual resembled ancient scapegoating, but most of Streicher's scapegoating was in the modern style. He drove through Nuremberg in an open car, searching for Jews. When he saw a man he took to be Jewish, he called out, "Hey, Jew!" and struck at him with a long whip.[36] And he founded the newspaper *Der Stürmer* (*The Attacker*) to fight Jews. Its pages were known for pornographic stories and drawings of Jewish men seducing Aryan girls and women and for the most bizarre statements about Jews, which Streicher pedantically claimed to be proved scientifically.

Streicher's obsession with Jews focused on the depraved sexuality he imputed to them. At the Nuremberg tribunal, asked why he had attacked Jews, he said:

Why it's all in the Talmud. The Jews are a circumcised race. Didn't Joseph commit *Rassenschande* [race pollution] with Pharaoh's daughter? And what about Lot and his daughters? The Talmud is full of such things.[37]

While he wrote much about protecting the Aryan family against sexual threats from Jews, Streicher was known and prosecuted for sexual offenses. Reportedly he tried to use his position as a Nazi leader to have adolescent girls made available to him for sex.[38] His imputing criminal sexuality to Jewish men was a transparent projection of his own desires. Nonetheless, he believed sincerely that Jewish men stole and polluted Aryan girls.

Reinhard Heydrich, an SS officer, had the reputation of being the most violent of Nazi leaders and was given the task of planning the extermination of Jews. When he was a child, schoolmates had called him Isi (Izzy)—short for Isidor—meaning he was a Jew, upsetting him badly. He had features considered Jewish—a long, aquiline nose, high cheekbones, and full lips. (Paradoxically, he was also considered the most typically Nordic among Nazi leaders because he was tall, blond, and long-headed.) And he was dogged by the story that his grandfather was a Jew named Süss. The allegation never failed to disturb him and, as an adult, he sued people who called him a Jew. He was also tormented by self-loathing. Reportedly on catching sight of himself in a mirror, Heydrich whipped out his pistol and shot his image.[39]

Himmler, his superior in the SS, said of him, "He had overcome the Jew in himself by purely intellectual means and had swung over to the other side. He was convinced that the Jewish elements in his blood were damnable; he hated the blood which had played him false. The Führer could really have picked no better man than Heydrich for the campaign against the Jews." Reportedly, Hitler also believed Heydrich had Jewish ancestry and that it made him exceptionally suited for exterminating Jews.[40]

Alfred Rosenberg, head of the Party's foreign affairs department, was the Nazis' chief theoretician on race. His ancestry is unknown; different sources cite German, Estonian, Latvian, Russian, and Jewish in various combinations. He was born in Estonia, grew up in Russia, and emigrated as a young man to Germany. In Estonia and Russia, Rosenberg was not considered a Jewish name, but in Germany it was. His name was the main source of allegations that he was a Jew, although some people said he looked Jewish. To counter the allegations and to establish himself as an Aryan, he denied all his reported ancestry and claimed to be Icelandic—purely Nordic.

During World War II, Rosenberg was made administrator of the conquered part of the Soviet Union, which included Estonia, Latvia, and part of Russia. One of his duties was overseeing the identification of Jews for shipment to death camps. He was directed to use a complex procedure, including detailed examination of suspected people's family trees. But he reportedly ordered that people named Rosenberg not be subject to the examination. Simply on the basis of having that name, he had them classified as Jews and sent to their deaths![41]

It makes no difference here whether Hitler, Streicher, Heydrich, and Rosenberg had Jewish ancestors. The key fact is that they were sorely troubled by the idea that they did. They went through life with divided identities, and Jewishness was a taint against which they struggled. Their obsession with purifying Germany's blood was linked to torment about having tainted blood themselves.

Hitler did "know perfectly well . . . that in the scientific sense there is no such thing as race." Intellectually, he also knew there was no such thing as Jewish blood. But his self-loathing pressed a different kind of truth on him: his blood was poisoned. This was a fixed idea, and intellect could not remove it, repeated blood tests could not remove it, and the nine investigations he ordered into his ancestry could not remove it. The obsession overpowered his reason, driving him to eradicate all Jewish blood from Germany. An obsession like Hitler's seems also to have driven Streicher, Heydrich, and Rosenberg.

Other important Nazis said to have been troubled by stories of Jewish ancestry were Eichmann, Frank, Odilo Globocnik, Goebbels (called "the rabbi" in college), Himmler (also said to have Black and Mongolian ancestry), and Robert Ley (whose "real name" was said to be Levy).[42] Information is lacking on how the stories affected their lives but, in the racism that preceded the Third Reich, innuendos of Jewish ancestry were enough to cause embarrassment. And during the Third Reich, accusations of Jewish ancestry were enough to cause investigation by the Gestapo, loss of job, and arrest. Innuendos and apprehension about being considered Jewish may have contributed to the anti-Semitic zeal of Eichmann, Frank, Globocnik, Goebbels, Himmler, and Ley. Eichmann, Frank, and Globocnik, along with Heydrich, Himmler, and Rosenberg, administered the extermination of Jews.

This does not mean that having Jewish ancestry or being accused of it was the origin of their racism. It means that being identified with an ethnic group of low status may contribute to spoiled identity. Self-loathing comes primarily from the way a child is treated as an individual. But once developed, it readily becomes focused on ethnic ancestry or physical features.

Craig's suggestion that hatred of one's double—that is, of oneself—was behind the Holocaust fits the personalities of the most fanatic Nazi anti-Semites. Self-loathing often rules the lives of people who suffer from it. One result is hatred directed against those who remind sufferers of the loathed part of themselves. As Poe's Wilson said of his double, ". . . nothing could more seriously disturb me . . . than any allusion to a similarity of mind, person, or condition existing between us." For Hitler, Streicher, Heydrich, Rosenberg, and others, it was Jews who reminded them of themselves in a way they found intolerable. For them, getting rid of Jews served the ancient purpose of scapegoating—cleansing themselves.

How many other Germans turned against Jews for the same reason cannot be estimated. People were scrutinized for Jewish names, Jewish facial features, Jewish mannerisms, Jewish ideas, Jewish acts, and Jewish relatives and friends. And the scrutiny was threatening. A Nazi newspaper carried the statement:

Whoever does what a Jew does is a scoundrel, a criminal. And he who repeats or wishes to copy him deserves the same fate: annihilation, death.[43]

Criteria of Jewishness were hardly clear. Most Germans could not be sure their names, faces, and so forth were free of it. At any moment they could be denounced to the Gestapo, whose investigations were frightening and brutal even when they ended in exoneration. Many people were falsely denounced as Jews. And the most trivial allegations were enough for the Gestapo. It investigated people accused of having business dealings with a Jew, of playing cards with a Jew, of buying in a Jewish store, or of living in an apartment house where a Jew lived. Even a single contact with a Jew could trigger an investigation, arrest, and confinement in a concentration camp. In addition, the allegation of being "soft on the Jewish question" was a serious one, especially for members of the Nazi Party. In the overwrought concern with race during the Third Reich, a great many Germans wondered uneasily whether they carried Jewish taints or had Jewish connections and feared others might think so. Many may have accepted and supported anti-Semitic measures to counter suspicions that they had Jewish taints or connections and to prove they were not "soft on the Jewish question."

CHAPTER 14

STRUGGLING WITH TEMPTATION

... I have always been ... in my private life more unfortunate than anyone I have ever known.[1]

—Adolf Hitler, c1932

On taking office, Hitler brought together a group of eugenicists to draw up a law for sterilizing people involuntarily. The law targeted people with hereditary health defects but, to Hitler and some of his eugenicists, non-Nordic features were health defects. Shortness, dark hair, and brown eyes were evidence that people carried Jewish or other defective blood. Germans with such features were *minderwertig*—inferior—and Hitler meant to stop them from having children. The sterilization law of 1933, later used against ethnic groups, was his first step toward racial purity, as the Third Reich pried into its citizens' sexual, marital, and reproductive activities, attempting unprecedented control.

While the sex-linked measures came from Hitler's conviction that Germany needed to be purified, they cannot be understood on that basis alone. They also reflected his own problems with love and sex, which were little known. A subject of much rumor and speculation then, they have remained a puzzle.

In private, Hitler said he scorned marriage. It was an arrangement needed only for having children. He loved youngsters and wanted a family, but he had decided against having children and had no need to marry. On the contrary, he had strong reasons not to. In order to fulfill his mission to the German people, he had to deny himself the happiness of family. He added, "I have another bride—Germany! I *am* married."[2]

Most revealing was his statement that his decision to remain childless was for Germany's benefit. If he had children, the likely outcome would be an unworthy son— "an encumbrance ... or a danger" to the nation.[3] His rationale was that famous men and geniuses often fathered cretins because they married stupid women, and boys took after their mothers. He also spoke of hereditary diseases associated with inbreeding that were common in the ruling families of Europe.[4]

Hitler also said young boys should be taken away from their mothers. If not they became spoiled "mamas' boys." The cause was mothers' intense, uncontrollable love for their sons. They pampered their sons and even did the boys' thinking for them. As a result, boys grew up to be tyrants, enslaving their mothers.[5]

The explanations Hitler gave were plausible and true to an extent. He was devoted to Germany and inbreeding did bring out recessive hereditary diseases. He may have had in mind that inbreeding was substantial in the region where he was born or that it had occurred in his family. And many boys were spoiled by their mothers. But the reasons did not account fully for his decision to remain a bachelor or for his future actions of state that these confidences foreshadowed.

What he said about famous men reflected his own preference for "naive" girls and "stupid" women. Such a preference comes from a feeling of inferiority and an apprehension of being unable to satisfy mature women. This was shown in Hitler's comments about being unable to marry because of impotence, because he was incapable of fidelity, and because his political duties would keep him away from home much of the time. Therefore, he could not give a wife what she would expect.[6] The reasons expressed only part of the inadequacy he felt. As he knew, they did not ordinarily stop men from marrying.

His argument that his son would be defective as a result of taking after the mother can be discounted. Hitler considered himself incapable of fathering a healthy child, as he hinted to Eva Braun when she pleaded to have children.

Hitler's conflict over intimacy began when he was young. His decision at eight to become a monk was a hint of the inhibition to come. Like many boys who thought of becoming monks or priests, Hitler soon gave up the idea, but it may have marked the onset of his ideas about not marrying or having children. By sixteen, when he made plans to live with his friend Gustl for life, he was projecting a future without a wife, a child, or even a lover.

Falling in love with Stefanie brought Hitler's inhibition into the open, but at seventeen his shyness still fitted his romantic ideals. Women were to be respected and protected. Sex should wait for love and marriage and, until then, desire should be suppressed. Such ideals were common among Austrian youths at the time. Middle-class young men, while trying to suppress their desires for "good" women, considered prostitutes suitable in meeting their needs and helpful in waiting for the proper time with the right woman. Hitler, however, shunned prostitutes, believing in self-discipline. After a negative experience with a prostitute, he renewed his efforts to control himself. His goal was to feel no desire.

Living in Vienna at eighteen, he attracted women. Gustl said Hitler usually seemed unaware of their interest and ignored them. One day, Hitler met a woman who tried hard to seduce him—an older woman, very attractive in Gustl's eyes. Hitler failed to grasp her intention, until she contrived to open her dressing gown in a seemingly accidental way, showing her breasts. Shocked, Hitler abruptly ended the encounter, angrily calling her "Potiphar's wife."[7]

The reference was from the Biblical story of Joseph, the Jewish youth sold into slavery in Egypt. His master Potiphar took a strong liking to Joseph and treated him as a son. Unfortunately, Potiphar's wife also took a strong liking to him and tried repeatedly to seduce him. As a result, Potiphar turned against Joseph and had him thrown in jail. The woman's seductiveness was dangerous to Joseph, even though he resisted her.

Thereafter, seductive women disgusted and frightened Hitler, and he avoided them. He said, ". . . a harlot; if you love her unsuccessfully, she bites your head off." Later Hitler would say he avoided promiscuous women because they carried disease—another danger in women.[8]

Especially revealing was Hitler's comment during another shocking experience. Visiting a museum with Hanfstängl when in his thirties, he saw a painting of Medusa. Hitler's reaction was extreme:

> "Those eyes, Hanfstängl! Those eyes. They are the eyes of my mother!"[9]

Medusa was so dangerous that any man who looked at her died—the ultimate forbidden seductress. And concern about others' eyes—about being looked at—is a mark of shame or guilt.

During the years in Vienna after he gave up his rented room, Hitler's circumstances and state of mind were unsuited to romantic or erotic involvements. To people who knew him then—men in similar circumstances—his lack of interest in women was unremarkable. His spirits improved with his move to Germany, but he remained uninvolved. Reportedly, he was troubled then and in later years by being particularly attracted to Jewish women.[10] His explanation was that he considered sex evil and, therefore, to be engaged in only with women who were already degraded. Such thinking was common among men who were inhibited with the "good" women of their own group. They found women of an out-group attractive, uninhibited, and evil.

In the Nazi Party, Hitler's lack of romantic relationships was no problem. A few associates found partners for him, while others preferred that he remain single and uninvolved—a rarity at the time—to attract women to the Party. Most Nazis, including married ones, had limited interest in women, and many were woman-haters. They routinely insulted women in crude terms. In Nazi publications, Rosenberg described them as a vegetable-like, inferior species, and Streicher described them as stupid, lustful, and deceitful.[11] Hitler expressed the same views in private.

Occasionally Hitler became infatuated with women without getting involved. He made declarations of hopeless, platonic love to a few, including Hanfstängl's wife:

> . . . he went down on his knees in front of my wife, proclaimed his love for her, said what a shame it was he had not met her while she was still free and declared himself her slave.[12]

Hitler also declared his love to a single woman, saying he could not marry her, while asking her to live with him.[13] Later he would try to tie other women to him, without committing himself to them.

And he started to date, at first briefly with Jenny Haug, the adolescent sister of his chauffeur. The first romantic relationship Hitler is known to have pursued occurred in 1925, when he was thirty-six. She was Maria (Mimi) Reiter, a girl of sixteen. They met while walking their dogs, and he was immediately taken with her and decided to approach her.

Hitler had considered himself below Stefanie, but with Mimi he was in a far superior position. Besides his age and worldly experience, he was a man of achievement, means, and enormous power. Famous in Bavaria as leader of the Nazi Party, he commanded its army of Storm Troopers. Nonetheless he was as inhibited with Mimi as he had been with Stefanie. A key to his inhibition was his observation that Mimi's eyes reminded him of his mother's.[14] Week after week he resolved to speak to her, but could not.

Finally, Hitler got around the barrier by having a subordinate speak to Mimi in his behalf. She accepted this overture, and they went together for some months. Then, Nazi associates urged Hitler to stop; the relationship was unseemly and an embarrassment to the Party because Mimi was a child. Hitler ended it abruptly.

Afterward Hitler accepted his inhibition, relying on friends to find women who suited him and to arrange meetings. It was easily done because he was an exciting public figure. Many women wanted to meet him and wrote letters offering to be his lovers and to have children by him. For dating, Hitler chose women a little older than Mimi—from eighteen to twenty-five. He later said:

> There is nothing finer than to be able to educate a young thing into one's ways— a girl of eighteen or twenty is as malleable as wax. A man must be able to impress his stamp on each girl. And that is all that a woman wants, too![15]

He needed malleable partners because his sexual demands, as noted below, were rather unusual.

He enjoyed going with women to cafés and the opera, and being seen with them got him the reputation of a Don Juan. An acquaintance said he fathered forty children out of wedlock, but Hitler usually limited the relationships to going out. At forty-three, he became infatuated with an actress from a dance she did in a movie but made no effort to meet her. Meanwhile, she attended a speech he gave, was fascinated, and wrote asking to meet him. He did not reply himself, but had an aide invite her to a meeting and ask her to make a movie for the Party. Then he arranged to walk alone with her. As she described it, in silence, without as yet having spoken a personal word to her,

> . . . he halted, looked at me, slowly put his arms around me, and drew me to him . . . He stared at me in some excitement, but when he noticed my lack of response he instantly let go and turned away. Then I saw him raise his hands beseechingly: 'How can I love a woman until I have completed my task?'[16]

The encounter shows his continuing inability to speak to a woman in initiating an erotic or romantic relationship and that his statements about being precluded from love by his commitment to Germany were rationalizations to cover his awkwardness.

Hitler's most intense and troubled relationship was with his niece. Her mother, Hitler's widowed half-sister Angela, was the only member of his family with whom he had resumed contact. Earlier, with the affluence that came from his position as head of the Nazi Party and royalties from *Mein Kampf,* Hitler had rented a country home—the Berghof (also called Haus Wachenfeld, Obersalzberg, and Berchtesgaden). In 1925, Angela had come there with her children to keep house for him, and he and his adolescent niece Angelika—Geli for short—became especially fond of each other.

Hitler had begun to give up the ascetic lifestyle he had imposed on himself. Besides the Berghof, which he later bought and had enlarged, he acquired expensive cars but continued to live in a tiny, meagerly furnished apartment in Munich. At forty-one he got a large apartment in a wealthy neighborhood there and offered Geli a room in it. By this time, she was twenty-one and living on her own in Vienna.

After she moved in with Hitler, the two became companions and were often seen together. In public, he held her hand, cuddled her, and kissed her. As to what happened in private, there were conflicting versions. Members of Hitler's domestic staff and some friends said their relationship was simply that of uncle and niece, which at first seems to have been true. Later, they evidently became intimate, and Angela thought they might marry, but the relationship was not exclusive. Geli had other lovers, and Hitler dated Eva Braun. Two points on which people who knew them agreed were that Geli was not in love with Hitler and that he loved her very deeply. One said, "I remember the emotion with which Hitler spoke of her . . . it was akin to the worship of a Madonna."[17] Friends called her the love of his life, and Hitler said she was the only woman he might have married.

A year after moving into Hitler's apartment, Geli died of a gunshot wound, which prompted many speculations. Some political enemies said he shot her or had her shot, while others said she killed herself in despair over being pregnant by him. Friends of Hitler said her death was an accident. The evidence was that she killed herself, and one view was that disgust over his way of making love drove her to it. Another was that conflict between Geli's willfulness and Hitler's attempt to control her life drove her to it. She was vivacious, on the wild side, stubborn, and able to stand up to Hitler. And he was very possessive and strict with her, with the result that they had vehement quarrels.

None of these speculations has an authoritative source nor are they sufficient motives for suicide. The possibility that Geli was pregnant by Hitler comes closest to the idea of being trapped in a hopeless life as a motive and fits the fact that Hitler pressured local authorities to forego an autopsy. Internal examination of her body probably had no bearing on the physical cause of death, which was already established. In that connection, there was no apparent need to suppress an autopsy. But it could have revealed an internal condition bearing on her motive. A revelation that she was pregnant, with the presumption that Hitler was the father, would have caused a scandal for him and the Nazi Party.

Pregnancy would explain suppressing her autopsy but not her suicide. Unwed pregnancy was common in Germany and in Austria, where Geli grew up. Although disapproved, it was not a reason for suicide. Having an illegitimate child reduced a woman's chances to marry and, especially among the poor, increased the hardship of her life. Geli and her family were poor, but Hitler was wealthy. Assuming abortion was out of the question, other solutions were possible. If Geli wanted to keep her baby, Hitler could easily have provided for her to live in comfort, and she could have moved away to minimize scandal. Or Hitler could have found a family to adopt the child, as he later arranged for thousands of women whom he induced to bear illegitimate children.

Insofar as Geli suffered under Hitler's strictness, the remedy was simple. She had already lived on her own and could have done so again. If Geli had been hopelessly in love with Hitler as well as disgusted by his sexual demands, she might have become desperate. But the evidence is that she was not in love with him.

Geli left no suicide note but only an unfinished letter to a friend saying she was moving back to Vienna. Reportedly, some weeks before her suicide, Geli had voiced her intention of returning to Vienna and resuming her music lessons. Hitler had objected on the grounds that her teacher was a Jew, and they had quarreled.

The day she killed herself, they had a another quarrel—a very long, loud one with some violence toward the end. The sounds were overheard by servants but not the words. Bridget Hitler, Alois, Jr.'s wife, gave an inside account of the quarrel—one that provides a sufficient motive for suicide. While her truthfulness has been questioned, her account is supported in key details by Hoffmann's memoir. He probably knew more about Hitler's sex and love life than any other friend, and Geli had confided in his wife about her situation before her suicide.

According to Bridget and Hoffmann, before moving in with Hitler, Geli had been involved with an artist in Vienna. Later she resumed the relationship and became pregnant. She loved the man and made plans to move back to Vienna and marry him.[18]

That could have been reason enough for a quarrel. Before Geli's suicide, Hitler had confided to Hoffmann:

> I love Geli, and I could marry her; but you know my views and you know that I am determined to remain a bachelor. Therefore I reserve to myself the right to watch over the circle of her male acquaintances until . . . the right man comes along.[19]

When he said this, added Hoffmann, "Hitler, of course, had no idea that Geli was deeply in love with someone . . . she had known in the old days in Vienna."

Earlier, Geli had been involved briefly with Hitler's new chauffeur and pal, Emil Maurice. Hitler considered Maurice unsuitable for Geli and angrily fired him. According to Hoffmann, Maurice was afraid Hitler was going to kill him.[20] Then Hitler gave Maurice a large sum of money not to see Geli again.

According to Bridget, the father of Geli's unborn child was worse than unsuitable in Hitler's eyes; he was a Jew. A few years later, Hitler went to extraordinary lengths to prevent Jews from impregnating or marrying Aryan women. Even kissing between Jewish men and Aryan women was an abomination to him, and he had Jews executed for it. What Geli was doing was an abomination and a personal betrayal of him. And by making her pregnant, the Viennese Jew had committed the foulest of all abominations. At the best of times, such a situation would have been intolerable to Hitler, and this was a bad time. Anti-Nazi newspapers were telling the story that a Jew had impregnated his grandmother—that Hitler was descended from that mating—and he was being blackmailed over it.

Bridget reported that on learning Geli's lover was a Jew, Hitler became enraged and forbade her to marry him or even to leave. That was what their quarrel was about, and neither one would yield. Hitler was to go on a speaking trip that day, which he did, breaking off the quarrel. As he was getting into his car, Geli shouted out the window an urgent plea to be allowed to go to Vienna. Hitler shouted back "No," and drove off. Her plea and his refusal were overheard by servants and neighbors, establishing that the quarrel was over Geli's intention to go to Vienna. Hours later, she shot herself.

Geli was neither a child nor a prisoner. Having already lived on her own, she could have resolved the issue simply by leaving without Hitler's approval, unless there was a compelling reason not to. Why did she need his permission? A few years later Hitler had an affair with a woman who then fell in love with a Jew. Reportedly Hitler ordered her to give up the Jew and, when she did not, sent the Gestapo after her lover to kill him.[21] At the time of Geli's death, Hitler was not yet chancellor and did not have a Gestapo, and Geli's lover lived in Vienna. But Hitler did have a branch of the Nazi Party in Austria, known for its violence. Before leaving on his trip, he could have threatened to have Geli's lover killed. Doing so would have been fully in character for him.

Geli's dilemma evidently was between submitting to Hitler's prohibition and leaving despite it. From Bridget's and Hoffmann's accounts, submitting meant giving up marrying the man she loved and the life to which she looked forward. Leaving meant risking the consequences of defying Hitler. Geli's unfinished letter suggests she was going to defy him and then changed her mind and committed suicide.

Hitler was called back from his trip by the news that Geli had shot herself. Arriving as she died, he cried out, "She's dead and I am her murderer," meaning he had caused her suicide.[22] Heartbroken, depressed, and suicidal, he went into seclusion. Later he told a friend:

> I loved Geli, my niece, so much that I thought I couldn't live without her. When I lost Geli I couldn't eat for days on end.[23]

He told another:

> Until now, I still had ties to the world . . . though I was unaware of it. Now everything has been taken from me. Now I am altogether free, inwardly and outwardly. Perhaps it was meant to be this way. Now I belong to the German Volk and to my mission.[24]

Recovering his political awareness, he had a physician say Geli committed suicide because of nervousness over an upcoming music recital she was to give. He then sent a letter to the *Munich Post* denying that he had quarreled with Geli before her death and that he had ever quarreled with her, denying that he had opposed her going to Vienna, denying that she meant to go there to get engaged, and denying that he opposed her engagement.[25]

He had her room made into a shrine, and he carried her picture for the rest of his life, looking at it daily along with his mother's. He saved her letters until, just before his suicide, he burned them. For years he spent Christmas alone in Geli's room. Others were forbidden to mention her name, and when Hitler spoke of her he wept.

A few other women with whom Hitler was involved sexually or romantically killed themselves or tried to. A popular explanation was that they were driven to suicide by his "demonic" lovemaking—his demands to be abused verbally, kicked, whipped, urinated on, and defecated on.[26] The evidence does not support masochistic demands as a motive. For example, Mimi Reiter, Eva Braun, and Unity Mitford attempted suicide over being abandoned by Hitler. Nonetheless, Hitler's masochism is important here because it spilled over into his acts of state.

Masochism, when limited to acts that are not humiliating or harmful and hardly painful, is very widespread. It appeals to people with problems in self-esteem, especially when the problems come to the fore in erotic or romantic relationships. Small bruises that may result, for example from being bitten, are accepted by most participants with only a little embarrassment or even with pride. Probably the most common masochistic fantasy is submitting to the power imputed to a partner, power that may be dramatized by trappings—costumes, bonds, or weapons. Many masochists need their special practices to enable them to proceed to a consummation they would otherwise not attain. Some people with very low self-esteem need extreme masochistic acts in order to participate in lovemaking or to reach orgasm, and that was reportedly the case with Hitler. Sex seems to have been the only activity in which he openly expressed his self-loathing, telling his partners he was unworthy of them and begging them to say degrading things about him.

Some of Hitler's masochistic demands are common enough. While hardly spoken of in his time, they have been studied recently. The more extreme ones are rare, and interpretations of them are largely inferential. The following suggests their meaning for male masochists with female partners.[27]

Being urinated on is called the Golden Shower and being defecated on the Brown Shower by people who engage in these practices. The names indicate that the acts are experienced as receiving special gifts. The negative connotation of urine and feces suggests receiving them, along with verbal abuse, is a penance by which a sinner becomes worthy of forbidden sex.

Research shows that masochistic surrender relieves shame and counters inhibition by reducing self-consciousness. Men are distracted from obsessive concerns about themselves; they lose themselves and concentrate on their partners and on fantasies of gratifying them by submitting to them. Some experience ecstasy, a spiritual sense involving communion, and worshipful feelings toward the woman.

In addition, the anticipation and experience of pain focus men's attention on their bodies. During masochistic acts some men lose awareness of everything except their bodies and their partners' bodies—a state involving "the denial of self."[28] Masochistic acts also focus awareness on the moment; the past and future recede from consciousness. Submission is especially appealing to men with spoiled identities. Submission to the partner, pain, extravagant fantasies, and altered consciousness—all have the effect of suspending the passive partner's identity. For the moment, he is not himself.

To masochists who fear punishment for sex, undergoing prearranged abuse is reassuring, giving them control of a dangerous situation. Even though masochists act as if they are submitting to powerful women, they are usually in control, as by telling their partners what to do. Engaging in conventional sex puts them at risk of delayed punishment—a period of anxious waiting for whatever consequences they fear—in Hitler's case, the symptoms of syphilis. Some seek relief from suspense by having blood tests done. Submitting to abuse and surviving it can serve as a symbolic test, providing assurance against delayed punishment. It is similar to Hitler provoking his father and submitting to beatings. Every beating Hitler provoked and lived through was proof of his power to survive. Inviting abuse during sex may have assured him of his power to survive punishment for it.

Hitler's masochism was related to a larger pattern that ran through his life—being a victim. Nursing injustices, defeats, and humiliations is very widespread and gives the victim moral superiority over others. In troubled relationships, both partners commonly allow themselves to be hurt, claim the position of victim, and accuse the other of being the perpetrator.

Hitler needed the moral superiority of being a victim to deal with his guilt, and he frequently provoked hostility against himself. During his early years in the Party, he led groups of Nazis in inciting violence against themselves. A deliberate purpose was getting attention and winning the public's sympathy and a high moral position by creating Nazi martyrs. In 1936, disregarding the warnings of his military staff, he violated the Versailles Treaty clause that prohibited Germany from having troops in the Rhineland. Hitler sent in troops and waited fearfully for an attack by French, Belgian, and British armies (which did not come). Hitler planned to retreat if those countries responded with force. He later said:

> We had no army worth mentioning. At the time it could not maintain itself even against the Poles. If the French had acted we would have been defeated in a few days.[29]

Thus, he invited an attack, risking foreign occupation of the Rhineland again. He even risked the possibility that foreign troops might not stop in the Rhineland but continue into the heart of Germany and topple his regime.

Hitler's greatest provocation was his declaration of war on the United States. He did it without the intention or possibility of invading the United States. On the contrary, he did it with the full expectation that it would lead directly to an attack by the United States. Then Hitler awaited a United States invasion eagerly, obsessing about when and where it would come, bracing himself mentally for it and bracing the nation by building fortifications in France and moving soldiers there from the eastern front. He said, ". . . the moment it starts will be a relief."[30]

Hitler's way of dealing with his father had become a basic approach to dealing with enemies. He provoked and waited to see whether he and Germany would survive the test. His preparations in France proved of little use when the Allied invasion began. They did, however, weaken Germany on the eastern front and help the Soviet Union turn the tide of war against Germany. Germany's destruction came partly from putting its fate in the hands of a man with an extreme need to be tested and punished.

Another effect of collecting injuries is the feeling of entitlement to hit back. The victim is in a position to inflict harm on others with a sense of righteousness, even when they are not the ones who inflicted the injuries on him. Hitler did this in the extreme, feeling justified in taking "revenge" on socialists, Jews, and others with little regard to whether they had actually harmed him or Germany.

A word analysis of *Mein Kampf* found it filled with metaphors of masochism and victimization.[31] Pride in the amount of suffering they can endure is common among masochists and habitual victims as a mark of physical and moral strength. Hitler boasted of how much he had endured from his father and about his willingness to suffer pain and death. In masochism and being a victim, "trauma becomes triumph."[32]

Given his inhibition, masochism, and sadism, it was logical that Hitler's main sexual pursuits were voyeurism and pornography. When he was in his thirties, the pornographic paintings of Franz von Stuck fascinated him and, when he became affluent, he bought some. The newspaper *Der Stürmer* was also pornographic, especially in its stories and drawings of Jewish men seducing, drugging, corrupting, and harming Aryan girls and women. The effect, insofar as readers identified with the victims, was masochistic. Friends said *Der Stürmer* was the one newspaper Hitler read eagerly and regularly, from first page to last.

Hitler also went to pornographic movies and amassed a collection of pornography. After becoming chancellor, he had movies shown in the Chancellery—one, two, or three a night, depending on his insomnia. Many were pornographic and he had pornographic movies made for him.[33] He visited art classes, interrupting them for long chats with nude women models. And he had women dancers perform for him alone at the Chancellery, often in the nude.[34] Watching pornographic films and live performers became Hitler's main erotic activities, probably because they were safe and dependable, did not bring up the problem of impotence, and did not involve him in sexual acts of which he was ashamed.

Geli was the last woman with whom Hitler was involved deeply. His conversations about marriage and children cited above occurred shortly after her death. Hitler also said he had come to believe he had long ago lost his passionate desire for women until Geli unfortunately awakened it. He renewed his resolve to get rid of his desire.

Hitler had met Eva Braun before Geli moved into his apartment. Although he liked Eva, he took little interest in her. He continued to go out with her occasionally and, after Geli's death, spent more time with Eva, and they became lovers. But he continued to keep her at a distance. He hid the relationship and did not appear with her in public. Months went by without her seeing him or even getting a call or letter.

Although others found her attractive, Eva hardly excited Hitler. She was a woman with whom he could control himself—one whom he could resist and ignore for as long as he chose. In the first years, he did not spend a night under the same roof with Eva. Then he invited her to stay at the Berghof, but she had to keep out of sight when he had visitors or to pretend she was his secretary—a sign of his continuing shame over erotic involvement. He did not acknowledge her as his lover even to his friends. And he continued to see other women.

Eva was in love with Hitler, wanting badly to marry him and have children with him. She also wanted more lovemaking, complaining to a friend that there was almost none. She was hurt by his refusal to acknowledge her, by his affairs, and most of all by his neglect for months at a time, complaining in her diary, "When he says he loves me, he means only at the moment."[35] Nonetheless, she was determined to accept his ways in hope of winning him, alternating between patient devotion and suicidal despair.

After one period of neglect, she thought she had lost him and tried to kill herself. Hitler asked the doctor who was called in whether her attempt was genuine or only a gesture to win his sympathy. On being assured it was genuine, he was touched, telling a friend that from then on he would have to take care of Eva.[36] He became more considerate, spent more time with her, and acknowledged her within his circle as his lover. But to outsiders, he continued to introduce her as his secretary or housekeeper.

By the outbreak of war when he was fifty, Hitler had given up other women, and Eva was the only one in his life. Nonetheless, when staying together at the Berghof or the Chancellery, they routinely slept in separate rooms. According to associates, he occasionally "obliged" her. Eva reportedly urged him to use drugs to increase his potency, begging his doctor to get them for him. Occasionally Hitler used them.[37]

After invading the Soviet Union, he spent long periods living at his military headquarters, directing the war in detail, not seeing Eva. And when they were together, he was not openly demonstrative. Finally, when the war was lost, when it no longer made a difference in his life, he acceded to her dearest wish. The day before they committed suicide, he married her. It was then that associates saw him kiss her on the lips for the first and only time. Reportedly, he was deeply moved by her insistence on spending the last days with him in the bunker and dying with him. Nonetheless, he then talked to a friend about her coming death in the same way he talked about his dog's coming death.[38] His casual tone in speaking of Eva continued until the end.

Thus, the last years of Hitler's love life were quiet and stable. He had dropped his voyeuristic pursuits and rarely engaged in sex, speaking of Eva as his good friend. But his sexual conflicts were unresolved. The less he was involved intimately with women, the more he meddled in other people's love lives. His conflicts were expressed in increasingly bizarre laws and programs that affected women and families on a mass scale.

CREATING THE MASTER RACE

After the successful revolution [the Jew] completely tore down the bonds of order, of morality, of custom, etc., abolished marriage as a lofty institution and instead proclaimed a general copulation with the aim of breeding a general inferior mishmash, by way of a chaotic bastardization . . .[1]

—Adolf Hitler, 1928

Hitler hid his most radical and destructive plans from the public. He proclaimed the importance of family, dedicating his regime to "put an end to the destruction of family, honor, loyalty" wrought by the Weimar Republic.[2] But fostering promiscuity and illegitimacy, which he imputed in the quotation above to Jews in the Soviet Union, turned out to be a good forecast of what he would do to Germany. To achieve his dream, he launched an assault on German values, family life, and loyalties.

Hitler had a life-long distrust of adults and their institutions, and his revolution was an attempt to transform Germany—its appearance, customs, institutions, and people. His minister of education said the Third Reich was instituting "*a process of transformation whereby the total life of the people was to be refashioned in harmony with the philosophy of National Socialism.*"[3]

The changes were directed most toward children. Hitler had written:

The crown of the *völkisch* State's entire work of education and training must be to burn the racial sense and racial feeling into the sense and intellect, the heart and brain of the youth entrusted to it. No boy and no girl must leave school without having been led to an ultimate realisation of the necessity and essence of blood purity.[4]

And he concluded *Mein Kampf* with:

A state which, in this age of racial poisoning, dedicates itself to caring for its best racial elements, must one day become the ruler of the earth.

This, the followers of our movement must never forget, even when the vastness of the required sacrifice misleads them to compare it in fear to the potential outcome.[5]

Accordingly, books were rewritten to educate children racially and eugenically. History textbooks concluded that intermarriage brought disaster to nations, while military victory went to pure-blooded ones, and that misfortunes were caused by Jews.

> The French Revolution had as its aim the extermination of aristocrats of Aryan blood. It was fomented by the Judeo-Mediterranean elements who wished to seize power in order to enslave the people.[6]

Germany's defeat in World War I was explained similarly:

> The Reich, which lacked at the time an Adolf Hitler, could not prevent the infiltration of certain disloyal elements into our government. Germany was betrayed.

> Erzberger, a Jew, signed a shameful armistice which bound us hand and foot.[7]

Science, in particular, had to carry the racial message, and even mathematics was recruited. Biology classes visited asylums so pupils could write essays on the effects of racial degeneration and their burden on the economy. A mathematics textbook gave the weight of a bomber with its bomb load and fuel, and then said, "The aircraft makes for Warsaw, the center of international Jewry . . . When it returns from the crusade there are still 230 kilos of fuel left." Students were asked to recalculate the bomber's weight.[8]

The new journal *German Mathematics* declared in its first issue that failure to judge mathematics by racial considerations "carried within itself the germs of destruction of German science." A scientist wrote that Aryan physics is "the physics of the reality-probers, the physics of the truth-seekers, the physics of those who founded natural science." The director of a physics institute wrote, "Modern Physics is an instrument of [world] Jewry for the destruction of Nordic science . . . True physics is the creation of the German spirit . . ." Another physicist said Albert Einstein was the key figure in a Jewish plot to pollute science "directed from beginning to end toward the goal of transforming the living—that is, the non-Jewish—world . . . and bewitching it into spectral abstraction in which all individual differences of peoples and nations, and all inner limits of the races, are lost in unreality" and the final goal of Einstein's Theory of Relativity was "Jewish world rule which was to force down German manhood irrevocably and eternally to the level of the lifeless slave." Still another wrote that physics was to be "cleansed of the outgrowths which the by now well-known findings of race research have shown to be the exclusive product of the Jewish mind and which the German *Volk* must shun as racially incompatible with itself."[9]

The attempt to purify science weakened Germany militarily. Hitler inherited a superb community of scientists and technicians, but his effort to rid German science and industry of Jews and "Jewish ideas" got rid of many and handicapped those who stayed. Hitler ignored complaints that science and industry were losing valuable contributors, saying, "If the dismissal of Jewish scientists means the annihilation of German science, then we shall have to do without science for a few years . . ." He reportedly stopped funding German scientists who were developing atomic weapons because he considered nuclear physics "Jewish physics."[10] Jews fled to Allied countries and contributed heavily to war technology there, including development of the atomic bomb. Aryans also left, and those who stayed, discouraged from using "Jewish ideas," did poorer work. (The *Hertz*, an electromagnetic unit, was prohibited on the grounds that Hertz was a Jewish name.[11]) In the end, Germany would be outproduced by nations scientifically and technically inferior to it before Hitler's rule. He believed purifying Germany racially would make it stronger militarily, but his racial policy achieved the opposite of what he intended.

To Rosenberg and Streicher, for whom race also came first, its central role in the Third Reich was taken for granted. But to most Nazis, the racial rhetoric was nonsense, and they hoped it would not play a significant part in Hitler's rule. To them the realization of how central race was came slowly. On trial at Nuremberg after the war, von Schirach, an avowed anti-Semite, surveyed the physical and moral destruction of Germany and concluded, "The whole misfortune came from racial politics."[12]

The racialization of life applied most to sex, marriage, and reproduction. Thus the most troublesome parts of his own life were at the center of Hitler's plans to control the nation's life, and his programs involving sex and marriage were especially self-contradictory. On coming to power, Hitler tightened restrictions on divorce and then loosened them. He outlawed pornography while continuing quietly to foster it. He proposed sterilizing promiscuous women while encouraging promiscuity. He outlawed prostitution while his government established brothels for various purposes. He banned abortion while secretly having newborn babies killed. His best-known programs fostered marriage and family life. Women were given monetary incentives to leave jobs, marry, and have children—the more, the better. And they were forced out of the civil service and the professions to persuade them to become homemakers. Meanwhile, Hitler began implementing programs that broke up families. The most bizarre and destructive of his programs affecting sex and the family are among the least known. Many were secret and one—involving sterilization—was the most carefully guarded secret of the Third Reich.

A major part of Hitler's appeal to the voters had been his promise to end disunity—to establish a community of Germans centered on family life, strong in its bondedness, proud of its identity, confident of its future. The promise had been undercut from the start by his threats to divide Germans by ethnics, politics, and health, for he had long meant to exclude from national life "alien" types (Jews, Gypsies, and Slavs), Communists and Social Democrats, and sick and "asocial" people. Divisiveness along these lines was to be expected of his regime, but his sex and family programs introduced still more divisiveness. His racial program was designed to unify the nation but did more to divide and demoralize it.

Hitler was particularly fond of children. Like many people traumatized by parents, he saw children as pure.

> We older ones are . . . rotten to the marrow. We have no unrestrained instincts left. We are cowardly and sentimental. We are bearing the burden of a humiliating past, and have in our blood the dull recollection of serfdom and servility. But my magnificent youngsters! . . . With them I can make a new world.[13]

Children needed protection from the influence of parents and churches to achieve the greatness for which they were born. To this end, Hitler organized the Hitler Youth in 1923, enrolling boys at the age of ten. A parallel organization, the League of German Girls, was formed later.

The Hitler Youth grew rapidly, becoming a powerful organization even before the Nazis came to power. By training and ritual pledges, members were required to be loyal to Hitler, to the state, and to each other more than to family and church. Under the Third Reich, an internal security unit of boys was established, backed by the power of the government, with the task of spying on other boys and parents. Reports were made to adult leaders of the Hitler Youth and other officials, who could invoke punishment for children and adults. Spying and reporting introduced a "suspicious and poisonous atmosphere into the family," as parental "caution and silence replaced candor and guidance" of children.[14]

A Youth Office was established with the responsibility of removing children from homes considered undesirable for political and religious reasons. Among grounds for removal were parents' friendship with Jews, membership in Jehovah's Witnesses, refusal to enroll children in the Hitler Youth or League of German Girls, and failure of children to give the Nazi salute.

Boys were encouraged to be arrogant and violent toward adults generally—particularly toward Jews—and were protected against consequences of assaulting them. Denigration of teachers and assaults on them by members of the Hitler Youth became common.

Surveillance became widespread, as the Gestapo intercepted mail, tapped phones, and hired informers. Goebbels joked, "The only individual with a private life in Germany is the person who is asleep."[15] Citizens were asked to spy on each other and denounce those suspected of criminal or political offenses to regular police and the Gestapo. Many who denounced people were given their jobs as a reward, and threats to denounce people were used to extort money. Family members were asked to spy on each other, and denouncing spouses became an easy way to get rid of them.

People were denounced to the police for traditional criminal and civil offenses but also for political, racial, social, and sexual ones. With the onset of war, more and more formerly innocuous acts came to be considered hostile to the state, and denunciations rose to a peak in 1941. Looking around to see that no one was near enough to eavesdrop before talking about politics or about someone who had been arrested became known as "the German glance," and "hardly anyone felt entirely safe, whether at work, play, during leisure activities, at school, or even in the privacy of the home." For, "Surrounded by spies, informers, zealots . . . the people live in an atmosphere of vague though ever-present terror . . ."[16] In short, while Hitler meant to establish a highly unified state, his programs alienated and separated children from parents and set citizens against each other.

Two incidents from 1940 show how life was affected. When the war began in 1939, the government prohibited listening to foreign broadcasts. Afterward, the air force informed a mother that her son was missing in action and presumed dead. She also heard from several friends and acquaintances that a British broadcast had reported her son captured and safe in England. She denounced them to the police for listening to a foreign broadcast, and they were arrested.

The parents of a submarine officer were officially informed that their son had died in action and been lost at sea. They arranged a church funeral. Among the early arrivals at church were friends who had heard on a British broadcast that their son had been taken prisoner. To avoid questions that canceling the funeral would raise—to protect their friends—the parents went ahead with the funeral.[17]

Hitler said that to achieve and maintain dominance in Europe, Germany needed a much larger population—double what it had. Besides measures to increase childbearing, people of German descent in other countries were invited to move to Germany. The results of these measures were small, and Hitler expected them to be more than offset by deaths once he began his war. Needing a large increase in births, he turned to illegitimacy and infidelity.

One campaign played on the strong sexual and romantic appeal Hitler had for women. Young women—including adolescents—were urged to have children for the *Führer* whether they were married or not. Single ones who did so were given special recognition and benefits for contributing children to the Reich, and their offspring were called state children, a mark of honor. Women and girls were encouraged to find racially suitable men to impregnate them, and education of school girls encouraged pregnancy without regard to marriage. Adolescents were told, ". . . virginity is treason to the race," and:

> All of us can now enjoy the rich emotional and spiritual experience of having a baby by a healthy young man without the restricting ties of the old-fashioned institutions of marriage.[18]

While girls and boys were schooled separately, they were brought together at times and encouraged to engage in sex. In 1936, members of the League of German Girls, also called Hitler Girls, were required to serve for six months in labor camps. The assistant leader of the Hitler Youth said:

> . . . what else are [League] girls for except to take them to bed. It is necessary since otherwise they might become lesbians.[19]

During their service, many girls became pregnant. One wrote to her parents, "Please don't thrash me when I come home with a baby, otherwise I'll report you." On learning her sixteen-year-old was pregnant, a mother rushed to the girl's camp, but the girl told her to go home or she would report her to the Gestapo for "sabotaging German motherhood." In 1936, one hundred thousand members of the League of German Girls and the Hitler Youth attended the Nuremberg rally of the Nazi Party. Nine hundred girls came home pregnant.[20]

Women and girls were urged especially to seek members of the SS as fathers for their babies. The SS had been planned as an elite and its members were screened for Nordic traits. They came under heavy pressure to have large numbers of children by their wives, but most were single. They were also urged to have children by whatever women of the Nordic type they could find outside marriage—married women, single women, and adolescent girls.

During World War II, as concern mounted over the population decline, women married to soldiers at the front were urged to get pregnant by SS men. Men chosen to be breeders were instructed:

> Persuade these German women that as it is their husband's highest duty to die in battle, so it is their own loftiest task to bear children for the Reich . . . Since their husbands are not in a position to become fathers, offer the women your services in the name of Germany's future.[21]

SS men serving at the front were given leave to impregnate soldiers' wives. This campaign aroused a storm of protest and was quickly abandoned.

In 1935, the SS established a semisecret breeding program called *Lebensborn* (The Fountain of Life).[22] To the public it was described as a shelter program for unwed mothers. Single, pregnant women could come to *Lebensborn* centers for prenatal care, childbirth, and aftercare, and a small number did. SS members also could bring their wives to the centers for these services, and some did. But the main function of *Lebensborn* was to provide racially ideal women for breeding to members of the SS and other selected men. A fantastic goal was the production of one hundred fifty million pure Aryan babies. *Lebensborn* recruited volunteers as young as fifteen. To disguise their use as breeders, recruits were called nurses, suggesting their function was caring for unwed mothers and their babies. Secrecy was maintained by SS guards at the centers. But despite deception and secrecy, people living near *Lebensborn* centers heard what took place in them and called them by derogatory names—"stud farm" and "brothel for the SS."

Some of the single women and girls of *Lebensborn* kept their babies, but they were encouraged to give them up for adoption or rearing in state schools. Visiting a *Lebensborn* center was by permission of the director, and fathers were often not permitted to visit. Thus *Lebensborn* also separated children from parents.

At first, enough women were recruited voluntarily, but the number of children produced was disappointing. Estimates range from twelve thousand to several hundred thousand. With a growing sense of urgency, as the population declined during the war, the number of *Lebensborn* centers was increased and women were coerced and kidnapped to serve in them. Thus, rape was another effect of the program.

As the population continued to shrink, Hitler established a program of importing children from conquered countries.[23] It began with offering Norwegian mothers incentives to give up their children, and then coercion was used. The children were taken to Germany to be given new names and reared as Germans. Some were then rejected as non-Nordic and sent to concentration camps, because returning them to their families was inconvenient. Those placed with German families or in schools who were old enough to remember their original families were brainwashed to believe they were the offspring of German parents who died in the war. Girls too old for "Germanization" were to be kept for breeding and then killed. The goal was thirty million children to be imported and kidnapped.

Hitler considered Norwegians pure Nordics. The idea of absorbing their children into the German *Volk* at least made sense by his racial theory. But the recruiting was then extended into France, a racially inferior nation, and Poland, a subhuman nation, in his eyes. The rationale was that some people in France and Poland were descendants of Nordic Germans.

Norwegians were considered so pure that no screening of their children was necessary. For the French and Polish, screening by physical traits and family trees was established. But as the program was extended, screening was reduced and sometimes not done at all. Children were simply taken from schools or seized on the street. In the end, by far the most children were taken from Poland—more than 200,000—and with little or no screening. Thus, a plan to infuse racially ideal blood into Germany had, by Hitler's standards, the effect of adding to the "mishmash" and "polluting" German blood. The *Lebensborn* breeding program and the importing and kidnapping of children did little to advance Hitler's racial plan or to add significantly to Germany's population. Their main effect was separating children from parents.

The *Lebensborn* and kidnapping programs were ill-conceived not only in relation to their racial goals, but also because they weakened Germany militarily. From 1943 on, Germany was losing the war. Without victory, Hitler's racial goals could not be met, and victory required all-out effort. Nonetheless, soldiers, SS men, labor forces, food and other material (all in short supply), and transportation (already overloaded) were allocated to these and other programs that did not help the war effort. Perhaps the oddest program came from Hitler's conclusion that Gothic letters, the prevailing form of print in Germany, were of Jewish origin. He ordered their replacement by modern type fonts and the reprinting of educational and official documents, street signs, and so forth—a job requiring major material and human resources—which shocked Nazis.[24] The concentration camp and extermination programs interfered most with the war effort.

Since 1920, the Nazi Party's program had called for removing Jews from Germany's political, economic, and cultural life, and Hitler's first measures followed it. He barred Jews from public office, the civil service, newspapers, radio, film, theater, teaching, and farming. In addition, he took nonlegal steps—boycotts enforced by violence against Jewish doctors and Jewish-owned businesses. Later, Jews were barred from the remaining professions, and their businesses were confiscated. According to an SS publication, a secret purpose of economic oppression was reducing Jews to poverty so they "would sink into criminality and could be wiped out by fire and sword."[25]

More difficult to formulate were measures based on Hitler's sexual agenda. Sexual restrictions he proposed were rejected by the Ministry of Justice as likely to disrupt people's lives. It anticipated correctly that prohibiting sexual acts would lead to "Extortion, denunciations, and so forth by partners from a broken relationship or third parties . . ."[26] For two years, Hitler put off measures to protect women from the sexuality of Jewish men. Meanwhile, government officials began refusing to marry Jewish-Aryan couples. When such couples sought help in the courts, judges upheld the refusal.

When Hitler took legal action, it was reportedly abrupt and impulsive. On September 12, 1935, the chief Reich medical officer, Gerhard Wagner, declared in a speech that further race mixing would be prevented by a "Law for the protection of German blood."[27] The next day, jurists summoned to Nuremberg began writing the law in haste. At 2:30 AM, Hitler approved a draft and had it printed immediately. The cabinet, including the minister of justice, did not get to consider the proposed law. The Reichstag, also suddenly summoned to Nuremberg, immediately approved it without dissent. Then, with special fanfare, Hitler announced at the Nazi Party rally on September 15 the Law for the Protection of German Blood and German Honor. Its preface was:

> Realizing that the purity of the German blood is the prerequisite of the continued existence of the German people, and animated by the firm resolve to secure the German nation for all future times, the Reichstag has unanimously passed the following law, which is being proclaimed herewith:[28]

The section barring marriage between Aryans and Jews applied only to full and three-quarter Jews, but it started a wave of regulations, as Hitler went on to control marriage and sexual behavior by people with smaller fractions of Jewish ancestry. For example, quarter Jews were forbidden to marry other quarter-Jews, three-quarter Jews, or full Jews. They could marry half-Jews only by special permission. And they were free to marry full Aryans. An observer said, ". . . Nazi legislation now forces [one-quarter Jews] to 'defile' the purity of German blood."[29]

The hodge-podge of laws and decrees proved difficult for the public and even the courts to apply. People were unclear about what was forbidden and judges were unclear about what to punish, because biological features of race were hard to define with legal precision. The Nazi Medical Association had reported in November 1933 its failure to find a test for Jewish blood—its failure to find a clear biological criterion on which Hitler could rely. The Chancellery said over and over that the Nuremberg Laws and other laws affecting Jews were a purely racial (biological) matter, having nothing to do with the practice of Judaism. The government insisted freedom of religion was guaranteed by the Third Reich, while punishing Catholics and Protestants as well as Jews for activities connected with their religions. Nonetheless, the government explicitly made the practice of Judaism a factor in enforcing the Nuremberg Laws. Part-Jews who practiced Judaism were officially classified as Jews, while those with the same ancestry who did not practice it were classified as Aryans. And Aryans who converted to Judaism were officially classified as Jews. "In the end Nazis were compelled to resort to the expedient of defining a Jew as anyone who regarded himself as a Jew or who was considered a Jew by the Nazi official in charge of his racial evaluation." Classification became increasingly arbitrary, and Himmler wrote, "I urgently request that no ordinance regarding the definition of the word 'Jew' be issued. We are only tying our hands by establishing these foolish definitions."[30]

The concept of blood pollution was not limited to sex and reproduction. A Jewish doctor gave emergency treatment to an Aryan. Lacking time to find elsewhere blood of the type needed for a transfusion, the doctor used his own. For polluting his patient's blood, the doctor was sent to a concentration camp. And the Ministry of Justice considered prosecution in a case it described as follows:

> A full Jewess, after the birth of her child, sold her mother's milk to a woman doctor and concealed the fact that she was a Jewess. With this milk, infants of German blood were fed in a clinic . . . The purchasers . . . have suffered damage, because the milk of a Jew cannot be considered food for German children.[31]

Sexual offenses involving Jews and Aryans were to be punished only when committed by men. Marital prohibitions were to apply to men and women, but police were instructed to enforce them only against men. This suggests again Hitler's preoccupation with the "crimes" of his grandfather and father. The penalty was imprisonment. In 1936 sex crimes by male Jews were broadened to include kissing Aryan women, dancing with them, and approaching them for the purpose of dating. Jews were punished for such acts even when they mistakenly thought the women were Jewish. And prohibited intimacies were made capital crimes. For example, a kiss could be punished by death if the court concluded that a Jew intended it to lead to "polluting" the woman he kissed, and such conclusions were reached with little or no evidence.[32]

Hitler had a lifelong aversion to intimacy and marriage, and his programs served to prevent intimacy and marriage. If he had gotten further with his plan of creating a pure *Volk*, he would have prevented intimacy and marriage on a much larger scale. He was a voyeur, obsessed with sex and with controlling his desires. His programs put the government in the position of observing and controlling people's sex lives.

As leader of the Nazi Party, Hitler had long taken upon himself controlling marriages of his subordinates. They were asked to submit information about their prospective brides and bring them for Hitler to see. Then he gave or withheld approval. His control ranged from the highest Nazis down to his chauffeur. Since those who applied to him already intended to marry, Hitler's approval did not increase the number of marriages, but withholding approval did prevent marriages. In 1931 strict control of marriage was applied to the elite guard. All SS members who wished to marry were required to submit family trees and photos of their intended brides to Himmler, who gave or withheld approval.

To friends, Hitler said having a mistress was better than marrying. The growing success of the Party made its leaders and Storm Troopers public figures. Because of their elevated status, middle-aged Nazis attracted young women as lovers and potential wives. With Hitler's encouragement, many indulged themselves at the expense of their wives, and some left their families. Hitler said the wives of Nazi leaders were "good, trusty wives who were entirely in place during the time of struggle but no longer suit their husbands today."[33] Hitler also took the opposite position when Goebbels was about to leave his family for a young lover, temporarily placing him under house arrest until he agreed to stay.

In *Mein Kampf* Hitler had pledged "to do away with the idea that what he does with his own body is each individual's own business" because:

> *A racial state will first have to raise marriage from its level of continuing racial disgrace in order to consecrate it as the institution which is called on to beget the image of God and not monsters halfway between men and apes.*[34] (Emphasis in original).

"Monsters halfway between men and apes" meant offspring of Aryans and Jews. After becoming chancellor he said, "*We* regulate relations between the sexes. *We* form the child."[35]

To carry out his racial policy, he called on the medical establishment to devote itself to controlling reproduction. In response, Bavaria's health commissioner declared that medical care for the sick and weak was becoming obsolete; medicine's paramount task was fostering the Aryan race. A professor told medical students that in the future their only task would be "selection, breeding, and elimination."[36]

"Elimination" was rarely mentioned in public, but "selection" was a word with which eugenicists were comfortable. What German physicians and scientists understood it to mean varied. To many physicians, conventional medical practice—improving the health of individuals, some of whom were uncooperative or incurable—was hardly satisfying. A Nazi leader said Hitler gave followers "the opportunity to create on a heroic scale" and the "euphoria of history-making activity."[37] To physicians, Hitler offered an end to difficult patients; he gave them instead the opportunity to create a super race. Caught up in the dream, they set aside medical and other ethics as killing became a form of treatment in the Third Reich.

To achieve the ultimate goal, physicians and eugenicists in the Third Reich sought to bring all reproduction under government control. While they never came close to that goal, they did increase control both publicly and secretly. The government established screening boards so that every couple could apply for approval to marry and have children. In 1935 approval became mandatory, although the criteria were not strict. The net effect was to reduce the number of marriages.

A Nazi periodical said:

> Every Aryan man should marry only a blonde Aryan woman with wide-open, blue eyes, a long, oval face, a pink and white skin, a narrow nose and a small mouth, and who under all circumstances must be a virgin.[38]

Nazis and soldiers were particularly urged to marry such women. The Party urged Aryans to divorce Jewish and partly Jewish spouses, and the courts recognized Jewishness in a spouse as grounds for divorce.

These policies came from Hitler's belief in the myth of the master race, by which pure Germans were "Nordic"—tall, long-headed, blond, and blue-eyed. Therefore, candidates for the SS were screened for those features. They also had to provide family trees to prove their ancestors were purely Aryan as far back as 1800 for men in the ranks and 1750 for officers. It was this "Nordic" fraction of Germany's population that Hitler meant to perpetuate. All other Germans were not only *minderwertig* (inferior) but also undesirable. By mating with the elite, they dragged them down.

Only a quarter of the German population was tall, blond, and blue-eyed. By Hitler's thinking, that was because centuries of race mixing had brought in Jewish, Slavic, and French blood. The Race Policy Office of the Nazi Party, established to prepare for racial purification, worked at compiling a eugenic register for all Germans so that a minority could be encouraged to have children and the rest discouraged.[39]

Most of the time, Hitler shared these ideas with only a few people, but occasionally he mentioned them in public. In 1927 he proposed openly that newborns with physical or mental defects be killed. Those who knew him best understood "defects" to include racially undesirable features. He revealed his full goal in a 1929 speech:

> If Germany every year would have one million children and eliminate 700,000–800,000 of the weakest, the end result would probably be an increase in strength.[40]

Hitler admired Sparta, known for pruning its population by killing infants, as "the most pronounced racial state in history."[41] His suggestion to kill most newborn children was not taken seriously, but he meant it seriously. For fulfilling Germany's grand destiny would have required preventing reproduction by at least three quarters of the population.

When he wrote *Mein Kampf*, Hitler recognized the difficulty of achieving a purely Nordic Germany and proposed a selective breeding program that would take 600 years. But when he was chancellor, he decided to change Germany's genetic makeup decisively during his lifetime.

Hitler hesitated to eliminate Germans he considered undesirable by systematic killing. In 1935, he told Dr. Wagner he was considering a program of involuntary euthanasia and would start it in wartime.[42] In 1938, he stopped waiting for war, deciding to use instead the cover of a health program and to keep the killing secret. Children were the first victims, as midwives and nurses were instructed to report births of defective infants (a category enlarged during the war to include "racially undesirable" ones). Thousands were killed by injection or deliberate starvation.

The killing was soon extended to adults, beginning with people in mental hospitals. A member of a government conference planning the extension said:

> Today registration forms are being sent to all nursing homes and mental hospitals along with a circular from the Minister of the Interior . . . No suspicion can arise as to the true purpose for which the registration forms are being filled out, for the reason given . . . is the need to consider everyone in the formation of our future economic plans.[43]

To maintain secrecy, victims were cremated and their families were given false explanations. But the deception was poorly managed at first, with families receiving the same form letter giving the cause of death as appendicitis. Some families were suspicious because their dead relatives had already had appendectomies. And when families who knew each other got the same letter, they also suspected their relatives had been killed. As a result, religious leaders learned of the program and objected vigorously, making it public knowledge. "Euthanasia" contributed heavily to suspicion of the government. "No one in Germany trusted anyone else anymore."[44]

Up to 1939, about seventy thousand adults were killed. The protest confirmed Hitler's belief that he could carry out mass killing only during war. With the invasion of Poland in 1939, he issued a secret order that Germans "suffering from illnesses deemed to be incurable may be granted a mercy death."[45] As in many other decrees, the wording was misleading. The purpose was getting rid of people, and "mercy" was irrelevant. "May be granted" meant killing people against their will. Victims were shot by SS squads and gassed by paramedical teams—in all about two hundred thousand. Hitler's minister of justice said, "This is murder by assembly line."[46]

By November 1940, the "euthanasia" program was a cover for killing political prisoners, slave laborers, Jews, half-Jewish children, and Gypsies. A physician designating people for "euthanasia" wrote his wife that in an afternoon session, he and his colleague made about fourteen hundred decisions, including:

> The second portion consisting of 1,200 Jews, who were not 'examined,' but for whom it was enough to take the reason for arrest . . . from the records and to put that down [as symptoms and diagnosis] on the forms.[47]

Examples of such symptoms and diagnoses were: "Fanatical Germanophobe and asocial psychopath." "Major Germanophobe. Agitator." "Jew from the Protectorate [Czechoslovakia]. Subversive behavior. Miscegenation."

In June 1940, the gassing of Jews in mental hospitals began. Later Bavaria's minister of the interior ordered Jews in all kinds of hospitals transferred for "euthanasia," and then the killing of nonhospitalized Jews was increased. Jews had already been killed in concentration camps but in small numbers. Under the "euthanasia" program they were killed in larger numbers.

The "euthanasia" program is important beyond the number of victims. Methods developed for killing people in small groups—including gas chambers disguised as shower rooms—would be used three years later in the Holocaust. And expert staff for the death camps would be recruited from the "euthanasia" program. These facts would lead historians to infer that Hitler intended "euthanasia" as an experimental preparation for the Holocaust. Whether so intended or not, the program showed that mass killing was technically feasible and that staff would carry it out when ordered.

At the turn of the century, a burst of interest in Darwin's theory of natural selection had given Aryan supremacists a pseudoscientific boost. They extended his theory of survival of the fittest to explain a paradox: Aryans were the greatest race on earth, yet Germany had been inferior militarily to nations around it throughout much of its history. The argument they developed was that nature had been prevented by civilization from taking its course in bringing Aryans to their destined position of world rule. Christianity and liberalism, by humane protection of the unfit, gave them a survival advantage over their superiors. Instead of dying out, the unfit in Germany multiplied and pulled Aryans down.

Such ideas coming from *völkisch* writers in the nineteenth century had impressed many lay people but not Germany's academic and professional community. *Völkisch* writers had sought university positions, but their intuitive, mystical approach and lack of academic credentials had stood in the way. Then, toward the end of the century, the biologist Ernst Haeckel became Germany's herald of Darwinism, attracting a large group of enthusiastic students and followers. Haeckel became known as the *völkisch* prophet and later as the Nazi prophet, as he and his followers presented a scientific-sounding basis for racist policies.[48]

While used in other nations also, the Darwinian argument caught on strongly in Germany. Eugenically minded anthropologists, geneticists, and physicians saw their mission as stopping civilization from interfering with nature. A moderate goal was ending public programs for people regarded as unfit. An extreme goal was stopping them from having children. Government control of childbearing was difficult; by relying on persuasion, purification of the Aryan race would take centuries or never be accomplished. Sterilization of the "unfit" became the preferred means for most eugenicists, while killing them appealed to a few.

The scientific concept of people who, through no fault of their own, were unfit for survival was rather different from the *völkisch*-Hitlerian concept of willfully evil people. Nonetheless, the scientists and Hitler found common ground. German eugenicists, long frustrated in their dreams of selective breeding, looked with hope to the Nazi Party, and many joined it. And Hitler used them to lend an air of respectability to his measures.

Involuntary sterilization had been proposed in the Reichstag before Hitler came to power but won the support of only one party—the Nazis. To Fritz Lenz, a leading eugenicist, outspoken anti-Semite, and Nazi convert, Nazism was "applied biology." He wrote in 1931 that millions—about 30 percent of the German population—should be sterilized. He meant not only people with hereditary diseases but also those who were "racially inferior." To Lenz, genetic purification was the nation's first priority. He declared Hitler to be the only political leader in tune with "racial hygiene" and wrote:

> The question of the genetic quality of the coming generations is a hundred times more important than the conflict between capitalism and socialism and a thousand times more important than the struggle between [Germany and other countries].[49]

Five months after the Nazis came to power, Minister of the Interior Wilhelm Frick established a Committee of Experts for Population Questions and Racial Policy. It was made up of anthropologists, geneticists including Lenz, Dr. Wagner, who was an extreme anti-Semite, and Nazi leaders Himmler and Walther Darré, who were devotees of breeding a pure Aryan *Volk*. The work of the committee and related organizations made clear that population (demographic) policy was not distinct from racial policy; they were the same. Addressing the committee's first session, Frick suggested that "as high as 20 percent of the German population" was unfit to reproduce and was to be sterilized.[50]

The law produced by the committee provided for involuntary sterilization of genetically diseased and retarded people and did not address Hitler's dream of changing Germany's racial makeup. A leading eugenicist said, however, "No one approves of the new sterilization laws more than I, but I must repeat over and over again, that they constitute only a beginning." To gain public acceptance for the law, official statements and propaganda focused on people with hereditary diseases. Meanwhile those who drafted and implemented the law anticipated its extension to ethnic groups in advancing the government's basic eugenic policy of racial purification.[51]

When the sterilization law was enacted, fear of how far it might go centered on Lenz's statement about sterilizing 30 percent of the people. As a result, he took pains to explain he had not meant to have 30 percent sterilized involuntarily. He said only a small fraction of the population should be sterilized by force and the rest divided into three groups. One group should be sterilized by government persuasion and pressure short of force. Another group should not be persuaded but be permitted to undergo sterilization on a purely voluntary basis. And the rest—about 30 percent—should be prohibited from being sterilized.[52] The reassuring part of his clarification was that forced sterilization applied to only a small fraction. The ominous part was that reproduction by only 30 percent of the population was desired.

After the law was enacted, a participating physician wrote that from his experience people unworthy to reproduce fell into seven groups:

> 1. Retarded, 2. Mentally disturbed, 3. Epileptics, 4. Antisocials (criminals), 5. Deaf-mutes, 6. Tuberculars, 7. Alien races."[53]

He added that, while the sterilization law did not cover people of alien races:

> The infiltration of foreign racial blood into the organism of our *Volk* we will prevent as far as possible. Jews, Blacks, Mongols, and equivalent peoples can be non-punitively sterilized voluntarily, quite equally, whether they are healthy or sick . . .

And he proposed such people be paid premiums as an inducement to accept sterilization.

In 1934, Lenz said at a meeting of the Committee of Experts:

> Our goal must be to establish a certificate of hereditary biology for every citizen and every inhabitant . . . Those who do not suffer from hereditary disease within the meaning of the law are not necessarily healthy and fit to breed . . .

As things are now, it is *only a minority of our fellow citizens* who are so endowed that their unrestricted procreation is good for the race . . .[54] (Italics added.)

"Citizen" meant Aryan; "inhabitant" meant Jew and Gypsy. A "certificate" referred to the eugenic registers being compiled by the Race Policy Office. Lenz's statement anticipated the law passed the next year that took away Jews' citizenship and rights, freeing the government to act against them.

Panels of judges and physicians that ruled on petitions to have people sterilized were urged by the administration not to be scrupulous about precision of diagnosis or whether a condition had been proved scientifically to be hereditary. For example, a woman was ordered sterilized as a hereditary deaf-mute even though the panel knew she still spoke and had lost her hearing as a result of an accident and an infection. In addition, Nazi psychiatrists coined the term "camouflaged feeble-mindedness" for people whose retardation was hidden by a "mask of cleverness." The concept of hidden retardation was used to justify sterilizing intelligent people.[55] And court applications to have people sterilized cited as supporting evidence that they had a reputation of being "work-shy" or had been members of the Communist Party. In these ways, the application of the sterilization law to people without hereditary diseases was soon apparent.

In all about four hundred thousand people were sterilized under the law. Besides the main effect of preventing people from having children, sterilization interfered with marriage, for the government went on to prohibit sterilized people from marrying and to annul new marriages among them. And already married couples wanting children sometimes divorced as a result of one of them being sterilized. Sterilization also caused injury and anguish; as a result of the surgery an estimated five thousand people died, and an unknown number committed suicide.

Meanwhile, racial sterilization began on a small scale. In 1934 involuntary sterilization was applied to Gypsies and proposed for several hundred children in the Rhine and Ruhr valleys fathered in the early 1920s by Black soldiers of the French occupation forces. In justifying the proposal, the government said the children were born as a result of rape but, according to a secret report, only one mother said she had been raped. In 1937 the sterilization was carried out quietly. Some of the children were sterilized under court decrees in technical accord with the sterilization law by giving them medical diagnoses. Others were sterilized secretly without legal proceedings.[56]

In 1935 "castration" of Jews was proposed. As health-related sterilization waned, consideration of other groups increased. One group proposed in 1939 was called *Gemeinschaftsfremden* (aliens to the community) or *Asoziale* (asocials). The concept was intuitively clear to Hitler, but it defied legal description, resulting in such vague formulations as:

> A person is an alien to the community if he/she proves to be incapable of satisfying the minimum requirement of the national community through his/her own efforts, in particular through an unusual degree of deficiency of mind or character.[57]

Proposed laws to sterilize them—never enacted—fell back on listing examples: do-nothings, ne'er-do-wells, confirmed dawdlers, disturbers of the peace, peevish people, beggars, tramps, wanderers in Gypsy fashion, promise-breakers, betrayers, swindlers, extortioners, seducers, pimps, abortionists, weaklings, unstable people, hysterical women, quarrelsome women, loose women, idle women, prostitutes, and so forth. In addition, the concept included Jews, Gypsies, Poles, Russians, and Ukrainians, all of whom were considered asocial by nature.[58]

Still another group considered for sterilization was people of partly Jewish ancestry, called *Mischlinge* (halfbreeds; the singular is *Mischling*). *Mischlinge* were a special group under Nazi law, which decided people's races by counting grandparents. Germans with three or four Jewish grandparents were Jews and had almost no civil rights. Those with no Jewish grandparents were Aryans. A *Mischling*—a German with one or two Jewish grandparents—was legally neither a Jew nor an Aryan. *Mischlinge* had many civil rights except in Austria, where their rights were taken away after annexation. To purify Germany racially, Hitler and Himmler meant for them not to have children, but there was no law to stop them. In 1936 an official commentary on the Nuremberg Laws said, "The aim of a legal solution to the *Mischling* problem must be the disappearance of the *Mischling* race."[59]

Various groups were considered further for sterilization between 1939 and 1941, when Dr. Walter Gross, chief of the Race Policy Office, again proposed *Mischlinge*.[60] A meeting of representatives of the Party, the SS, and government ministries rejected the proposal as likely to arouse unrest in the nation and infeasible during wartime because it would require ten hospital days per person—a consideration showing that only women were targeted at the time. Then sterilization took a turn that ended in a mystery.

By the time Hitler and his eugenicists extended sterilization to ethnic groups, public opposition to even health-related sterilization was mounting. As a result, in 1937 government eugenicists discussed finding a method that could be used surreptitiously on large numbers of people. In 1941, Himmler started a major experimental program to develop such a method, employing dozens of physicians. Hundreds (perhaps thousands) of concentration camp inmates—mostly Jewish and Gypsy women—were sterilized in the experiments.

At first Himmler told researchers the goal was sterilizing Russian prisoners of war or exterminating Poles and other enemy peoples. Later he said it was exterminating Jews or limiting the populations of subject peoples (Slavs). He also told them criminals were to be sterilized. Participating researchers and historians who later described the experiments did not question Himmler's statements, but the goals he presented were misleading. While the stated goals changed, depending on whom he was telling, Himmler's requirements, listed here, remained constant.

1. Quickness and ease. The need was to sterilize millions of people. Specific numbers mentioned by Himmler's staff were between two million and three million.[61]

2. Undetectability. Himmler required that people not know they had been sterilized. Accordingly, surgical sterilization was ruled out because it left a visible scar.[62] Much consideration was given to using hidden X-ray machines on men transacting business in offices. The main problem with X rays was that a dose sufficient for sterilization caused other damage. After a series of experiments, Victor Brack, Himmler's deputy in the research, reported that:

. . . as it is impossible unnoticeably to cover the rest of the body with lead, the other tissues of the body will be injured . . . [and those sterilized will] sooner or later realize with certainty that they had been sterilized or castrated by X-rays.[63]

Also seriously considered was a method to render women sterile by secretly inserting something into their wombs as part of routine medical office examinations.

3. Haste. Caladium seguinum, a chemical derived from a South American plant, was considered ideal, for it could be given to people without their awareness. The plant could not be obtained in quantity from South America during the war, and hothouses were established to produce it. Their output was disappointingly small, and there was no way to synthesize the chemical. Therefore caladium seguinum was abandoned in favor of a method that could be used during the war, and the experiments were rushed. The difficulties in using X rays on men and inserting substances into women without their awareness were never mastered. By contrast, caladium seguinum was considered a proven method of sterilizing people, was undetectable, and was very easy to use. It could have been used. The problem with caladium seguinum was the limited supply, restricting its use during the war.[64] Himmler was evidently interested only in a method for mass use before the war ended.

4. The highest secrecy. Caladium seguinum was virtually unknown in Germany. Dr. Gerhard Madaus, who was not involved in Himmler's project, had published articles on sterilizing *animals* with the chemical. When Himmler decided to experiment with caladium seguinum, he told Madaus to publish no more articles about it. Dr. Karl Tauboeck, one of Himmler's researchers, was told falsely the target was mental patients, and he was given a false name to use when getting information about sterilization from physicians who were not part of the project.[65] The sterilization experiments were more secret than any of the programs described in this chapter and much more secret than the Holocaust. All people below Himmler were misled about who the targeted group was.

The reason Himmler gave the project staff for the secrecy of the sterilization experiments was that bad publicity would result from discovery by enemy governments. This was hardly plausible. By 1941 the Third Reich had openly sterilized hundreds of thousands of Germans. Since that was widely known, there was no apparent need to keep sterilization research itself secret.

The statements that Russian prisoners of war and Poles were the targets did not fit the situation. Prisoners of war were almost all men, while the experiments were done mostly on women. And Soviet prisoners were segregated by gender and hardly had a chance to reproduce. Reportedly, Hitler had decided to rely on segregation for preventing their procreation. Also, they and Poles were treated with such arbitrariness, open cruelty, and disregard for their feelings that, if they were to be sterilized, a method to be used without their awareness was unnecessary.

The goals of extermination or long-term population control of conquered Slav nations also did not fit. Such uses involved many tens of millions of victims, generation after generation. It was not feasible during the war and could well have been put off until afterward. And for such an extended project, secrecy was impossible so, again, sterilization without the victims' awareness was unnecessary.

Jews were an even less likely target. They too were treated with open cruelty and disregard for their feelings. In addition, when the sterilization experiments began, *the decision to kill all the Jews had already been made.* According to Brack, Himmler's interest in a new sterilization method was not for use on Jews after 1941 because Hitler had specifically decided against sterilization as a means to eliminate them.[66] *Nonetheless, Himmler continued to tell doctors performing sterilization experiments that Jews were the intended target.*

Why the secrecy and misdirection? Measures against Jews had been accepted along with propaganda to the effect that they were aliens and subhumans, not Germans. And measures against Russians and Poles seemed acceptable. Therefore, statements that Jews, Russians, and Poles were intended targets would not raise problems for the researchers, who were members of the SS. The secrecy, the misdirection, and especially the settings in which sterilization was to be done—on men in places of business, on women in medical offices—suggest that those to be sterilized were not prisoners, but people enjoying freedom of movement and civil rights.

The rush to develop a sterilization method and the implied need to complete sterilization before the end of the war are especially puzzling. The idea that sterilization was intended for a large group in Germany who had civil rights could explain the extreme secrecy of the research, the requirement that victims not know they had been sterilized, and perhaps the rush. Conditions of war provided a cover for government actions that would not be tolerated in peacetime. War might also provide a bizarre cover against postwar repercussions. It takes time for people to discover they are sterile. If millions of Germans later discovered they were sterile, an explanation would have been necessary. The fact that they had all become sterile in a short time during the war could have been blamed on a secret chemical or bacteriological weapon used by the enemy.

In 1942 when the experimenters thought they had found a method of secret sterilization, Goebbels spread a hoax throughout Germany. He claimed discovery of a secret plan
by Great Britain and the United States to sterilize Germans. Described as a Jewish plan,
it was published in every newspaper, and several million copies were printed and distributed to the public, ending with, "German People! You now know what your eternal
enemy has prepared for you."[67] The hoax may have been designed to prepare the public
for later discovery of sterility. Hitler had already perpetrated hoaxes on Germans by
which citizens were harmed and killed and the blame put on enemies. With his control of
the media and the boldness of his lies, he had enjoyed success with those hoaxes. The
idea of sterilizing Germans and putting the blame on "international Jews," which may
seem farfetched today, was the kind of scheming that appealed to Hitler.

The most logical target for a new method of sterilization were *Mischlinge*. Giving
people a chemical secretly, having men sterilized while doing business, and having women
sterilized during routine medical visits—all the schemes fitted *Mischlinge* and dealt with
both obstacles that caused their sterilization to be rejected in 1941. In theory at least,
surreptitious sterilization was feasible to use on them.

The problem with concluding that *Mischlinge* were the target is that there were too few
of them. The 1939 census for Germany (including Austria) reported only 115,000, not the
millions projected in the experiments.[68] While the main office responsible for the elimination of Jews used a similar figure, some Nazis believed the actual number was far higher.
They reasoned the official Christian population included many descendants of Jews who had
converted to Christianity over the centuries and Jews passing as Christians. An official
estimate was 775,000 *Mischlinge*—still short of millions.[69] Perhaps the category of *Mischlinge*
was to be broadened for the purpose of sterilization to include people with less than a quarter
Jewish ancestry, and some evidence supports the possibility.

Two documentary pieces of evidence that bear further on the purpose of secret sterilization have been found. A letter from a K. Gund to Himmler in August 1942 described
the purpose of the experiments as "the prevention of reproduction by the congenitally
unfit and racially inferior . . ."[70] Gund's letter also mentioned related experiments by a
Dr. Fehringer on inducing impotence with chemicals to advance "our demographic policy."
Fehringer was head of the Regional Office of Race Policy of the Lower Danube region,
responsible for "the prevention of procreation among racially inferior groups" inside
Germany. Reportedly, he was the one who brought to Himmler's attention Madaus's
experiments with caladium seguinum, saying they were "of extreme interest from the
viewpoint of population policy."[71]

The innermost circle for decisions about racial policy consisted of Hitler, Bormann,
and Himmler. They destroyed their records at the end of the war and died before they
could be questioned. On the possible target of the experiments, only one of their documents has been found—a 1941 note in which Himmler wrote to Bormann:

> I regard such investigations as being absolutely necessary, perhaps not only in
> quarter-Jews but also *in persons with even less Jewish blood*. We must follow a

similar procedure to that which is used in breeding plants and animals, but this must remain between us. For several generations (at least 3 or 4), the offspring of such mixed families must be racially examined by independent institutes, and, if racial inferiority is shown, they must be sterilized, and thus prevented from passing on their traits further . . .[72] (Italics added.)

By "racial inferiority" he meant non-Nordic traits. Himmler was trained in plant and animal breeding, in which traits are the most important consideration. By Hitler's racial theory, the physical traits of most Germans were proof that, regardless of their family trees, they were carriers of non-Aryan blood. Himmler's note stressed racial traits as a basis for sterilizing people—*as even more important than the proportion of known Jewish ancestry.* And his note cautioned Bormann to tell no one.

By law, quarter Jews were free to marry only Aryans. The descendants of quarter Jews and Aryans after three generations would include people with 1/32 Jewish ancestry—people 97 percent Aryan. If one started with a parent less than a quarter Jewish and if descendants beyond the fourth generation were included, *Himmler's proposal meant sterilizing Germans with more than 99 percent Aryan ancestry.*

Apparently, Germans who were officially Aryans but descendants of Jews who converted to Christianity were not considered for sterilization by people below Himmler. They were, however, the people most important to eliminate if Hitler's goal of a pure race were to be achieved. Aryans had been forbidden to marry or engage in sex with Jews and discouraged from such relationships with *Mischlinge.* But Hitler had taken no measures to discourage their mating with Christians whose great-grandparents or more remote ancestors were Jews. It was infeasible for him to order such Christians killed, to sterilize them openly, or to prohibit them from having children. And, as he saw it, Aryans would be unable to recognize these people as Jews. They would allow these "secret Jews" to seduce, marry, and pollute them.

When Christianity arose, people were already members of other religions. All Christians were converts or descendants of converts, and the first Christians were largely Jews. Until the nineteenth century, Germany did not distinguish Christians by whether their ancestors had been Jews .

To Hitler, it made no difference whether people's Jewish ancestors were their grandparents or their forebears fifty generations ago. The only important question was whether they carried Jewish blood. If they did, they were a menace. To most of the nation, however, descendants of converts were not Jews at all. If a group with fractions of Jewish ancestry as small as in Himmler's note to Bormann were known to be targeted for sterilization, most Germans could not have been sure they were safe. If descendants of Jewish converts from the distant past were known to be targeted, no Germans could have been sure they were safe. That could account for the project's extreme secrecy and for misleading the researchers.

Identifying descendants of Jews who had converted in the distant past and given up their ancient Jewish family names was difficult and often impossible. The failure of Nazi scientists to find a laboratory test for Jewish blood left Hitler with criteria he knew to be inaccurate. To identify "secret Jews," Nazi anthropologists devised criteria based on physical traits, sometimes using precise (although invalid) distinctions. For example, aquiline noses were divided into curved (Jewish) and bent (Aryan).

How many official Christians were descended from Jews is unknown and cannot be estimated, but one can estimate how many Hitler's scientists thought there were. In the early 1930s, there were nearly 600,000 Jews in Germany and 200,000 in Austria. Hitler's scientists projected an additional 300,000 "secret Jews" in Germany. Using the same ratio would make 100,000 "secret Jews" in Austria. By census there were about 85,000 *Mischlinge* in Germany and 30,000 in Austria. The scientists projected an additional 690,000 "secret *Mischlinge*" in Germany.[73] Using the same ratio would make 230,000 in Austria. Let us assume they also projected that for every *Mischling* (official and secret) there was a Christian whose ancestry was less than a quarter Jewish—775,000 in Germany and 260,000 in Austria. Excluding official Jews and combining the other groups gives about 2,470,000 people whose reproduction Hitler needed to prevent.

Excluding women who were past childbearing would lower the total. Including people in Bohemia and Moravia (annexed to Germany) and Alsace and Lorraine (to be annexed) would raise it. Including people from the annexed part of Poland would raise it considerably.

Based on the thinking of his scientists, when the sterilization experiments began, the number of Germans carrying Jewish blood whom Hitler had no means to prevent from having children was probably between 2.5 million and 3 million. With the population annexed early in the war, the number probably exceeded 3 million. The idea that Hitler and Himmler meant to sterilize people ordinarily considered Christians fits their racial program and makes sense of aspects of the research that have remained puzzling.

CHAPTER 16

CONQUEST AND ANNIHILATION

> The next war will be unbelievably bloody and grim . . . the most inhuman war
> . . . which makes no distinction between military and civilian . . .[1]

—Adolf Hitler, 1932

Hitler's long-range goals were to bring lost territories back into the Reich, to fight a great war and win a great empire, to get rid of Germany's Jews, and to change the genetic composition of Aryans. It may not have occurred to him that conquest and purification could be incompatible and that his racial obsession would prevent military victory. Conflict between the goals would cause him to take heavy risks at the onset of World War II and become crucial after the defeat of France.

Hitler's general war strategy was to destroy France and then the Soviet Union. Conquest of the Soviet Union was his main war goal, but France came first to prevent the disaster expected in fighting on the eastern and western fronts at the same time, for he expected France to aid the Soviet Union. Great Britain's role was unclear in Hitler's mind at first. His grandest idea was an alliance by which Germany would rule mainland Europe, and Britain would rule much of the rest of the world, after taking over the colonial empires of France and other European countries. Many people said Hitler never meant to go to war with the English. But he made only feeble efforts toward an alliance with them and declared in a speech to Nazi leaders, senior military staff, and the war minister in 1934 that France and Britain must be defeated before conquering territory in the east. According to Speer, Hitler equivocated about Britain until 1935, when tension between Britain and Italy reached a peak. He then concluded that he had to choose one of them as an ally, making the other an enemy, and he chose Italy. After that he counted on war with Britain and that it would be Germany's most formidable enemy. In 1937, laying his plan before his military leaders, he included England among Germany's first targets, and he told Party leaders, "Our Enemy Number One is England."[2] And the minutes of Hitler's speech to his military leaders in 1939, informing them of the imminent invasion of Poland, include:

> The Führer doubts the possibility of a peaceful settlement with England. We
> must prepare ourselves for the conflict. England sees in our development the

foundation of a hegemony that would weaken England. England is therefore our enemy and the conflict with England will be a life-and-death struggle.[3]

The invasion of Poland was preceded by a heavy propaganda campaign promoting hatred of Poles. But even then, hatred of Poles came third in Hitler's propaganda, after hatred of Jews and the English.[4] And a few weeks after the invasion of Poland, he told his military staff he planned to invade England soon.

Earlier, during the years in which he armed the nation and spread hate to inspire Germans for a war they opposed, Hitler anticipated a preemptive invasion by Britain and France before Germany was ready. He therefore presented himself as a peacemaker. As he prepared secretly to invade and annex Austria, he said:

> Germany neither intends nor wishes to interfere in the internal affairs of Austria, to annex Austria, or to conclude an *Anschluss* [union].[5]

As he prepared secretly to invade Poland, he said:

> . . . war brings suffering and misfortune to people . . . National Socialism knows no policy designed to change borders at the expense of other peoples . . . We shall never attempt to conquer foreigners who hate us by a process which requires that we sacrifice millions that are dear to us, and whom we love, on the field of battle.[6]

And while menacing Austria and Poland, Hitler gave heavy assurances to other nations that he meant them no harm. In Great Britain, the main recipient of the assurances, he was most successful. Chamberlain was convinced Hitler wanted peace and even some historians concluded Hitler became involved in war with Britain unwillingly.

The invasion of Poland was a departure from Hitler's plan to destroy France first. The change seemed understandable; people accepted as sincere his territorial demands of Poland—the city of Danzig and a corridor of land to connect East Prussia with the rest of Germany. He also justified the invasion by claiming the Polish government was castrating Germans in Poland, whose protection was necessary. (There was no evidence for his claim, but Hitler was castrating Germans.) Thwarted in his wish to start a war by invading Czechoslovakia, Hitler was determined not to be thwarted again. To his staff he said:

> I shall give a propagandistic reason for starting the war—never mind whether it is plausible or not. The victor will not be asked afterward whether he told the truth or not. In starting and making a war it is not right that matters, but victory.[7]

The prospect of a German invasion of Poland alarmed the government of Germany's new ally, Italy. Foreign Minister Count Galeazzo Ciano asked von Ribbentrop, the new German foreign minister, "Well, what do you want? The Corridor or Danzig?" Von Ribbentrop replied, "Not that any more. We want war!" After their conversation, Ciano wrote in his diary:

> The decision to fight is implacable. He rejects any solution which might give satisfaction to Germany and avoid the struggle. I am certain that even if the

Germans were given more than they ask for, they would attack just the same, because they are possessed by the demon of destruction.[8]

High Nazis confirmed Ciano's conclusion. Hitler's wish was that Poland reject his demands, for Danzig and the corridor were unimportant to him. To prevent another Munich, he kept raising his demands and, during the last month before the scheduled invasion, ordered his ambassadors in Warsaw and London to be unavailable. He later said, "I needed an alibi, especially with the German people, to show them that I had done everything to maintain peace."[9]

To his military leaders Hitler did not stress his public demands of Poland, saying Danzig was unimportant; the vital goal was conquering territory so that Germany could expand.[10] Hitler had long ago taken up the nationalist cry for *Lebensraum*—a need for living space owing to Germany's heavy population density—and carried it further, for he meant to double Germany's population. Later events would show *Lebensraum* was less important than conquest and racial purification in his war decisions. He also told his generals that Germany needed Poland's agricultural resources and added a personal consideration: "No one knows how long I have to live."[11] His expected lifespan had no bearing on the Polish campaign itself. At the time, perhaps no one except Himmler and Heydrich knew the reasons behind the invasion of Poland.

The decision to invade Poland was Hitler's alone, according to his chief of staff, Gen. Alfred Jodl:

> There is absolutely no doubt about it! In this case it was Hitler's will alone that forced the issue. I can only assume that he had his mind dead set on it and all the negotiations were bluff.—I don't know, but it certainly looks that way. Nobody really knows what went on in his mind.[12]

A few months before invading Poland, Hitler told his military staff, in the words of the minutes taken:

> We cannot expect a repetition of the Czech affair. There will be war. Our task is to isolate Poland. The success of this isolation will be decisive . . . There must be no simultaneous conflict with the Western Powers.[13]

The "Western Powers" were France and Britain. Hitler was sure war would occur because he had decided on it. No matter what concessions the Poles and their allies might make, he meant to invade Poland. This he did not tell his military leaders. Rather, he said that if Poland could not be isolated, he would invade France first. Otherwise, he risked a two-front war, for France and Britain were committed to Poland.

His statement to them was a lie—the same lie he had told them in 1938 when directing them to draw up plans for invading Czechoslovakia. His intention then had been to invade even if France and Britain came to the defense of Czechoslovakia. Only Czechoslovakia's capitulation prevented the invasion.[14]

Hitler's efforts to isolate Poland failed; France and Britain renewed their commitments emphatically. Nonetheless, Hitler went ahead with the invasion of Poland. He calculated a two-front war could be avoided by subduing Poland quickly, before France and Britain attacked Germany. Knowing France and Britain were not well prepared for war, he still could not be sure they would hold back. He said, "We must accept the risk with reckless resolution."[15]

In April 1939, when Hitler had ordered the invasion of Poland for September, the risk had been even greater. The Soviet Union, fearing a German invasion, had sought an alliance with France and Great Britain—an effort that failed. If Hitler's invasion of Poland had brought the Soviet Union, France, and Britain together, he would have faced an alliance that his generals considered overwhelmingly strong. The Soviet Union had by far the largest army in Europe, and Germany's military power was well short of the peak it would reach in 1941. Tentative gestures toward an alliance between Germany and the Soviet Union were exchanged early in 1939, but it was not until August, a few weeks before the scheduled invasion of Poland, that Hitler pursued them. He meant to invade Poland whether or not Stalin agreed to the nonaggression pact that was then signed.

This time, the planned pretext was used. Germans from a concentration camp were dressed in Polish army uniforms and "invaded" Germany. Their bodies were exhibited to the press as evidence. Announcing that Poland had attacked Germany, without waiting for a declaration of war by the Reichstag as required by the constitution, Hitler ordered the invasion that began World War II. In his address to the Reichstag, broadcast to the nation, he said the Poles had misunderstood his peaceful intentions and refused to send a representative to talk peace. Instead, they had mobilized and attacked, and "we are only shooting back."

Behind Hitler's decision to risk French, British, and even Soviet intervention was his primary objective. His main goal in starting the war combined purification of Germany with destruction of Poland. He had decided it was time to start the bloodletting, and part of it would be military casualties, for war was a way of pruning Germany's racial stock. It was a strange way, for he believed war removed the best stock—the warriors. Nonetheless, he saw war as essential in elevating Germans, saying, "Victories without loss of blood are demoralizing."[16] Himmler said Hitler believed that "War makes men stronger and more virile" and "The world cannot know real peace until it has been purified by war." Later in the war, when aides would bring Hitler news of heavy German casualties, he would say, "But that's what young men are there for!" and "Losses can never be too high! They sow the seeds of future greatness." And toward the end, in his last address to the nation, he would say, "The more Germans suffer, the closer they are on their way to victory."[17] War would purify Germany, for death was redemptive and regenerative; the more blood, the greater the rebirth that would follow.

Hitler had long meant to destroy some or all the Polish people. One idea was to kill a large fraction and reduce the survivors to a primitive existence suitable for slaves. The opportunity for mass killing of Poles tempted him strongly, but the idea closest to his heart was using Poland as a place to send and dispose of Germans who were carriers of poisoned blood. As he planned the invasion of Poland, he said privately, "We are going to destroy the Jews."[18]

Poland was home to more Jews than any European country except the Soviet Union and to the worst Jews, as he saw it—the "caftan-wearers" (Hasidic men) who reproduced like vermin and poured into Germany. They especially were to be killed. As he ordered his armies into Poland, Hitler gave his generals an idea of what was to come:

> I have sent to the east my Death Head units with the order to kill without mercy all men, women and children of Polish race or language.[19]

And in justifying the extermination, he cited genocide by Turkey in 1919: "Who still talks nowadays of the extermination of the Armenians?"[20]

In fact, the killing was much more limited. Horrified army officers complained about the slaughter of civilians, and it was narrowed mainly to Polish political leaders, clergy, gentry, intellectuals, and Jews. In all about 1,250,000 were killed by the death squads. Incidentally, they also killed Poles of German ancestry—the Germans Hitler said he was invading Poland to protect—by mistaking them for Jews.[21]

It was the opportunity to begin the extermination that made invading Poland Hitler's first choice. His ideas about invading France did not involve extermination. And he believed correctly that, if he died before launching it, there would be no Holocaust. The men Hitler had designated as his successors—Hess and Göring—did not share his genocidal intentions. In May 1941, Hess would take himself out of the picture by flying to Scotland in hope of negotiating an end to the war. He would do it just when Hitler was about to enlarge it and establish the death camps. And Göring would oppose the Holocaust directly. Knowing how little support he had for geno-cide, Hitler was determined to complete it during his lifetime. To his generals he could not urge accepting the danger of a two-front war in order to exterminate Poles and rid Germany of Jews.

Weeks after the successful invasion of Poland, Hitler told his military staff to hurry preparations for invading France, saying:

> As a final factor I must, in all modesty, list my own person: irreplaceable. Nei-ther a military nor a civilian personality could take my place. Attempts on my life may be repeated . . . the fate of the Reich depends on me alone. I shall act accordingly.[22]

If any of his staff understood in what way the fate of the Reich depended on him, they did not say. Some of them were aware of the extermination already going on in Poland, but there is no indication they connected it with Hitler's claim of being indispensable.

About the coming invasion of France, he said:

> Every hope of compromise is childish . . . I have to choose between victory and destruction. I choose victory.[23]

Compromise was impossible because he had ruled it out. Later he said about the invasion of Poland:

> . . . it was not only fortunate there was no compromise; at the time we would have had to regard it as harmful, and I should therefore have struck in any case.[24]

On another occasion he said:

> Basically I did not organize the armed forces in order not to strike. The decision to strike was always in me.[25]

He added:

> I believe that German might is such as to make the triumph of Germany inevitable but, if not, we will all go down together. Whether that be for better or for worse.[26]

He was a gambler, driven to go for all or nothing, and it would turn out that all and nothing were inseparable. Over the next five years, he would often mention victory and the destruction of Germany in the same breath, and it would become apparent to some of his associates that for him there was no basic difference between them. Victory over the part of himself he loathed would come only with his death. And since he had identified himself with Germany, victory for the nation would become inseparable from its destruction. He would turn a run of easy conquests with minimal German casualties and the prospect of an early end to the war into a bloodbath threatening the existence of Germany.

Hitler enjoyed a remarkable string of successes from 1932 to 1941—electoral wins, domestic and diplomatic feats, and military victories. After Poland, he easily conquered Denmark and Norway and then Holland, Belgium, and Luxembourg on the way to crushing France. The string then turned into defeats. Up to 1941, he kept his wish to exterminate the Jews in check, but once he committed himself to the main phase of the Holocaust—the death camp program—it overshadowed his other goals. He then gave up public appearances and speeches, lost interest in domestic government, stopped pursuing diplomacy, and made the worst of his military decisions. Keeping in view Hitler's obsession with racial purification makes sense of decisions that have been a puzzle for half a century.

During his easy conquests, Hitler's timing was apt and his preparations more than adequate. In World War I, four years of combat with millions of German casualties were not enough to defeat France. In 1940, France fell in six weeks at a cost of only 27,000 Germans. That left Great Britain standing alone against Germany. Although still dominant on the seas and formidable in the air, Britain was at a severe disadvantage on the ground. Germany, nearly at peak strength, was allied with Italy and Japan and would shortly be joined by Hungary, Bulgaria, Romania, and Yugoslavia. Of Britain's forces in Europe, most had fallen or been captured in France, and the remnant that escaped was incapable of warfare for some time. Tanks had been abandoned in France, and those in

England were mostly obsolete models used for training.[27] The time for invading the only nation still at war with Germany would never be better.

In fact the best time had just passed. In late May, Britain's decimated ground forces were in a disorganized retreat through Belgium and France, and its air force was occupied in France. Hitler had more than enough troops in reserve to invade England, and he favored surprise attack. An invasion then would have caught the British in the worst position.[28]

Estimates made at the time by Hitler's generals and later by some historians were that, if German armies had landed in England, in its badly weakened condition, with its main forces far away in Africa, the country could have been overrun in two weeks. The "if" is a large one, but the point is not that an invasion would have succeeded. It is that Hitler and his generals had full confidence. They concluded a quarter million troops would be enough to conquer Britain, in contrast to the three and a third million they would send to conquer the Soviet Union, with little confidence in the outcome of that invasion.

Had Hitler conquered Britain, his dominance of Europe would have been secure. He would then have had ample time to organize the manpower and production of most of Europe for conquering the Soviet Union. Germany's army was adequate for the kind of campaign invading England required but unequipped for war in the Soviet Union, whose enormous population and area and harsh climate posed special problems. Victory over Britain would have given him time to retool for invading the Soviet Union. Total victory rested on conquering Britain first.

Hitler's decision to invade the Soviet Union instead of England changed the war drastically. Besides leading to a multifront war, it resulted in the alliance that beat Germany—the alliance that the leaders of Britain, the Soviet Union, and the United States had tried but failed to create for themselves. The decision to invade the Soviet Union began a chain of events leading to Germany standing alone against an alliance of dozens of nations. It turned victory into defeat.

Hitler's decision against invading England was not made in haste. It has been explained by his love of the English as opposed to his hatred of Russians. But he did not love them; his attitude toward them combined hatred with admiration for what he saw as their exceptional nationalism, racial purity, and political skill. His hatred of them was clear in World War I and runs through his thinking until his death. And his admiration of them was hardly a barrier to invading England. It was matched by his admiration of Norwegians, and he had readily invaded Norway.

The decision has also been explained by the military difficulties of invading England. With Germany's overwhelming ground forces, there was only one major obstacle to crushing Britain—crossing the English Channel. The question is whether that obstacle—large as it was—was what decided Hitler against the invasion.

Hitler ordered an invasion plan involving crossing the Channel in ships and boats. His staff presented one with reservations centered on the crossing. Meanwhile, Hitler said the British would realize the utter hopelessness of their position and make peace without an invasion, but he did not take significant peace initiatives. General Albert Kesselring would later say:

> . . . we commanders at the front could not conceive how Hitler could hope to reach an agreement with the English when day after day and week after week went by without anything happening.

and,

> . . . the utter neglect of the invasion idea, obvious to every soldier, is incomprehensible.[29]

Before France fell, Hitler had put out peace feelers to Britain through Switzerland, while telling a member of his foreign office that no real basis for peace negotiations existed.[30] In the summer of 1940, he made the vaguest of peace suggestions to Britain's new prime minister, Winston Churchill, and waited. On June 18, Churchill declared the Empire would fight on and then attacked the French fleet to prevent it from falling into German hands. Hitler still waited and then on July 19 proposed before the Reichstag that Britain negotiate peace with Germany, but he laced his speech with pointed insults of Churchill—a ridiculous nonentity, a political misfit of nature. Churchill was known for his tenacity, and Hitler's words fitted better with goading him to fight than persuading him to yield. These gestures were Hitler's efforts for peace with Great Britain. Reportedly, in August the king of Sweden offered to mediate a settlement between Germany and Britain, but Hitler refused.[31]

Before ordering an invasion plan, Hitler had ignored for weeks his generals' proposals to invade England.[32] And after endorsing it, he postponed designating a specific landing site or date. In July he selected sites and a date—September 15, 1940. An invasion fleet was assembled along the French side of the Channel and both sides waited. Many historians concluded that, despite the specific invasion plan he had approved and the massive preparations to carry it out, Hitler had not reached a decision on invading England, and subsequent events support the conclusion.

In September, Hitler postponed the invasion for days. Then he postponed it again and again, as he talked about the weather, military considerations, and the possibility of bombing Britain into submission without an invasion. The British air force's success against the German air force—"winning the Battle of Britain"—has been credited with turning Hitler against the invasion plan. Without detracting from Britain's courage and remarkable achievements, evidence presented below indicates that Hitler was turning against the invasion before the Battle of Britain.

Meanwhile, Britain bombed Hitler's invasion fleet and built up ground forces. On October 12, Hitler postponed the invasion until spring, and it became a dead issue. Two months later, he told his staff of his decision to invade the Soviet Union instead.

Historians assumed that military considerations were decisive for Hitler, and much was made of his military staff's reservations as souring him on invading England. Later, Hitler voiced regret over not having done it and blamed his staff for talking him out of it, contributing to misinterpretation of his decision. His military staff did not talk him out of it. They had opposed him on invading Poland and then on invading the Low Countries and France. Between those campaigns, they had opposed him most on invading Norway. The sea to be crossed to Norway was far greater than the English Channel and patrolled by the British navy and air force. Fearing destruction of the invasion force en route, Hitler's staff had pronounced invading Norway impossible.[33] Conquering Norway (of great racial value to Hitler) had little military value compared to conquering Britain, and Hitler had considered it the riskiest of his military ventures. Nonetheless, he had brushed the objections aside.

In May 1940, Kesselring had presented a plan for an air invasion of England, which would have made the choppiness of the Channel and Britain's naval superiority irrelevant. Germany was equipped for airborne landings and had had successful experience with them. Nonetheless, Hitler ignored Kesselring's plan.[34]

Hitler's generals strongly opposed invading the Soviet Union; therefore, in the fall of 1940, he worked to convince them. To those who insisted Britain be defeated first, preventing a two-front war—a position he also had taken earlier—he promised to do it. Meanwhile, he used an incredible argument on them: invading the Soviet Union was the best way to defeat Great Britain. The argument his military staff found more persuasive—although it was also false—was that German intelligence had learned Britain and the Soviet Union were concluding a pact against Germany and a Soviet invasion of Germany was imminent. Therefore a preemptive strike against the Soviet Union was necessary. In December he told them the decision to invade the Soviet Union was final, ending the argument.

In parallel developments, Benito Mussolini, Italy's leader, reminded Hitler in June 1940 of their prior agreement for a joint invasion of England and said he was ready to proceed with it, but Hitler put Mussolini off.[35] At the same time, Hitler dropped a hint to his generals about invading the Soviet Union and to Himmler that Himmler was going to carry out the total extermination of the Jews.[36] At the end of July, he told Jodl he was planning to invade the Soviet Union and hinted he might do so before invading England. In October, after talking with Hitler, the Italian foreign minister inferred that Hitler was no longer interested in invading England.[37]

Of all his proposed ventures, it was the invasion of England that had the most support among his military staff. According to Gen. Wilhelm Keitel, invading England was what they urged on him, and Gen. Günther Blumentritt said, "He showed little interest in the plans and made no effort to speed up the preparations. That was utterly different to his usual behavior."[38]

Hitler's lack of enthusiasm for invading England was clear, but the reason was not. His decision not to invade England was foreshadowed by earlier decisions that allowed

British forces in France to escape. In May 1940, rapid advances in Belgium and France had trapped several hundred thousand troops, mostly British, between German armies and the English Channel. With those troops in a desperate retreat, Hitler ordered tank units pursuing them to slow down on May 17. Boulogne was cut off on May 22 and Calais on May 23, and the British navy evacuated a small number of troops from those ports to England. That left most of the trapped forces on a shrinking slip of land near the port of Dunkirk. Knowing the evacuations at Boulogne and Calais were going on, with his troops ten miles from Dunkirk, Hitler halted the advance, and it remained halted for three days.

Most German generals who spoke about it said it was Hitler who ordered the halt. Another version is that Gen. Gerd von Rundstedt, the area commander, initially ordered a one-day halt, which Hitler extended to three days. Von Rundstedt first said he initiated the halt and later that the decision was entirely Hitler's. That Hitler and von Rundstedt discussed the halt is not in question. Basil Liddell Hart commented, "If Hitler had felt that Rundstedt had prompted him to halt the [tank] forces, he would almost certainly have mentioned it after the British escape among the excuses he gave for his decision, for he was very apt to blame others for any mistakes."[39] Before the halt, Göring, commandant of the air force, had urged that his bombers be given the chance to destroy the enemy pocket around Dunkirk, and Hitler agreed. But according to Blumentritt, Hitler restricted even air attacks on the trapped troops.[40] These actions were unusual in Hitler's conduct of the war.

After the halt order, Gen. Ewald von Kleist's tank unit entered the town of Hazebrouck, behind enemy lines, cutting their flight toward Dunkirk. Hitler then ordered von Kleist to retreat, which he did.[41]

During the halt, the British navy began to ferry Allied troops from Dunkirk across the Channel. Four hundred thousand had been trapped there, of whom 350,000 were evacuated. And another 200,000 were evacuated from nearby French ports.

The decision to halt the advance on Dunkirk shocked most of Hitler's generals. Commander-in-Chief Walther von Brauchitsch, Chief of Staff Franz Halder, and Heinz Guderian objected vigorously and persistently and were soon joined by Kesselring, von Kleist, Günther von Kluge, Wolfram von Richtofen, Fedor von Bock, Wilhelm von Thoma, and von Rundstedt. Hitler did not argue with them on strategic grounds, but said that continuing the advance would destroy part of Flanders inhabited by Flemings, whom he admired. He also said that the area, crisscrossed by waterways, was unsuited to tank warfare and time was needed to repair tanks.[42] After interviewing the German generals, Liddell Hart said, "The motives behind the Dunkirk halt-order have remained a puzzle to all the generals concerned. The [tank] generals are the most puzzled . . . for they saw the ground at the time and could see no justification for halting . . ."[43] And the tanks were not especially in need of repair. Most generals believed that Hitler was sincere in the military reasons he gave but had made a mistake in judgment.

To others, Hitler gave a variety of contradictory reasons. To his naval adjutant, he said that the British in France would fight to the last man; therefore, his plan was to contain them until they ran out of ammunition and take them prisoner. To his personal and administrative staff, he said, "The army is England's backbone . . . If we destroy it, there goes the British Empire," adding that the Empire was a stable element in an unstable world and should be preserved. To his valet, he said, "It is always good to let a broken army return home to show the civilian population what a beating they have had." And to some generals, he said that a humiliating defeat of the British would be an obstacle to concluding a satisfactory peace with them, which was what he wanted. On hearing this, von Rundstedt said, "Well, if he wants nothing else, then we shall have peace at last."[44] But Hitler did want much more.

A few years later, Hitler would say:

> Churchill was quite unable to appreciate the sporting spirit of which I had given proof by refraining from creating an irreparable breach between the British and ourselves. We did, indeed, refrain from annihilating them at Dunkirk.[45]

The last sentence was true. As to sportsmanship, he had contempt for it. As to his concern for Great Britain and its empire and his regard for the Flemings, at best Hitler's statements were irrelevant. Such considerations had not limited his destructiveness in the past, nor would they deter him in the future. "What is clear is that Hitler's reasons . . . were complex, illogical, and very personal. The official reasons he gave . . . were obviously spurious, and the real reasons may never be known."[46]

After the Dunkirk evacuation, Hitler did not punish or scold his staff. On the contrary, he sent congratulations to von Kluge over the campaign in that area and visited von Rundstedt "in a very good humour," seemingly untroubled by the British escape.[47]

Militarily, advancing on Dunkirk and invading England were the obvious choices and by far the best choices for winning and ending the war. These were the goals of Germany's military leaders and its people. The projected invasion of England was the only one that had popular support.

But winning and ending the war were not Hitler's priorities. While stalling on invading England, Hitler was moving secretly toward his decision to exterminate the Jews. Later events would show that the decisions to invade the Soviet Union and exterminate the Jews were linked. The steps leading to the extermination can be traced by documents and testimony from people who worked on it. The evidence shows that the Holocaust was in Hitler's mind when he postponed and then gave up the idea of invading England. A quick victory over Great Britain, the key to winning World War II, would have prevented, or at least postponed carrying out the Holocaust, which required the cover of war. Hitler and those who administered the Holocaust anticipated that two or three years would be needed to complete it, which would prove to be a serious underestimate.[48]

Up to 1939, Hitler's goal was disposing of Germany's Jews, but then he began to consider all of Europe's Jews. By the time he came to his final decision, he probably had Europe's Jews in mind. Estimates of when he made it range from 1938 to 1942. The year 1938 is probably too early, and 1942 is certainly too late. The Wannsee Conference of

January 1942 has been cited as when the decision to kill the Jews was made. However, the conference was held not to make a decision, but to work out details for doing what had been decided earlier.

In 1919, Hitler said his goal was total elimination of Jews from Germany by deportation. In 1922, he said to a journalist, "Once I am really in power, my first and foremost task will be the annihilation of the Jews."[49] In 1924, while writing *Mein Kampf,* he was asked by a Nazi whether he had softened his position on violence against Jews, and he answered:

> . . . I have been far too soft up to now! While working on my book, I have finally come to realize that the harshest methods of fighting must be employed in the future if we are to win. I am convinced that this is not only a matter of life and death for our people but for all peoples.[50]

Over and over he said the Jews were to be gotten rid of. In public he often used the word *Entfernung* (removal). In some contexts it meant coerced emigration or deportation; in others, as in *Mein Kampf,* he said it could only be accomplished "by the sword"— by a "bloody" procedure.[51] For twenty years, he alternated between the two and sometimes combined them, considering deporting some Jews and killing the rest. His words about World War I in *Mein Kampf* were to prove prophetic:

> If at the beginning of the War and during the War, twelve or fifteen thousand of these Hebrew corrupters of the people had been held under poison gas . . . the sacrifice of millions at the front would not have been in vain.[52]

Enormous losses would have been worthwhile if Jews had been killed. And two months after becoming chancellor he said:

> I don't know whether my name will be held in high repute in Germany . . . no matter what I am hoping to achieve for my people, but . . . I am absolutely certain . . . the name of Hitler shall be glorified everywhere as the person who once and for all had extirpated the Jewish pest from the world.[53]

Hitler's personal preference was to kill the Jews but, constrained by popular opposition to violence against them, he gave priority to emigration during the 1930s, using terror to motivate Jews to leave Germany. His threat to the Jews in his oft-quoted speech of 1939, prophesying their complete annihilation, had the same function and increased Jews' flight. But during the 1930s Hitler also put obstacles in their way, increasing the cost of leaving to a confiscatory level. Jews were allowed to take only ten marks with them, ensuring that other countries would refuse to admit most of them. In addition, the government took away their passports and required special exit permits. Jews who tried to leave without permits were arrested. In Austria after annexation, most Jews who tried to leave failed.

The annexations of Austria and part of Czechoslovakia added a half million Jews, and the invasion of Poland added two million more, giving Hitler a different situation to consider. The invasions of Norway, the Low Countries, and France added still more. Starting with fewer than 600,000 Jews in 1933, Hitler had four million under his control by the summer of 1940. This probably contributed to enlarging his purpose from getting rid of Germany's Jews to getting rid of Europe's.

Heydrich had been assigned to help German Jews emigrate to the British protectorate of Palestine (now Israel), but in 1939 Great Britain ordered Jewish emigration there sharply curtailed. Heydrich then cooperated with Zionist groups to smuggle German Jews into Palestine and worked on emigration of German Jews to other countries. Hitler delegated Göring to meet with an international committee whose task was enabling German Jews to emigrate. But when Göring submitted a proposed agreement on emigration, Hitler rejected it.[54] At about the same time, Heydrich reported the emigration plan was failing because countries were refusing to take in Jews. The invasion of Poland brought an end to negotiations with other countries on emigration of German Jews, and Heydrich was directed to devote himself to a plan for deporting them.

Lucy Dawidowicz concluded that Hitler had decided before the invasion of Poland on killing Germany's and perhaps Europe's Jews.[55] She cited public remarks by some Nazi leaders in 1938 and 1939, anticipating the killing of all German Jews who did not leave, but the remarks seem to have been used as threats to get Jews to leave. Eichmann clearly used threats for the purpose. In charge of ridding Bohemia and Moravia of Jews, in 1939 he told the Jewish Council in Prague that 70,000 must emigrate within a year. The council said the number was impossibly high, and Eichmann replied that if they did not leave he would send 300 a day to Dachau "where they will become very keen on emigration."[56]

Dawidowicz also cited Heydrich's 1939 briefing to leaders of the death squads sent into Poland. It referred to a two-stage process: in the first, Jews were to be collected in ghettos and concentration camps and many of them killed as preparation for the second stage—"the final goal"—which was not specified. According to later testimony by Eichmann, who was present at the briefing, it meant extermination. But there is evidence "the final goal" in Heydrich's briefing meant resettlement of Polish Jews in the "Lublin Reservation," a large area to be established for them in Poland, with their ultimate fate not yet decided.[57] Later documents include extermination as one of the possible final dispositions for Polish Jews. And Heydrich's briefing applied to them only, not to German Jews. Centuries earlier, Martin Luther had proposed burning Jews' homes and deporting them from Germany as "the final solution" to the evil he saw in them. When Hitler first spoke of "the final solution" in 1939, he referred to deporting German Jews, killing them, or both. And Heydrich continued to work on deporting German Jews. Another reason 1939 is too early is that after Poland was conquered, Hitler had many Polish Jews expelled to the Soviet Union.

A vague plan for deporting German Jews to the French colony of Madagascar had been under consideration since *Kristallnacht*. After Palestine and other countries were out of consideration, Madagascar came to the forefront. In May 1940, as the invasion of

France began, Himmler prepared a detailed plan for settling German Jews in Madagascar. It required French cooperation, and Hitler expected to have it after the fall of France.

When France surrendered in July, Germany occupied the northern part, leaving an autonomous government in the south (Vichy), which administered the colonies. Hitler then ordered Jews from Alsace and Lorraine (still part of France but designated for annexation) and from Germany deported to Vichy France for later shipment to Madagascar. In all, the order slated 275,000 Jews for deportation to Madagascar. On October 6, the deportation of German Jews to Poland began. The likelihood that they were to be killed was high but not yet certain. On October 22, the Vichy government protested deportation of German Jews to France for reshipment, and Hitler suspended it. That was the end of the Madagascar plan, but not of the deportation of German Jews. Designating the Lublin Reservation for their resettlement, Hitler sent more and more of them to Poland.

Meanwhile, emigration of German Jews was stopped in March 1940 by an unpublished order. Permits were no longer given, although a written order banning their emigration was not issued until the next year. Written orders stopping emigration of Jews from occupied western lands, however, were issued in 1940. One from September included the phrase ". . . in view of the doubtless imminent final solution of the Jewish question." In October, the emigration of Polish Jews was also prohibited.[58]

If we assume Hitler stopped Jews from leaving in order to kill them, the orders of March, September, and October 1940 take on heavy meaning. They place steps toward total extermination of the Jews at the time when he postponed invading England and even earlier, when he ignored urgings by his generals and Mussolini to proceed with an invasion.

Meanwhile, the killing of Jews had been increasing. In September 1939, mass killing of Polish Jews by death squads had begun, followed in June 1940 by killing of Jews in German mental hospitals, followed in August by killing of Jews in German nonmental hospitals. Then, in November 1940, Hitler ordered that the Jews who had been collected in Polish ghettos and concentration camps were to be starved to death.

According to a member of the SS, Hitler discussed with SS leaders in December 1940 the gassing of all Jews. In the same month, gassing equipment for the Auschwitz concentration camp was ordered. In January, Himmler told SS leaders the invasion of the Soviet Union would occur in the summer, along with mass extermination of Jews. Eichmann and two other officials said that during that month, they saw a plan for the death camps approved by Hitler. A meeting like the Wannsee Conference of January 1942, but for officials in occupied France and Belgium, was called in January 1941. And Heydrich wrote in the same month about "Auschwitz II," which did not then exist.[59] It would be the name of the main death camp, also called Birkenau, built the next year. January 1941 was marked by much preparation for the Holocaust.

Göring continued to oppose extermination as late as May 1941, and what he said is most apt here:

It is more important that we win the war than carry out racial policy.[60]

Undeterred, Hitler ordered his generals to cooperate in the killing of all Soviet Jews once the invasion began.

Meanwhile, Himmler had given orders for construction of Auschwitz II. By July, Göring's opposition ended, and he signed an order authorizing Heydrich to proceed with the Holocaust—an order Heydrich could show in commandeering administrators who had not been privy to the decision. By then *die Endlösung* (the final solution) was officially the code phrase for extermination. That summer, Himmler told Rudolf Höss, a concentration camp commandant and later commandant of two death camps, "The Führer has ordered that the Jewish question be solved once and for all, and that we, the SS, implement that order."[61] In September 1941, specially fitted vans using automotive exhaust were gassing Jews at some locations and *Zyklon B* (cyanide), which would be the main tool of the Holocaust, was being tested on them at Auschwitz. Chelmno, the first death camp to use *Zyklon B* regularly, was operating by December. Ordering a reluctant Himmler to proceed with gassing on a mass scale, Hitler said, "The war will soon be over, and I have given the world my word that at the end of it there will not be one Jew left on earth. We must move quickly and vigorously."[62] Months later, the death camps were in full operation.

By this reconstruction, when Hitler allowed the British to escape at Dunkirk and hesitated over invading England, he was approaching his decision on the Holocaust. In or about October 1940, when he gave up on invading England, he made it.

The decision to invade the Soviet Union also included exterminating other peoples. Himmler had written in May 1940:

> . . . within a few years . . . the concept of the Kashubian race will have disappeared, for then a Kashubian people will no longer exist . . . Over a somewhat longer period it should also be possible to eliminate from our territory the concepts of such races as the Ukrainians, the Górale, and the Lemki. The same that can be said about these splinter races applies, on a correspondingly grander scale, to the Poles.[63]

The Kashube and Górale were ethnic groups in Poland, the Lemki in the Ukraine.

Once he made his decision to kill the Jews, Hitler stuck to it at the expense of other goals. To associates who complained that the extermination program hindered the war effort, Hitler replied, "The Jewish question takes priority over all other matters."[64] In 1942, Gen. Baron Kurt von Gienanth, army commandant in occupied Poland, sent a memo to his superior, Jodl, listing delays in the war effort caused by the priority given to killing Jews. Von Gienanth urged only that Jews be eliminated "as promptly as possible without impairing essential war work." Hitler relieved him of command. In a follow-up memo to army commandants, Himmler wrote:

> I have issued instructions that steps be ruthlessly taken against all those who think it their business to intervene in the alleged interests of the war industry, but who in reality want only to support the Jews . . .[65]

Toward the end of the war, after millions of casualties at the front, when Germany was facing defeat, Hitler would say privately to Himmler about the Jews:

> Should we lose, then we shall at the very least have hit decisively these subversives . . . I am determined, out of a higher responsibility, to translate this recognition of mine into action, whatever the consequences.[66]

Historians have questioned the conclusion that Hitler compromised the war effort in order to exterminate Jews, and one said, ". . . the Nazi regime diverted almost nothing in terms of real military resources for [the] offensive against the ghettos."[67] It is true the death camps, the extermination squads operating outside the death camps, and the liquidation of the Polish ghettos involved army troops and material only on a small scale. But if we consider allocation of resources having military value, it is also true that the war effort was compromised. The death camps, death squads, and liquidation of the ghettos used guns, bullets, fuel, and other resources. They also employed several hundred thousand men—members of the SS and Order Police and men recruited from Estonia, Latvia, Lithuania, and the Ukraine. Most of them could have served at the front. Among the SS alone, over a quarter million worked on finding, arresting, and guarding Jews and others being sent to death camps. The number being sent to death camps became so great that—even with the larger camps killing thousands a day—not all victims could be taken in. To house people delayed en route to death camps, a thousand transit camps were built, also staffed by the SS. Still other SS men worked on transporting Jews and operating the death camps. In all, about 2,400 camps served the extermination program. In addition, shipment of army units and military supplies was often delayed because trains were commandeered by the SS to ship Jews and others to camps.[68] Further still, the extermination program required much construction, labor, and material and was supported by a bureaucracy, all of which could have been devoted to military projects.

The Soviet Union had long tempted Hitler. Of the invasions he launched, the Soviet campaign was by far the most important one to him—the titanic battle of good versus evil, the chosen Aryan people against the Jewish Bolsheviks. Hitler's instructions to his generals were laced with this rhetoric, common in Nazi circles but strange in military conferences. He described the campaign to come as matching the greatest invasion force ever assembled against the greatest enemy force of all time. It was to be the war of wars, the ultimate gamble.

The invasion of the Soviet Union was only part of his expansion of the war. During the winter of 1940–41, he sent an army to Africa, where Mussolini was invading Egypt, and committed troops to fight a planned war in Turkey that did not take place. He then invaded Yugoslavia (where a coup had toppled the government friendly to him) and sent troops in support of Italy's invasion of Greece. By the time he invaded the Soviet Union in June 1941, said his chief of the general staff, ". . . he scattered the formations of the German Army from the North Pole to the Libyan desert . . ."[69]

As the invasion of the Soviet Union began, Hitler said:

> I feel as if I have opened a door into a dark, unseen room—without knowing what lies behind the door.[70]

This was true, reflecting his often-stated view of himself as a gambler. He had opened the door with little study and—even though a year had passed since he first hinted to his generals of the coming invasion—with shockingly little preparation.

General Walther von Reichenau's invasion plan called for a *Blitzkrieg* (lightning war)—a campaign of a few months to be completed in warm weather. He and Hitler agreed that there would be no combat during the winter. To overcome the general staff's objections to the invasion, Hitler promised the Soviet Union would be crushed in weeks—at most in a few months. He told them the invasion would occur only if Germany could shatter the Soviet Union "with one blow. Holding part of the country alone will not do. Standing still for the following winter would be perilous."[71] And he promised Nazi district leaders victory within eight weeks.

But Hitler told Göring, who was now in charge of the economy and its integration with the war effort, and Admiral Erich Raeder, to prepare for a long war, keeping this from the generals.[72] Not until two months after the invasion did he let hints drop to them that they were in for a long war. In fact, Hitler prevented his armies from delivering the "one blow" and, at the same time, gravely neglected preparations for a long war.

Compared to the Soviet Union and Great Britain, Germany underused human and factory resources in its war effort. Until 1943, mobilization was only partial and an unusually large part of the German army was in offices and war production rather than in combat units. Hitler underused women in war production and refused to include them in the military. And he repeatedly refused suggestions to operate factories around the clock. As a result, Germany was outproduced. Hitler considered the Soviet Union incapable of matching Germany's production and, when German intelligence reported the extent of Soviet production to him, he dismissed it as false and impossible—enemy propaganda. The Soviet Union would gain tank supremacy, and Great Britain would gain airplane supremacy.

The features of Germany's ground and air forces that had made them so effective up to this point were less suited to a long war over a vast terrain. Hitler's personality inclined him to bold, fast strikes, and the army that he inherited in 1933 and enlarged was designed for *Blitzkrieg*. Ironically, the limitations imposed on Germany's army at the end of World War I were a main cause of its success in World War II. Other European countries retained the type of army they had had—massive numbers of slow-moving soldiers with enormous fire power—while Germany was sharply limited in number of men and size of weapons. Unable to compete on customary terms even with small neighbors like Belgium and Czechoslovakia, the German army was redesigned for high mobility—built around fast tanks to fight best in headlong rushes. And the key part of the air force became its Stuka dive bombers—small, slow, low-flying craft ideal for working in proximity to advancing troops and targeting enemy ground forces but having a short range compared to the Soviet Union's vast distances. The tank-led ground forces and Stukas worked excellently together. They were the key to the quick victories over Poland, the Low Countries, and France. And with his armies so equipped, Hitler entered his long, great war.

The Soviet population, area, and climate were, of course, known to Hitler and his generals. The invasion began in warm weather, and at first it too was a sweeping success. But the Soviet Union was so rich in population and territory that it could take enormous losses without being knocked out. To end the war quickly, the German command sought to draw Soviet armies into decisive battles and destroy them. The Soviet command avoided such battles, fighting a few but mostly retreating deep into the interior. Within two months German armies were approaching Moscow and Leningrad (St. Petersburg), the main cities. But the end of the war was not yet in sight, and German armies were unprepared for winter combat in the Soviet Union. In addition, the sheer number of Soviet troops would become important because the front was enormous. At the border of the Soviet Union, it was 1,000 miles wide and German advances soon doubled its width.

Another problem was sharp disagreement between Hitler and his generals. From the outset, the army command considered capture of Moscow, the capital, to be the first priority, but Hitler insisted on rapid advances along the entire front. In the compromise adopted, 29 divisions were allocated to Army Group North (directed toward Leningrad), 50 to Army Group Center (Moscow), and 42 to Army Group South (the Ukraine). For stretching German forces along the entire front, the number of available soldiers and tanks—reduced by campaigns in Africa, the Balkans, and Italy; by forces positioned to defend France against an expected invasion by Britain and the United States; and by troops used to control occupied countries—would prove insufficient. In Norway alone, an occupation force of 300,000 would remain until nearly the end of the war. Jodl's assistant, Gen. Walter Warlimont, would write in 1942, "Against *Norway* there was no threat; yet as always it absorbed a high proportion of our shrinking forces and resources."[73]

The first problems owing to lack of preparation involved heavy dust plus fleas, lice, and diseases endemic to the Soviet Union. Lacking dust filters, engines wore out. Lacking supplies to deal with parasites and diseases, troops and medical officers had to improvise. The army was also unprepared for the rainy season, beginning in October, which turned dirt roads into heavy mud. Vehicles lost traction, men and equipment fell into mud holes, and units became immobilized. Even paved roads were inadequate for German heavy equipment and crumbled under it.

The first freeze in late October improved vehicle traction briefly, but gouges in mud roads became hard bumps. Vehicles with low carriages had their gas tanks smashed by the bumps. Soldiers' boots were stiff and close-fitting, making walking on bumpy roads painful. For relief, they cut open their boots—a hazard when the cold became severe.[74]

Because the official plan was to conquer the Soviet Union before winter, the army had only warm-weather lubricants and light clothes. With the coming of snow and ice, trucks and tanks again lost traction, and cold-climate fittings for tank treads were unavailable. Fuel froze, lubricants congealed, and artillery and smaller weapons began to fail. In November, Gen. Guderian, a hero of the campaigns against Poland and France, wrote home:

> The icy cold, the lack of shelter, the shortage of clothing, the heavy losses of men and equipment, the wretched state of our fuel supplies—all this makes the duties of a commander a misery, and the longer it goes on the more I am crushed by the enormous responsibility I have to bear . . ."[75]

For the first time in the war, his troops panicked.

Guderian commanded an army approaching Moscow from the southwest, not the coldest part of the front, and the worst of winter lay ahead. Congealed lubricants on shells prevented soldiers from loading them into weapons and had to be scraped off. Lubricants were also removed from weapons, enabling them to fire but causing them to wear out. Brittle from temperatures of forty degrees below zero, firing pins snapped. To be able to start engines when needed, drivers started them every hour when not in use or left them running, even all night. When fuel became too scarce for that, bonfires were built under vehicles. Seventy percent of train locomotives broke down. Bread and other rations carried by the troops froze hard. Hot meals, prepared at kitchens a mile behind the troops, froze before reaching them. Worst of all were the direct effects of the cold on soldiers—chills, freezing to death, frostbite, gangrene, and other conditions. A soldier wrote, "We urinated into our numbed hands to warm them, and, hopefully, to cauterize the gaping cracks in our fingers."[76] The first severe cold spell alone caused 100,000 cases of frostbite. That winter, wounded soldiers being sent to hospitals froze to death on stalled trains. Angry about the obvious neglect in supplying them, reduced to despair, soldiers began committing suicide and deserting on a substantial scale.

Afterward, Guderian wrote about the terror of "the endless expanse of Russian snow . . . the icy wind that blew across it, burying in snow every object in its path" and about his "half-starved men." By painful contrast he noted the "well-fed, warmly clad and fresh Siberians, fully equipped for winter fighting."[77] Describing the situation of his troops to Hitler, Guderian requested permission to halt his advance and take up a defensive position. Hitler said Guderian was exaggerating and insisted his troops had already received winter clothes, denying the request.[78] Guderian then halted the advance of his army without authority.

With the onset of winter, the Soviets launched heavy attacks, endangering and decimating German armies, pushing them back and leading Hitler's generals to lose hope in Germany's victory. Nonetheless, Hitler proposed to them a campaign across the Caucasus into the Middle East, intending to kill the Jews in Palestine.[79] Later, when Hitler sought scapegoats for the winter losses, he relieved Guderian and other generals of command.

Soldiers commonly have to fight under miserable conditions, but neglect of preparations for the campaign in the east had been extreme. Winter came early in 1941 and was the hardest in years, but Hitler had been urged by his staff as early as June to prepare for cold weather. In turning them down, he assured them the campaign would be over before the cold came.[80] Before snow and frost arrived or after, he could have halted the advance to equip vehicles, weapons, and soldiers properly, at least to an extent. Winter uniforms had not been manufactured, and he still did not order them to be manufactured.

When December came, Goebbels directed an appeal to Germany's civilian population for warm clothes for the troops, collecting a large supply. But because of limited available transport, the clothes did not reach the front until March. According to Guderian, the warm clothes his soldiers got that winter came from captured and killed Soviet soldiers—a dangerous improvisation because Germans in Soviet uniforms were occasionally mistaken by comrades for enemies and shot.[81]

About 80 percent of Hitler's soldiers fought through the winter with light clothes. A quarter million fell victim to frostbite and other illnesses caused by exposure, which also claimed 1,100 horses daily.[82]

General von Brauchitsch was one who had urged Hitler to provide winter clothes. After the reverses that winter, he asked to be relieved of command. Hitler relieved him and then blamed him for the lack of winter supplies, making him one of the scapegoats for the losses.

The famous Russian winter and its role in the defeat of Napoleon's powerful armies were well known. There should have been nothing surprising about conditions—nothing for which the German armies could not have been prepared. Why did Hitler not have them prepared? He alone decided when to invade the Soviet Union, and he directed the invasion in detail. He had access to intelligence and advice and to control of German resources—to what was needed for running a better campaign. He would blame his intelligence service for giving him insufficient and inaccurate reports and his generals for mishandling the invasion, for that was his way. Still later he would blame the Italians:

> [They] had the nerve to plunge into the totally senseless campaign against Greece without asking us, without even informing us . . . That forced us, contrary to all our plans, to intervene in the Balkans, which in turn resulted in a catastrophic delay for the beginning of the war against Russia . . .[83]

But he had known in advance, and German preparation for the invasion of Greece had begun in the fall of 1940.[84]

Hitler had said *Blitzkrieg* was the most merciful type of war, because a quick end kept casualties of both victor and vanquished to a minimum. But his talk about the campaign in the Soviet Union before and after it began and the actions he took showed that being merciful was furthest from his mind. His goal was maximum destruction. He gave orders that Soviet cities not be permitted to surrender—that fighting go on until they were destroyed.[85] These and orders to kill Soviet civilians and prisoners of war were obstacles to early victory. There is substantial evidence that his talk of *Blitzkrieg* was deliberately misleading in order to persuade his generals to accept the invasion and that his secret plan was for a long war. Besides what he told Göring and Raeder, he wrote in a secret memo shortly before the invasion, "The war can be continued only if, by the third year, all Armed Forces are fed from Russia."[86] The idea that this memo represented his true intention is supported by details from military conferences that took place after the invasion began.

In July 1941, Hitler proposed diverting tank units from the advance on Moscow to the campaign in the south, and the next month he ordered that done. He then diverted other tank units toward Leningrad, stripping Army Group Center of its tanks. Hitler told his staff that the first priority was capturing economic targets in the south. His generals disagreed vigorously, insisting that capture of Moscow would seriously disrupt, if not crush, Soviet resistance. Hitler's angry reply was that Moscow was nothing more than "a geographical expression" and "Only completely ossified brains, absorbed in the ideas of past centuries could see any worthwhile objective in taking the capital."[87] In August, only two months after the invasion started, with German armies already near Moscow and the Soviet Union's situation precarious, Hitler's generals urged sending additional armies from the south to help capture the capital, administering a knockout blow. Hitler replied in a directive (written for him by Jodl):

> The principal object that must be achieved yet before the onset of winter is not the capture of Moscow, but rather, in the South, the occupation of the Crimea and the industrial and coal region of the Donets, together with isolation of the Russian oil regions in the Caucasus and, in the North, the encirclement of Leningrad . . .[88]

He ordered the advance on Moscow halted.

Let us bring together four questions that have been raised many times without a satisfactory answer:

> Why did Hitler allow the British to escape at Dunkirk?
> Why did he not invade England?
> Why did he invade the Soviet Union instead?
> Why did he prevent the capture of Moscow?

Historians have tried to explain these decisions on military grounds—as intended by Hitler to win and end the war. But the opposite goal—prolonging the war—makes more sense of them. John Lukacs wrote that getting rid of the Jews "was the principal purpose of his life . . . [and] influenced not only the course of his actions against Jews but also his course of action in the war."[89] Nonetheless, like others, Lukacs omitted that purpose in explaining Hitler's key war decisions, accepting Hitler's stated purpose of ending the war quickly.

Generals von Bock, Guderian, and Halder conferred in a last attempt to get Hitler to reconsider and authorize an attack on Moscow. They designated Guderian, who then was still a favorite of Hitler, to be their spokesman. Guderian had an extraordinary conference with Hitler in which they argued for five hours. Guderian's summary argument, reminding Hitler of his original plan of *Blitzkrieg*, was:

> Moscow is not only the head and the heart of the Soviet Union. It is also its communications centre, its political brain, an important industrial area, and above all it is the hub of the transport system of the whole Red empire. The fall of Moscow will decide the whole war. Stalin knows this . . . And . . . he will employ his entire military strength before Moscow. He is already bringing up everything he has left . . . Outside Moscow we shall encounter the core of the Russian military might. If we want to destroy the vital force of the Soviets it is here we shall encounter it . . .

Hitler lost patience and replied:

> My generals . . . understand nothing of economics . . . We need the grain of the Ukraine. The industrial area of the Donets must work for us, instead of for Stalin. The Russian oil-supplies from the Caucasus must be cut off, so that his military strength withers away.[90]

Shortly after, when his armies reached Leningrad, Hitler ordered them to surround it and not take it. The Soviet Union's second most important city, under siege for 900 days, would never be taken.

In rejecting his generals' arguments, Hitler also referred to *unspecified* goals to be accomplished before the capture of Moscow, goals about which one can only draw inferences. His most important goal, the extermination of the Jews, was the one he avoided discussing with his generals. At this time in August 1941, the gassing of Jews in death camps was just about to begin, and it was to be completed before the war ended. A victory by autumn would have interfered with the Holocaust.

By September, Hitler's orders made clear to his staff that the war would continue into 1942. In October, Hitler ordered the offensive on Moscow resumed, and units reached its outskirts by December. But that was too late to capture the capital before winter conditions paralyzed German armies. A German soldier reported that infantry, immobilized by cold, their weapons useless, were slaughtered by workers from a Moscow factory using picks and shovels.[91] The capital, seemingly in Hitler's grasp during the summer of 1941, also would never be taken.

Meanwhile the war was changing crucially. The time Hitler projected to carry out the Holocaust was enough for Great Britain to arm itself fully and the Soviet Union to reorganize its armies effectively. Stalin had purged his military command in the 1930s, putting loyalty to himself ahead of competence. When the Soviet Union was invaded, its armies were poorly led. By winter, Stalin had installed better commanders, and the Soviet Union was being supplied by Britain and heavily by the United States. By spring, its armies had grown from additional mobilization and from transfer of armies positioned in Siberia anticipating a Japanese invasion. Stalin's conclusion of a pact with Japan and Japan's attack on the United States in December reduced that risk. Soviet troops were now better equipped and led, and their resolve was stronger.

Hitler's invasion plan had called for his armies to pose as liberators, and during the first months of war many Soviet people had welcomed German armies—people suffering under oppressive government measures, and Ukrainians and other national groups suffering under domination by Russians. Soldiers had surrendered readily, and civilians had greeted the invaders "with flowers, bacon, and vodka."[92] But the deliberate killing of Soviet prisoners of war and civilians—estimates run as high as three million the first year—changed that. In addition, Stalin used Hitler's words about Slavs being subhuman to unify and rally the Soviet people against the invaders. Realizing they were facing extermination, Soviet soldiers fought harder and civilians formed partisan units.

Meanwhile German morale fell. Besides relieving generals that winter, Hitler began demoting, retiring, and executing them for lost battles. Other generals, demoralized by having their authority reduced as Hitler directed the campaign down to small details and by being blamed and ridiculed, became depressed. General Erich von Manstein wrote:

> It is, I think, understandable that one should have wished to be relieved from responsibilities rendered almost unbearable by the interminable, nerve-racking battles that had to be fought with one's own Supreme Command before it would accept the need for any urgent military action.[93]

And von Rundstedt complained that "my authority to move troops is limited to changing the guard at my office . . ."[94] Some generals resigned, and others committed suicide, adding to a high turnover in army leadership. And despite the lessons of the first winter in the Soviet Union, despite recognition of how inadequate preparations had been and how long the war was likely to last, Hitler still did not prepare sufficiently. The next winter a substantial part of the army in the Soviet Union again lacked warm clothes. And serious shortages of tanks and planes developed. By the end of the war, his once dominant air force would be reduced to impotence.

We come now to a major war decision involving no battle campaign. Hitler did not need to sell it to his military staff in order to have them draw up a plan. He did not even need to give them a reason, and apparently he gave them none. Hitler's Nazi associates and military staff considered the United States' entry into World War I to be the turning point against Germany. They urged that the United States be kept out of World War II, to which Hitler agreed. He, however, scorned the United States and its military power, seeing it, along with the Soviet Union, as a Jewish-dominated nation. When his invasion of the Soviet Union slowed down in the fall of 1941, he urged his ally Japan to help him by invading Siberia instead of U.S. territories. But then, in a sharp reversal, he encouraged Japan to go to war with the United States and offered to join it.[95]

President Franklin Roosevelt had been trying and failing to manipulate his unwilling nation to join Britain against Germany. He seized German assets and ships in the United

States, sent armies to occupy Greenland and Iceland (belonging to Denmark, which Germany had conquered), and had his navy attack German ships on the seas in hopes of provoking an incident that could lead to war. In September 1941, he thought he had his incident. A German submarine exchanged fire with an American destroyer, and Roosevelt gave a militant speech, saying, "America has been attacked . . . the shooting has started."[96] But the American public remained unwilling to go to war with Germany.

Even after Japan's attack on Pearl Harbor in December 1941, it is unclear whether the U.S. Senate would have declared war on Germany. There was much sympathy for Germany in the United States and fear and hatred of the Soviet Union. Hitler did not wait to find out; he declared war on the United States, saying that the United States was about to declare war on Germany and that he was beating it to the punch. This was the kind of statement he often made, but it hardly explained this invitation to disaster.

Historians explained the declaration of war by Hitler's obligation to honor Germany's pact with Japan, but two considerations argue against that. The pact with Japan called for German intervention if Japan was attacked, not if Japan initiated a war. In addition, as Hitler said to military staff in 1939, "Agreements are to be kept only as long as they serve a certain purpose."[97]

During the 1930s, Hitler had thought about Germany's destruction, and during the war he talked about it more and more:

> . . . in this war there can be no compromise, there can only be victory or destruc-
> tion. And if the German people cannot wrest victory from the enemy, then they
> shall be destroyed. Yes, then they deserve to perish . . . Germany's end will be
> horrible . . .[98]

At the end of 1941, with his declaration of war on the United States, he tipped the balance decisively toward destruction of Germany.

Hitler's efforts to overcome his "weakness"—to transform himself into a destructive superman—had unintended consequences. With the invasion of the Soviet Union, he gave an order of no retreat. Not a foot of captured land was to be yielded, regardless of military considerations of the moment. On urgings of his generals to allow retreats when necessary to save armies, Hitler permitted some exceptions, while insisting generally on adherence to his order. The order of no retreat became critical at the battle of Stalingrad, the major turning point of the campaign in the Soviet Union. Without detracting from the well-disguised, well-executed Soviet plan to trap German forces at Stalingrad, the disaster there was the result of Hitler's compulsive need to appear strong.

With the arrival of mild weather in the spring of 1942, German armies resumed the offensive in the Soviet Union. Although not as successful as the year before, they made considerable advances, incurring moderate casualties. By the fall of 1942, army dead and missing exceeded a half million. Then by an irrational stroke, 300,000 were lost— the greatest single German loss of the war.

The Sixth Army under Gen. Friedrich Paulus, which had enjoyed extraordinary success up to this point, entered the city of Stalingrad on the Volga River. Overextended, it was exposed to encirclement. Paulus requested permission to retreat to a defensible position—a request endorsed by Hitler's military staff. Hitler refused, saying that to allow a retreat would show weakness. He demanded instead the complete capture of Stalingrad.

According to an aide, Hitler came near a breakdown during the battle of Stalingrad and, if he had yielded to the advice of his generals and gone back on his order of no retreat, he might well have suffered the breakdown.[99] For him, the situation had developed into a clash of wills, with his pitted not only against that of the Soviet forces but also of his own generals. His personal integrity was tied to beating his generals, and he did.

During the weeks that followed, he was urged repeatedly and vehemently to allow the Sixth Army to retreat. Hitler held firm but took the odd measure of requiring Paulus's divisional commanders to sign receipts for a full supply of winter clothing, although they had received only a partial supply.[100] Perhaps he was preparing to deal with blame for the coming disaster. The Sixth Army was encircled by the end of November and cut off from supply. Most of its men had to fight their last battle without winter clothing.

Hitler informed his military staff that Gen. Ferdinand Heim alone was responsible for the encirclement of the Sixth Army. Heim commanded a tank corps positioned southwest of Stalingrad. Hitler had ordered it to attack toward Stalingrad and block the southern part of the Soviet pincer movement. But the Soviets had attacked Heim's unit, forcing it to give up its advance and save itself. Hitler dismissed Heim from the army, stripped him of his decorations, and imprisoned him without trial.[101]

The Sixth Army was running out of gas for its tanks and trucks as well as ammunition. This situation resulted in a new series of requests and urgings—to allow the Sixth Army, facing east, to turn and attempt a breakthrough toward German armies in the southwest and thereby escape annihilation. Hitler refused, trying to bolster the Sixth Army's morale by a series of messages including, "Sixth Army must know that I am doing everything I can to help and to relieve it."[102] His assurances were hardly true, as he made only partial efforts to supply and relieve it—efforts he knew were unsuccessful—while saying:

> Our generals are making their old mistakes again. They always over-estimate the strength of the Russians. According to all the front-line reports, the enemy's human material is no longer sufficient. They are weakened; they have lost far too much blood . . . the Russians will simply come to a halt . . . Meanwhile we shall throw in a few fresh divisions; that will put things right.[103]

His refusal to allow a breakout aroused the most vigorous objections by his generals. Kurt Zeitzler, new chief of the Army High Command, argued with him daily and often vehemently.

Zeitzler: . . . there is no way of keeping Sixth Army supplied.
Hitler: Reich Marshal Goering has just said that he can keep the army supplied by air.
Zeitzler: That's rubbish!

Hitler: I am *not leaving the Volga.*

Zeitzler: It would be a crime to abandon Sixth Army at Stalingrad.[104]

General Walter von Seydlitz, a commander under Paulus, radioed to headquarters, ". . . deliberately to remain where we are is not only a crime from the military point of view, but it is also a criminal act as regards our responsibility to the German nation."[105]

Neither was punished, but the pressure of his staff pushed Hitler to his most irrational responses. Noting that horses of the Sixth Army were too emaciated to haul artillery or even to travel and would have to be left behind if Paulus attempted a breakout, he added, "If these were Russians I would say: One Russian eats another. But I cannot make one horse eat another."[106] The grotesque words were a bad omen for the Sixth Army.

In January 1943, Paulus radioed to Hitler:

> Troops without ammunition or food . . . Effective command no longer possible . . . 18,000 wounded without any supplies or dressings or drugs . . . Further defense senseless. Collapse inevitable. Army requests immediate permission to surrender in order to save lives of remaining troops.

Hitler replied:

> Surrender is forbidden. Sixth Army will hold their positions to the last man and the last round and by their heroic endurance will make an unforgettable contribution . . .[107]

To stiffen their morale, Hitler promoted 118 Sixth Army officers, making Paulus a field marshal, saying that in all German history no field marshal had ever surrendered. The next day, the Sixth Army—1 field marshal, 24 generals, 2,500 other officers, and a remnant of 100,000 soldiers—began its surrender without permission.

On being informed of the surrender, Hitler said:

> They've just simply thrown their hands in! If they hadn't, they'd have got together, fought on, *and kept the last round for themselves.*[108] (Italics added.)

Paulus had disappointed Hitler by not committing suicide.

> . . . I promoted him to Field-Marshal. I wanted to give him this final satisfaction . . . He could have freed himself from all sorrow and ascended into eternity and national immortality, but he prefers to go to Moscow.[109]

Hitler philosophized:

> What is life? Life is the Nation. The individual must die anyway . . . But how anyone could be afraid of death, with which he can free himself of this misery, if his duty does not chain him to this Vale of Tears. Na![110]

The words of contempt for Paulus touched on Hitler's thoughts about his own future. The next year he would say he looked forward to death as:

. . . a release from my sorrows and sleepless nights and from this nervous suffering. It takes only a fraction of a second—then one is cast free from all that and rests in eternal peace.[111]

Meanwhile, speculating about Paulus and his generals, Hitler revealed more of himself:

You'll see: they will now walk down the slope of spiritual bankruptcy to its lowest depths. One can only say that a bad deed always produces new evils . . . the fundamental thing is always character, and if we don't manage to instill that . . . we're never going to get a race that can stand up to the heavy blows of destiny.[112]

The words recall Hitler's thoughts about himself as a mama's boy, unable to stand up to a blow from destiny, and his growing need with each crime he committed to commit more. Paulus had conducted himself with honor. The defective character was Hitler's; he was the one on the slope.

What had made Stalingrad so important to justify sacrificing the Sixth Army? The initial plan for the 1942 campaign, drawn up by the high command at Hitler's direction, gave first priority to invading the Caucasus in the extreme south. It included advances in the Stalingrad area to protect the northern flank of armies in the Caucasus. *Capture of Stalingrad was not included.* Hitler ordered its capture later when the Sixth Army, meeting little resistance at first, was advancing rapidly near Stalingrad. He told Paulus that Stalingrad was necessary to acquire the Caucasus with its oil supply, that without its oil he could not continue the war. He told others he needed to deprive the Soviets of a large tank factory in Stalingrad.

It was true that Hitler anticipated running low on oil, but Stalingrad was unnecessary for capturing and holding the Caucasus. The Caucasus armies' flank could be protected by maintaining forces near Stalingrad, not necessarily in the city. And without Stalingrad, Germany did capture much of the Caucasus and was then driven back, as the tide of war turned in favor of the Soviet Union. But loss of the Caucasus did not lead Hitler even to consider ending the war. It was also true that tank supremacy had shifted to the Soviets, but most of the Sixth Army was lost after the tank factory, along with the rest of Stalingrad, had been destroyed.

By staying in Stalingrad, the Sixth Army did perform the military function of tying down Soviet forces that could have been used against other German armies. But if the Sixth Army had withdrawn or broken out, retaining its mobility and fighting power, it could still have tied down Soviet forces and had other, varied, and lasting military uses. In short, *after entering Stalingrad and before being surrounded, the Sixth Army had accomplished its mission and could have been withdrawn.*

The explanations Hitler gave do not explain the action taken, and we are left with no good reason for the loss of the Sixth Army. After realizing that the main German advance in 1942 was not directed at Moscow, the Soviet high command had decided to shift armies toward Stalingrad and make destruction of the German forces there its first priority. That decision gave Hitler a stake in holding on to the city. Another reason for holding it was his need for bloodletting. A year later, he would say to his generals:

> Some think me heartless to insist on fighting to the last man just because the enemy will also let more blood that way . . .[113]

Still another reason was his need to maintain his posture as a military expert in front of his generals. A few months before the battle of Stalingrad, frustrated by the slow progress of his armies in the Caucasus, Hitler had sent Gen. Jodl to ensure that his orders were carried out there. Jodl came back and reported the Caucasus armies' commander, Gen. Wilhelm List, had followed Hitler's orders faithfully, but his forces were insufficient for the task. Hitler accused Jodl of letting List deceive him, and an argument ensued.

Jodl, the closest to Hitler among his military staff, had long ago concluded that "a dictator, as a matter of psychological necessity, must never be reminded of his own errors, in order to maintain his self-confidence" and had become a yes-man to Hitler. This time, however, Jodl flared up and vehemently cited Hitler's orders, arguing that List had indeed tried to carry them out. Hitler screamed, "You're lying! Never have I given such orders, never!" and stormed out.[114] Afterward, he stopped being cordial to Jodl and eating with his generals, turning to his dog for companionship. In addition, he ordered everything he and his generals said at staff conferences be taken down in case of future disagreement.

These events probably confirmed Jodl's conclusion about not shaking Hitler's self-confidence. Later, during the three months before the Sixth Army's surrender, when Zeitzler and other generals argued persistently with Hitler to change his orders to Paulus, Jodl kept silent. He thus contributed to the sacrifice of the Sixth Army in order to maintain Hitler's mental balance.

General Keitel was similarly concerned with maintaining Hitler's balance and went further than Jodl. He met with commandants about to report to Hitler and advised them to say nothing that might upset him, even if that meant withholding vital information. Once, after Guderian argued vehemently with Hitler for two hours, Keitel reproached him: "How dare you contradict the Führer like that? Couldn't you see how perturbed he was getting? What if he'd had a stroke?"[115] During the arguments about saving the Sixth Army, even though he shared the views of Paulus, Zeitzler, and the others, Keitel took Hitler's side.

Hitler was aware that the fiasco of Stalingrad had discredited him with his generals, including some who had had faith in him to this point. This time, he did not choose a scapegoat, but took the extraordinary steps of apologizing to them, working hard at regaining their support, and recalling to command Guderian and others he had dismissed.

Hitler did win back a measure of their support but did not give up his stubborn conduct of the war. His chief of staff said:

It is a fact, characteristic of the overall direction of the German war effort, that from the end of 1942 planning was confined strictly to minor details.[116]

From the fall of France on, Hitler's direction of the war consistently served to prolong it. The overall strategy became holding fast, and other armies were lost or decimated because Hitler did not allow them to retreat. The next winter, deciding against Gen. von Manstein's request to let his army group near Kiev save itself by retreating, Hitler said, "If it is possible at all, we are duty-bound to defend this second Stalingrad," and added, "I am worrying myself sick for having given permission for retreats in the past. It couldn't have been worse if they had remained in the forward position, on the contrary . . ."[117]

The idea that retreat was disastrous did not reflect experience in the Soviet campaign, but may have come from Hitler being nearly killed when he tried to run away from home. He continued adhering to his position of no retreat despite vigorous urgings of his military staff. The story of Stalingrad was repeated until little remained of Germany's armies and the nation lay in ruin.

According to Jodl, Hitler realized the war was lost after Stalingrad, which was early in 1943, yet he continued the war two more years. To his generals he spoke more and more of delaying actions. They were to hold their positions, preventing enemy advances until the means to return to the offensive was forthcoming. He promised them reinforcements by shifting units from other fronts, by mobilizing more men, and by transferring men from offices to the front. They got some reinforcements but not enough to offset losses, and the ranks of their men continued to grow thinner. He promised them additional and better equipment but failed to improve production. New equipment often was inferior to the old, and shortages increased. He promised secret weapons but pursued their development only to a limited extent. He spoke of dissension among the Allies and the prospect of saving Germany by concluding a separate peace with Great Britain or the Soviet Union—with either one so he could then crush the other—but he stopped subordinates from pursuing negotiations with them. During the last two years of war, Goebbels, von Ribbentrop, and other associates urged him to end it. He usually agreed with their suggestions but put them off, saying the time had not yet come. First Germany needed to win a major victory so he could negotiate from a position of apparent strength. His friend, Ambassador Hiroshi Oshima of Japan, also urged him to make peace with the Soviet Union, and to him Hitler replied that the idea was out of the question.

Germany's strength was ebbing and, the more Hitler delayed, the less there was. The army came down to drafting 14-year-old boys and even some 12-year-olds, the militia came down to drafting 8-year-olds as well as old men, and oil and other supplies were running out. The children and old men of the militia "were barely equipped with weapons, were without communications equipment, almost without supplies. But with high sounding orders they were thrown against a well-equipped enemy and given tasks for which even elite formations in full battle order had proved inadequate."[118]

While armies suffered from lack of material, the death camps remained supplied, and trains needed for shipment of army troops and supplies were still used by the SS for the Holocaust. As Germany's fighting forces became severely undermanned, SS guards at concentration and death camps increased into the hundreds of thousands. The way Hitler conducted the last two years of the war and the priority he gave the Holocaust showed that what he wrote in 1924 and what he said to Himmler were true. To him it was literally worth the sacrifice of millions of Germany's soldiers, loss of the war, and destruction of Germany in order to exterminate Jews.

By the end of 1943, as German armies in the east were being routed, Hitler became impatient for an Allied invasion of France. He said to associates that he welcomed the invasion; it would save Germany! His explanation was, as British and American forces landed in France, his soldiers would fight harder, throw them into the sea, and turn with renewed strength to crush the Soviet enemy. He hardly rationalized this fantastic idea. Its essence was that Germany would be saved by suffering more attacks. Later, when Germany's destruction was further advanced, he said:

> History shows that for Germany misfortune and adversity often constitute an indispensable prelude to a great renaissance. The sufferings of the German people—and in this war they have suffered incomparably more than any other people—are the very things which, if Providence wills, will help us to rise . . .

While still devoting himself to small details of the war, he found decisions harder to make, procrastinating more. By the end of 1944, his first situation conference of the day with military staff began at five in the afternoon, his second at midnight or later. This was a hardship for officers accustomed to rising early and presumably reduced their efficiency.

The longer the war continued, the more unrealistic Hitler's thinking became. He had long taken pride in what he saw as his ability to reduce complex issues to a single factor:

> I have the gift of simplification, and then everything works itself out. Difficulties exist only in the imagination.[119]

He was aware of neglecting factors but hoped that by finding a key simplification he could afford to ignore the rest of a situation. In confronting his father, he had reduced the situation to a clash of wills and won. It was a lesson for life. As Nazi leader, he often dealt with problems inside and outside the Party by reducing them to a clash of wills. During the war, he insisted on a strategy of meeting every enemy attack and concluded conferences with military staff by saying, "I shall not give in," once declaring:

> One word I never recognized as a National Socialist in my battle for power: capitulation. That word I do not know and I will never know as Führer of the German people and as your Supreme Commander: that word again is capitulation; *that is the surrender of the will to another person.* Never! Never![120]
> (Italics added.)

This deeply personal carryover from childhood prevented him from dealing flexibly with military situations.

While his soldiers fought and died under increasingly hopeless conditions, for Hitler the war became a matter of moving markers around on maps. He put considerations of armaments, logistics, and numbers of soldiers and their physical fitness into the background, believing, as he had said in 1924, the key to victory was willpower: "What we lack in weapons . . . the will must take the place of."[121] The nation with the will to win would win, for the problem was that simple. And Germany's good fortune was having a leader with a will of iron—a leader who could literally stare down leaders of other countries, who could intimidate them, who could maintain his position no matter what happened. That ensured Germany's victory.

Hitler's responses to frustration became increasingly petulant. He ordered an attack by General Theodor Busse and, when it failed, Hitler complained to Guderian, Busse's superior, "It was stupid generalship. In World War I . . . it was customary to fire at least ten times as many shells" before an attack.

When Guderian replied that Busse had not fired more shells because he had no more, Hitler shouted, "Then you should have arranged for him to have more." Guderian then told Hitler that all the shells Hitler had allocated to Guderian had been given to Busse, and Hitler shouted, "The troops let us down!" Guderian showed Hitler the extremely high casualty list for Busse's troops, indicating they had given all they could. Hitler abruptly left the meeting but, when Busse arrived, resumed blaming him. Again Guderian defended Busse, and again Hitler relieved Guderian.[122]

As the war was drawing to an end, Hitler continued to order armies to stand fast and occasionally to mount attacks. Some of the armies he ordered hardly existed except on paper. Decimated, they had too few soldiers to fill the roles required for them to function as armies. And many soldiers were wounded so badly they could not fight or even march when ordered to new positions. Hitler ordered an army group south of Berlin to attack toward the city with every tank it had and bring the battle of Berlin to "a glorious conclusion." His staff pointed out the group had no tanks, no fuel, and little ammunition and was desperately defending itself against superior forces. Hitler replied, "The Army Group can very well do it, only they will not."[123] He continued to believe that willpower would enable a handful of soldiers to perform the function of a division and enable cripples to march and fight. The markers he moved were symbols for armies, but as the war progressed, some of the markers no longer represented fighting forces. Hitler's conduct of the war increasingly became an exercise in fantasy. In directing it, he largely went through the motions, while devoting himself to drawing up detailed plans for rebuilding Germany's cities—plans he would never be in a position to use.

Hitler experienced each defeat as a betrayal, and not simply from paranoia. On many occasions he thought his subordinates were plotting against him, and sometimes they were. But most military defeats were betrayals of another sort, stemming from having based his life on willpower. The loss of a battle meant the commander had not had the will to win. It meant he had violated his solemn oath to do whatever it took to carry out Hitler's orders. Every defeat was, therefore, a betrayal, and when a battle was lost, Hitler ordered the commander or units of soldiers shot.

His orders to shoot officers and men were usually expressions of momentary frustration, and he did not keep after his subordinates to carry them out. He did, however, establish a Flying Special Tribunal to go immediately to places where German armies were defeated, to try soldiers of all ranks, and to carry out its judgments on the spot. Its first task was to try the "cowards and betrayers" who failed to blow up the bridge at Remagen before it fell into Allied hands. Four officers were executed.[124]

Early in 1945 Hitler ordered:

> All military, transport, communication, industrial and supply facilities, as well as material assets within Reich territory which the enemy might in any way whatever make use of . . . are to be destroyed.[125]

The order included bridges, dams, and utilities. Speer protested to Hitler that the resources to be destroyed would be needed for survival in the postwar period. If Hitler's order had been carried out, mass starvation and disease epidemics would have added to Germany's destruction. Hitler answered:

> If the war is to be lost, the nation also will perish. *This fate is inevitable.* There is no need to consider the basis even of a most primitive existence any longer. On the contrary, *it is better to destroy even that, and to destroy it ourselves.* The nation has proved itself weak . . . Besides, those who remain after the battle are of little value; for the good have fallen.[126] (Italics added.)

During the last days, Hitler concluded mistakenly that Göring had betrayed him and was leading a coup. He removed Göring from all his posts and ordered him shot, saying:

> Now nothing remains. Nothing is spared me. No allegiances are kept, no honor lived up to, no disappointment that I have not had, no betrayals that I have not experienced, and now this above all else! Nothing remains. Every wrong has already been done me![127]

Göring was arrested and then released.

Hitler later said, "All the failures in the east are due to treachery" and told a friend he was going to commit suicide: "The time has come. My Generals have betrayed me; my soldiers don't want to go on . . ." and "on my tombstone they ought to put the words: 'He was the victim of his Generals!' "[128]

Just before the end, thousands of Berliners, mostly women, children, and wounded men, sought refuge in subways and other tunnels. On learning of it, Hitler ordered the tunnels flooded.

An associate pleaded with him to authorize surrender to American and British forces, averting the devastation expected from Soviet forces. Hitler replied:

Devastation . . . is just what I want. The better to illuminate my finish.[129]

Hitler's last military directive was to soldiers facing Soviet troops now at the gates of Berlin:

> For the last time the deadly Jewish-Bolshevik enemy is going over to the attack with his hordes. He is trying to destroy Germany and exterminate our people. You soldiers of the East already know yourselves . . . what fate is threatening . . . The old men and children are murdered, the women and girls are reduced to camp whores. The remainder go to Siberia.[130]

Stalin had years ago purged the Communist (Bolshevik) Party of the Soviet Union, removing Jews from positions of importance in the government. The "Jewish Bolsheviks" with their aims of destruction were creatures of Hitler's mind. He himself had used German women and girls as whores, ordered Germany reduced to ruins, and wished annihilation on its people. What the Soviets intended he did not know. The intentions he imputed to them came from his own heart.

On April 29, 1945, Hitler was informed that Soviet troops would probably overrun his bunker the next day, and responded:

> Too bad, really. I had sincerely hoped to make it until May fifth. Beyond that date I have no desire to live . . . May fifth is a red-letter day all soldiers should remember and circle in their diaries. Napoleon died on St. Helena on May fifth, eighteen twenty-one. Another great career that ended in total disappointment, disillusion, betrayal, despair. The fickle Europeans did not really understand the French emperor and his great plans, as they have not understood me and mine. We were both men born before our times. Well, so much the worse for Europe. History will be my only judge.[131]

He added that no other leader in history had been stuck with more incompetent military officers who did not know their jobs and were intent on sabotaging the leader's plans. He seems never to have thought he had betrayed his followers, his soldiers, or the nation.

Early on, Hitler had spoken of sacrificing millions of Germany's best for a glorious victory that would secure the nation's future for a thousand years. Such thinking was traditional and in itself raises no question. But most of the millions of Germany's best were sent to their deaths after Stalingrad, in a lost cause. It was the prospect of sending millions to their deaths in a lost cause that had prompted Germany's leaders to sue for peace in 1918—a decision for which Hitler never forgave them. World War I had been his first grand opportunity for revenge, and he had lost it. World War II was another chance—his greatest and last one—and he was determined not to lose it. Given the circumstances and given Hitler's repeated statements that Germans did not deserve to live if the war were lost, he probably sent most of them to their deaths not for victory but for revenge—revenge on the generals and soldiers who had not fought hard enough, revenge on the Jews, and, ultimately, revenge on his father.

Hitler's struggle to free himself from his conscience succeeded; he became a person of extreme destructiveness and took much of Germany with him. When the self-hatred that propelled his rise to power turned to killing scapegoats, his guilt increased, and he needed still more scapegoats. Eventually, all of Germany was his scapegoat. The war aided his struggle against inhibitions by enabling him to focus his personality in its dominant trait. When it began, he stopped having young women entertain in the Chancellery and gave up movies and pornography. He saw rather little of Eva Braun and of most friends. He gave up the opera, the theater, and other pleasures. During the last four years, he increasingly buried himself in the underground bunkers that he made his home. His dealings were mainly with military staff, and his life was war. He lived only to destroy and to die.

The end of the war closed the circle of his life. As a boy, betrayed and abused by his father, his main objective had been to stand up to him. Now he saw himself betrayed and abused again, and by everyone. But this time he was in a position to make people pay. At the last, he took with him those he valued most—the boys he had reared to become gods, to whom he gave the task of standing up to the better-armed, seasoned Soviet men at the gates of Berlin. As the Soviets approached his bunker, Hitler's last victory over his enemies was depriving them of the opportunity to take him prisoner and humiliate him. It was also a victory over sorrow, sleepless nights, and nervous symptoms. He told his secretary:

> I'm no longer afraid of death. It will be a deliverance for me. For since my youth, misery and anguish have been my constant companions.[132]

Looking ahead to peace of mind and immortality, he killed himself.

AFTERWORD

Those who cannot remember the past are condemned to repeat it.

—George Santayana

Peoples and governments have never learned anything from history.

—Georg Hegel

The opportunity to perpetrate the Holocaust came from a breach in political and social structures, which began during World War I and was exacerbated by the economic chaos that followed. Germany's more responsible political leaders stopped cooperating with each other or respecting the law, widening the breach. Into it stepped a man recovering from a mental breakdown, offering himself as Germany's savior. He found doors open to him, and his paranoid vision became the order of the day. Breaches can be mended, and the surgery has been done in Germany, leaving enough scar tissue to make a new holocaust less likely there than in most countries.

Only fairly recently in the history of civilization did we take away fathers' legal right to kill their children. Only very recently did we recognize society's need to control nonlethal cruelty to children, reducing conditions that foster serial and mass killers. With education and laws against child abuse, fewer children grow up with the hatred that drove Hitler. But it takes only one person to lead a people in genocide. The main tasks in guarding against new holocausts are to reduce our acceptance of charismatic would-be killers and our reliance on scapegoating to solve national problems.

Learning from the Holocaust, like all learning from the past, requires making changes not based on our own experience but on the experience of others. The capacity to profit from others' experience has been increased by developments in communication and information storage. Unfortunately, what we learn that way is not immediate; it affects us less than our own experience.

Unlike other species, we lack inborn, biological inhibitors of destructiveness, making moral and social inhibitors vital. The lack of inborn controls lays a heavy burden on

217

education, moral training, and socialization. But the simple fact that the need is crucial has limited impact. A lesson of the Holocaust is that we need new methods of learning to enable us to be less bound by our own early experiences and to profit more from others' experiences. Until that happens, we will go on repeating mistakes others have made.

A requirement for a holocaust is self-exaltation by would-be perpetrators.

> . . . modern, premeditated genocide [is] the choice by a ruling elite of a myth or "political formula" . . . legitimating the . . . destiny of the dominant group, whose members share an underlying likeness, from which the victim is excluded by definition. Such a formula requires a myth exalting the origins of the group and idealizing the people . . .[1]

Finding such a myth in the *völkisch* movement, Hitler adopted it as the basis of his solution to the nation's problems.

According to legend, in the thirteenth century a mysterious stranger in pied (black and white) clothes came to the German town of Hamelin with an offer to get rid of its plague—rats. The Pied Piper, who ended by taking Hamelin's children, has been interpreted as representing the specter of death and the legend as portraying the fascination such figures arouse.

Thoroughly disillusioned after the war, Hans Frank called up the image of the Pied Piper to describe Hitler:

> It is as if Death put on the mask of a charming human being, and lured workers, lawyers, scientists, women and children—everyone—to destruction![2]

Hitler, a mysterious stranger, came to Germany with an offer to get rid of its plague—referring to Jews as Germany's rats—and in the end did take many of its children. His offer of racial purification, war, and death was what set him apart from other candidates.

Did Germans know he was a figure of death? Only a handful realized it consciously. If we ask the question the way lawyers ask—Should Germans have known he was a figure of death?—the answer is yes. He revealed himself in *Mein Kampf* on page after page and in countless speeches in the early 1920s. And as chancellor he repeatedly told Germans they would die for him. He presented himself as an agent of devastation and, despite the fears this aroused, it added to his appeal.

Known murderers are not normally chosen as government leaders. The challenge is to recognize and take seriously the signs of charismatic killers before they are given power. People discounted Hitler's threats of bloodbaths to come as political bombast or as wild tendencies that the responsibility of office would moderate or conservatives in the cabinet would control. They ignored beatings and killings that did not involve them, especially when the victims were held in low esteem.

Since most Germans did not support the policies that set Hitler apart from his rivals, why did they support him? The main reason was his charisma, but people who were not mesmerized also supported him. The German National People's Party, led by Alfred

Hugenberg, and conservatives of the center, led by Franz von Papen, gave Hitler the support he needed to become chancellor. And Communist leaders privately welcomed Hitler's government as a breach in the prevailing order that they might exploit to come to power themselves. Leaders across the political spectrum, unable to gain power on their own, tried to use Hitler as a means to it, and the public relied on him to free the nation from the oppressive Versailles Treaty and restore national power. Baldur von Schirach made a key point: in using Hitler to meet their own needs, people gave him power. The moral of the legend is that those who employ the Pied Piper will pay an unexpected price.

Throughout history the hero has been a figure of death.

> The hero's strength . . . resides in his dying first to [the] simple joy in existing; his power is rooted in his emphasis on "the very kiss of our annihilation"; his charisma is dependent on his "love of the fate that is inevitably death." Valorous, abnegating his own selfhood and severed from that of others . . . recognizing only the redeeming ecstasy of a tragic death. *The hero already lives as a dead man.* As a dead man he is fearless, because as a dead man he is unconquerable . . .[3]

Discounting that part of his appeal has enabled people to accept him, admire him, and choose him as a savior. "Why do we ever trust leaders who were terrorists before the mantle of respectability descended on their shoulders . . . ?"[4] The danger of Pied Pipers is easily ignored when we feel desperate. As the 20th century comes to an end, it is still hard even to imagine not being attracted to heroic figures.

To restrain destructiveness, we have a moral system based on shame and guilt. It is unreliable and may even contribute to destructiveness, for shame and guilt sometimes undermine individual responsibility. The ancient custom by which citizens permit and even condone crime by their rulers continues. And foremost among defects of our civilization, highlighted by Hitler's career, are the practices of dividing people into "us" and "them," using scapegoats, and taking vengeance.

The shame and guilt fostered by our moral training contribute to feeling rejected and alone. When shame and guilt become oppressive, we find quick relief by identifying others as the problem. Degrading them brings us together and gives us the feeling that we number among the good people. And calling them evil justifies harming them, which becomes a virtue and can add to feeling good about ourselves. The same act, evil when they do it, is good when we do it, especially when we do it to them. Scapegoating continues to relieve shame and guilt; harming innocent people is justified over and over.

On trial for his role in the Holocaust, Alfred Rosenberg said the Jews were to blame for their extermination. His rationale typified a way of thinking that prepared the way for the Holocaust. In 1930, as the possibility of Hitler becoming Germany's leader emerged, many Germans cited his anti-Semitism as a reason against supporting him. Others said it was "crazy" to hold his anti-Semitism against him since "the Jews themselves were to blame for anti-semitism."[5] Most people who deplored and even actively opposed violence against Jews, sometimes risking their lives to save them, were at least somewhat anti-Semitic, and many of them believed that improper behavior by Jews caused the animosity toward them. Hjalmar Schacht, minister of finance and president of the Reichsbank, disobeyed Hitler's orders to remove Jews from banking. Nonetheless, he said German culture belonged to Aryans, and therefore Jews' prominence in the arts was a reasonable cause of anti-Semitism. Others said Jews should stay out of politics, not be aggressive in business, or not marry Aryans, and that such actions were the cause of animosity toward them. And it is a small step—although a crucial one—from seeing people as the cause of animosity toward them to justifying harming them.

Destructiveness in the Third Reich was facilitated by a decline of individual responsibility. Although highly valued in our civilization, responsibility is undermined by conventional training in obedience. The great majority of Germans brought to trial after the war did not take responsibility for their own actions. General Wilhelm Keitel said:

> I did not have any inner conviction of becoming criminal . . . since after all it was the head of the state who, as far as we were concerned, held all the legislative power. Consequently I did not consider that I was acting criminally.[6]

By "legislative power," Keitel meant Hitler had assumed the power to pass laws—to make acts legal or illegal. A former member of the Gestapo said:

> I took part in the murder of many people. I often asked myself after the war whether I had become a criminal . . . and found no answer.[7]

Many people seem not even to have asked the question.

Among social patterns that undermine individual responsibility, blaming and scapegoating are most serious. In addition, responsibility and unquestioning obedience do not go together. Stanley Milgram concluded from his experiments, "The disappearance of a sense of responsibility is the most far-reaching consequence of submission to authority."[8] Authority and obedience to it are necessary for organized life to be efficient. Nonetheless, ". . . those of us who heedlessly accept the commands of authority cannot yet claim to be civilized . . ."[9] The key word is "heedlessly." Responsible behavior requires individual judgment about when to obey. Hitler had no problem in demanding blind obedience; he knew he did not want his subordinates to act responsibly.

Parents still scold and beat children for disobedience and threaten them with more severe consequences. "As long as you live in my house, you will abide by my rules. If you don't accept that, there's the door." Many parents show little tolerance for having their authority questioned, unaware that they are undermining the very responsibility they want their children to develop. Teachers and clergy also have limited tolerance for it. Children who question established ways or beliefs seriously or persistently are labeled troublemakers. Parents, teachers, and clergy who are serious about fostering responsibility need to reconsider their demand for obedience. The problems in fostering unquestioning obedience remain to be addressed seriously.

Wanton acts are restrained by laws and institutions. The Third Reich provided a horrifying case of what happens when laws and institutions are rendered dysfunctional. Von Papen wrote about Hitler, "No previous ruler had set out to undermine the rule of law."[10] A Nazi wrote that the Third Reich offered "surface discipline and order beneath which the destruction of all elements of order in the nation" proceeded.[11] Unfortunately, law-breaking by leaders excites followers, contributing to leaders' charisma, while preserving the law makes for dullness.

Our system of justice rests on the principle of rule of law, as opposed to rule by people. Judges and administrators are required to apply laws and not substitute their own judgment about what is just or desirable. In the long run, laws and the experience on which they rest are a better guide to justice than individual judgment, no matter how wise a judge may be. That is the principle. It restrains judges and others who administer the law from arbitrary uses, protecting people's rights.

Hitler's hero Frederick the Great wrote that a ruler's first duty is to the law. The principle seems out of date; modern leaders stress internal security and national security—Hitler's priorities—as their primary duties. Hitler's lawlessness was so frequent that his subordinates were often in conflict between obeying him and upholding the law. Military officers, judges, prosecutors, police, and civil administrators realized that, in obeying orders, they were violating their duties to the nation. Hitler deliberately fostered personal loyalty above loyalty to the nation and its laws, succeeding so well that few of his subordinates considered him a traitor. It was people who upheld their duties to their office, the constitution, and the public by opposing Hitler who were called traitors.

The cult of leadership is unnecessary for such misplaced loyalty. In democracies as well as dictatorships, subordinates illegally obey their rulers. Subordinates who remain true to their oaths of office by opposing their rulers are rare.

Baron Ernst von Weizsäcker, a career diplomat before Hitler came to power, served him and rose to a high position. Tried at Nuremberg, Weizsäcker justified his service. After Weizsäcker's death, his son Richard, later president of West Germany, said, ". . . the German people were led by criminals and let themselves be led by criminals."[12]

In the quotation at the beginning of this book, a historian asked what had happened to Germans for them to accept a criminal government. Unfortunately, nothing needed to happen. In nations across the world, people accept government crime.

The lessons of history are summarized in customs, social rules, moral codes, and laws. One of the most important lessons is that the rule of law is vital. Even though specific laws are sometimes faulty and in need of revision, the principle of the rule of law is sound and needs to be upheld over urges by rulers to substitute their own judgment. We worry about crime by individuals and small groups. But it is acceptance of government crime that allows for genocide.

CHRONOLOGY OF HITLER'S LIFE

1889	April 20	Birth
1895	June 25	Father's retirement
1903	January 3	Father's death
1905	Summer	Withdrawal from school
1907	September	Arrival in Vienna
	October	Rejection by Academy of Fine Arts
	December 21	Mother's death
1908	September	Second rejection by Academy
1909	November	Living on the street
1910	February 9	Arrival in Männerheim (men's residence)
1913	May 24	Arrival in Munich
1914	January 14	Arrest for draft evasion
	August 16	Enlistment in Bavarian army
1918	October 14	Gassing and hospitalization
	November 7	Mental breakdown
1919	August	Lecturing for army
	September 12	Encounter with German Workers Party (later known as Nazi Party)
1921	July 26	Assumption of dictatorial power in Nazi Party
1923	November 8	Attempted coup against Bavarian government
	November 11	Arrest for coup
1924	April 1	Conviction, continued imprisonment, writing *Mein Kampf*
	December 20	Release from prison
1925	Summer	First stay at Berghof (country home)
1929	September	Move to upscale apartment in Munich
1931	September 18	Suicide of beloved niece
1932	July 31	Nazi victory in national election
1933	January 30	Appointment as chancellor, first pogrom
	February 27	Reichstag fire
	July 14	Enactment of sterilization law

1934	June 20	Purge of Storm Troopers and political opponents
1935	September 15	Enactment of Nuremberg Laws
1936	March 7	Deployment of troops in Rhineland
1937	November 5	Presentation to army of plans for conquest
1938	February 4	Purge of army
	March 11	Annexation of Austria
	September 29	Munich agreement, annexation of part of Czechoslovakia
	November 9	*Kristallnacht* pogrom
1939	(early in year)	First killing under "euthanasia" program
	March 15	Annexation of more of Czechoslovakia
	August 23	German-Soviet pact
	September 1	Invasion of Poland, first killing by death squads
1940	April 9	Invasion of Denmark and Norway
	May 10	Invasion of Holland, Belgium, Luxembourg, and France
	May 24	Halt order enabling British escape at Dunkirk
	June 22	Fall of France
	October 12	Cancellation of invasion of England
1941	April 5	Invasion of Yugoslavia and Greece
	June 22	Invasion of Soviet Union
	September	First gassing of Jews in special vans
	December	First death camp operating at Chelmno
	December 11	Declaration of war on United States
1943	February 3	Surrender of German army at Stalingrad
1944	June 6	Landing of American and British troops in France
	July 20	Attempted assassination of Hitler
1945	March 19	Order to destroy Germany's resources
	April 29	Marriage
	April 30	Suicide

NOTES

ABBREVIATIONS

Hitler's writings and spoken words:

L & N	Hitler's Letters and Notes
MK-E	*Mein Kampf,* English edition
MK-G	*Mein Kampf,* German edition
MNO	My New Order
Quotations	Adolf Hitler Quotations
SB	Hitler's Secret Book
SC	Hitler's Secret Conversations
S & P	Hitler: Speeches and Proclamations
Testament	The Testament of Adolf Hitler
Words	Hitler's Words

Nuremberg trial records

Trial	The Trial of the Major War Criminals (blue set)
Trials	Trials of War Criminals (green set)

Archives

NA-DC	National Archives, Washington, D.C.
NA-FDR	National Archives, Hyde Park, N.Y. (Franklin Roosevelt Museum)

PREFACE

1. Arendt, *Men in Dark Times,* 34.
2. Rosenbaum, "Explaining Hitler," 50.

CHAPTER 1. THE ENIGMA

1. "Introduction" in Speer, *Inside Third Reich,* xi.
2. Snyder, *Hitler's German Enemies,* vii.
3. "Foreword" in Jetzinger, *Hitler's Youth,* 10.
4. Blackburn, *Education in Third Reich,* 6.
5. Lukacs, *The Duel,* 224.
6. Jäckel, *Hitler in History,* 1.
7. Bullock, *Hitler* (1961), 342.
8. Lukacs, *The Duel,* 223.

CHAPTER 2. THE PHANTOM JEW

1. Patrick Hitler in Toland, *Adolf Hitler,* 245.
2. Koehler, *Inside Information,* 146 ff.
3. Frank, *Angesicht des Galgens,* 330–331.
4. Waite, *Psychopathic God,* 149.
5. Proctor, *Racial Hygiene,* 125. As additional protection in 1937, Jews were excluded from spas and hotels that employed Aryan women under 45 as domestics (Hilberg, *Documents of Destruction,* 35).
6. *SB,* 76
7. Waite, *Psychopathic God,* 149; John Steiner, *Power Politics,* 287.
8. Schramm, *Hitler,* 49.
9. Kubizek, *Young Hitler,* 41.
10. Jacob Burckhardt in Fest, *Hitler,* 13.
11. Bunting, *Adolf Hitler,* 11.

CHAPTER 3. THE BIRTH OF A CHAMPION

1. Payne, *Life and Death,* 12.
2. Ibid., 13.
3. Toland, *Adolf Hitler,* 142–143. See also Hanfstängl, *Unheard Witness,* 86.
4. Eitner, *Der Führer,* 245; Grün, *Howl Like Wolves,* 57; Irving, *War Path,* 92; Gallagher, *By Trust Betrayed,* 49.
5. Emanuel Lugert in Jetzinger, *Hitler's Youth,* 45.
6. Waite, *Psychopathic God,* 156.
7. Dolan, *Adolf Hitler,* 5; Schenck, *Patient Hitler,* 302; Bloch, "My Patient Hitler." See also Jetzinger, *Hitler's Youth,* 86.
8. Traudl Junge in Galante & Silianoff, *Voices from Bunker,* 125.
9. Kubizek, *Young Hitler,* 34.

10. *NA-DC*, Investigative Records Repository, Box 87A, Paula Hitler; Waite, *Psychopathic God*, 169, 187; *NA-DC*, Investigative Records Repository, Box 87A, Bloch, 21.

11. *MK-G*, 1: 30.

12. Wagener, *Hitler*, 294.

13. Binion, *Hitler Among Germans*, 56.

14. *NA-DC*, Investigative Records Repository, Box 87A, Bloch, 21.

CHAPTER 4. THE TURN TOWARD NIHILISM

1. Kubizek, *Young Hitler*, 31.

2. *MK-G*, 1: 251. The sexual problem could be countered by sports and gymnastics (activities absent in his own life) and was pronounced in idlers who stayed at home (another apparent reference to himself).

3. Toland, *Adolf Hitler*, 9.

4. *NA-DC*, Investigatory Records Repository, Box 87A, Paula Hitler; Jetzinger, *Hitler's Youth*, 51.

5. Bridget Hitler, *Memoirs*, 170.

6. Fest, *Face of Third Reich*, 265.

7. Stierlin, *Adolf Hitler*.

8. *NA-DC*, Investigatory Records Repository, Box 87A, Paula Hitler.

9. Langer, *Mind of Hitler*, 104; *NA-DC*, Record Group 226 (microfilm), 925.

10. Bridget Hitler, *Memoirs*, 170.

11. Seligman, *Helplessness*.

12. *SC*, 197–198, 200.

13. Gervasi, *Adolf Hitler*, 14.

14. Goldston, *Life and Death*, 24.

15. Kubizek, *Young Hitler*, 30, 15.

16. Heinz, *Germany's Hitler*, 12.

17. Jetzinger (*Hitler's Youth*, 32) argued *Hitler* and its variants could only be of Czech origin because in German *Hüttner* (dweller in a cottage or worker in a foundry) can be derived from *Hütte*, but *Hüttler* cannot be. The argument was overstated. In Austria, a small cottage was called a *Hüttl*, and from this word the name *Hüttler* (dweller in a small cottage) can be derived.

18. Kubizek, *Young Hitler*, 100.

19. Ibid., 101.

20. Ibid., 96.

21. Ibid., 153.

22. *NA-DC*, Record Group 226 (microfilm), 384; Bromberg & Small, *Hitler's Psychopathology*, 42.

23. Kubizek, *Young Hitler,* 59.
24. Ibid., 108.
25. *NA-DC,* Investigatory Records Repository, Box 87A, Paula Hitler; Maser, *Hitler,* 41.
26. Bloch, "My Patient Hitler," 39.
27. *MK-G,* 1: 26.
28. Kubizek, *Young Hitler,* 157.
29. Gerald Fleming, *Hitler and Final Solution,* 11.
30. Kubizek, *Young Hitler,* 176.
31. Maser, *Hitler,* 48.
32. Kubizek, *Young Hitler,* 83.
33. Weiss, *Ideology of Death,* 100.
34. Strom & Parsons, *Holocaust and Human Behavior,* 121.
35. Deuel, *People Under Hitler,* 272.
36. *Assault on Arts,* 7.
37. Pope, *Munich Playground,* 47.
38. Kubizek, *Young Hitler,* 168.
39. Ibid., 174.
40. Ibid., 126.
41. Ibid., 266.

CHAPTER 5. THE WASTELAND

1. Fest, *Hitler,* 64.
2. *MK-E,* 29.
3. This section is based largely on Jones, *Hitler in Vienna*; Heiden, *Der Fuehrer*; Jenks, *Vienna and Hitler.*
4. *MK-E,* 38.
5. Jones, *Hitler in Vienna,* 225.
6. *MK-E,* 67.
7. Schenck, *Patient Hitler,* 124.
8. Gerald Fleming, *Hitler and Final Solution,* 6; Bullock, *Hitler,* 36.
9. Waite, *Psychopathic God,* 103 ff.
10. *MK-E,* 68.
11. This section is based on Jones, *Hitler in Vienna.*
12. Fest, *Hitler,* 64.
13. Hanfstängl, *Unheard Witness,* 76.
14. *MK-G,* 1: 165.
15. Ibid., 167, 165.
16. Ibid., 165.

CHAPTER 6. THE CALL

1.   Rauschning, *Voice of Destruction,* 6–7.
2.   Tolischus, *They Wanted War,* 53.
3.   Baird, *Die for Germany*; Pascal, *German Novel,* 297. See also Stierlin, *Adolf Hitler,* 84; Goodricke-Clarke, *Occult Roots,* 49 ff.
4.   *L & N,* 88.
5.   Ibid., 51.
6.   Ibid., 57.
7.   Ibid., 62, 75.
8.   Ibid., 52.
9.   Heiden, *Der Fuehrer,* 31.
10. Gervasi, *Adolf Hitler,* 27.
11. *MK-E,* 264; Langer, *Mind of Hitler,* 156.
12. Schwaab, *Hitler's Mind,* 126.
13. *MK-E,* 300.
14. Ibid.
15. Binion, *Hitler Among Germans,* 2.
16. Ibid., 138.
17. Karl Wilmanns, a psychiatrist and professor at Heidelberg University, told the story to his classes. When Hitler became chancellor, Wilmanns was dismissed and arrested (Müller-Hill, *Murderous Science,* 168–169, 207). According to Wilmanns' daughter, Ruth Lidz (letter to author, 1992), the story of Hitler's hallucination and hysterical blindness "was all over town . . . in Heidelberg . . ." See also Langer, *Mind of Hitler,* 156.
18. Fest, *Hitler,* 81.

CHAPTER 7. THE MAN

1.   Gerald Fleming, *Hitler and Final Solution,* 18.
2.   Gustave Gilbert, *Nuremberg Diary, 108.*
3.   Ibid., 129.
4.   Speer, *Slave State,* 305.
5.   Murray, *Personality of Hitler,* 18.
6.   *NA-DC,* Record Group 226 (microfilm), 597.
7.   Smith, *Last Train from Berlin,* 31.
8.   Dietrich, *Hitler,* 162.
9.   Traudl Junge in Galante & Silianoff, *Voices from Bunker,* 121.
10.   Gustave Gilbert, *Nuremberg Diary,* 61.

11. Waite, *Psychopathic God,* 57.
12. Hanfstängl, *Unheard Witness,* 82.
13. Rempel, *Hitler's Children,* 51; Stachura, *German Youth Movement,* 132; Siemson, *Hitler Youth,* 117; Bleuel, *Sex and Society,* 96; Heiden, *Der Fuehrer,* 218.
14. Görlitz, *German General Staff,* 283.
15. Waite, *Psychopathic God,* 48.
16. Traudl Junge in Galante & Silianoff, *Voices from Bunker,* 71.
17. Waite, *Psychopathic God,* 94.
18. Payne, *Life and Death,* xii, xiii; Schwaab, *Hitler's Mind,* 132.
19. Waite, *Psychopathic God,* 21.
20. Irving, *War Path,* 144, 6.
21. Langer, *Mind of Hitler,* 30.
22. Haffner, *Germany,* 21; Haffner, *Meaning of Hitler,* 19; Waite, *Psychopathic God,* 449.
23. Bellow, *Dangling Man,* 82.
24. Gordon, "Fascination Begins," 3.
25. Murray, *Personality of Hitler,* 193.
26. Picard, *Hitler in Our Selves,* 38.
27. Baynes, *Germany Possessed,* 156.

CHAPTER 8. IN POWER

1. Rauschning, *Voice of Destruction,* 3–4.
2. Hanfstängl, *Unheard Witness,* 50; Jäckel, *Hitler in History,* 8.
3. Shuster, *Mighty Army,* 75–76.
4. Göring, *Germany Reborn,* 121.
5. Johnson, *Modern Times,* 284.
6. Goebbels, *Tagebücher,* 2: 362.
7. Grün, *Howl Like Wolves,* 62.
8. Papen, *Memoirs,* 269.
9. Hoffmann, *Hitler My Friend,* 72.
10. Hanfstängl, *Unheard Witness,* 212.
11. Hoffmann, *Hitler My Friend,* 72.
12. Tobias, *Reichstag Fire,* 82–84, 89–91, 224–225.
13. Ibid., 60, 65.
14. Fest, *Hitler,* 413. Here "protective custody" probably should read "preventive custody." In German the same word is used for both. Nazi's misleading use of "protective custody" for preventive and punitive custody created a problem for translators.
15. Tobias, *Reichstag Fire,* 179 ff.
16. Ibid., 47–49.

17. Ibid., 137–140; Shirer, *Rise and Fall,* 193.
18. Ibid.
19. Papen, *Memoirs,* 271.
20. Tobias, *Reichstag Fire,* 49; Reed, *Burning of Reichstag,* 250.
21. Manvell & Fraenkel, *Göring,* 396; *Reichstag Fire Trial,* 174.
22. *Trial,* 12: 252; Manvell & Fraenkel, *Göring,* 102, Manvell & Fraenkel, *Hundred Days,* 224; Reimann, *Goebbels,* 162; Gisevius, *Bitter End,* 72 ff; *Trial,* 9: 433–434.
23. Wheeler-Bennett, *Knaves, Fools, Heroes,* 71.
24. Schacht, *Account Settled,* 251–252.
25. Kogon, *Theory of Hell,* 24.
26. Koehl, *Black Corps,* 99.
27. Rauschning, *Voice of Destruction,* 91.
28. Bleuel, *Sex and Society,* 4.
29. *S & P,* 1: 567.
30. Ibid., 488–489.
31. *MNO,* 265.
32. Ibid.
33. Irving, *War Path,* 39.
34. Papen, *Memoirs,* 306.
35. Görlitz, *German General Staff,* 326.
36. Neumann, *Black March,* 79; Holt, *Command and Control,* 25.
37. Liddell Hart, *German Generals Talk,* 32–33.
38. Walsh, *Total Power,* 105.
39. Shirer, *Nightmare Years,* 323.
40. Procktor, *Nazi Germany,* 105.
41. *Testament,* 84.

CHAPTER 9. TRANSFORMING THE SELF

"The Twisted Road to Auschwitz" is the title of Schleunes' book.

1. Waite, "Hitler's Anti-Semitism," 203.
2. Rauschning, *Voice of Destruction,* 11; Speer, *Spandau,* 158; *SC,* 55.
3. Röder & Kubillus & Burwell, *Psychiatrists,* 3.
4. Rauschning, *Voice of Destruction,* 137.
5. Ibid., 80.
6. Ibid., 175.
7. Irving, *War Path,* 120 (my modification of his translation). See also Rauschning, *Voice of Destruction,* 66–67.
8. Murray, *Personality of Hitler,* 148.

9. Waite, "Hitler's Anti-Semitism," 283.
10. Munch, *Norse Mythology,* 290.
11. Waite, *Psychopathic God,* 77–78. Deuel (*People Under Hitler,* 57) said Hitler copied the moustache of Nazi leader Gottfried Feder. But pictures show Hitler with the moustache before meeting Feder.
12. Lucas, *Last Year of German Army,* 136.
13. Rauschning, *Revolution of Nihilism,* 45.
14. Rauschning, *Voice of Destruction,* 80.
15. Stierlin, *Adolf Hitler,* 102.
16. *Testament,* 57.
17. Irving, *War Path,* 170.
18. Waite, "Hitler's Anti-Semitism," 203.
19. Grün, *Howl Like Wolves,* 117.
20. Schwaab, *Hitler's Mind,* 21.
21. Stierlin, *Adolf Hitler,* 94.
22. Murray, *Personality of Hitler,* 151.
23. Speer, *Inside Third Reich,* 121.

CHAPTER 10. EXHIBITING CHARISMA

1. Lüdecke, *I Knew Hitler,* 13. Another who described Hitler's speeches as lashing was Riefenstahl, *Leni Riefenstahl,* 123.
2. *Trials,* 5: 27.
3. Milgram, *Obedience to Authority.*
4. Jäckel, *Hitler in History,* 96; John Steiner, *Power Politics,* 292. See also Kitterman, "Those Who Said 'No!' " 241. For an excellent analysis see Buchheim, "Command and Compliance" in Krausnick, Buchheim, Broszat & Jacobsen, *Anatomy of SS State,* 371 ff.
5. Browning, *Path to Genocide,* 173 ff; Browning, *Ordinary Men.*
6. Ibid., 185.
7. Lewin, *Hitler's Mistakes,* 109.
8. Goebbels, *Diaries,* 131.
9. Paul Schmidt in Maltitz, *Evolution of Hitler's Germany,* 321.
10. Julius Streicher in *Trial,* 12: 309.
11. Baynes, *Germany Possessed,* 23.
12. Proctor, *Racial Hygiene,* facing 51; Baird, *Nazi War Propaganda,* 47.
13. This section is based on Conger, *The Charismatic Leader*; Willner, *The Spellbinders*; Reichmann, *Hostages of Civilization*; and Stern, *Hitler.*
14. John Dos Passos in Hofstadter, *American Political Tradition,* xxxiii.
15. Broszat, *German National Socialism,* 41. On intellectuals embracing Nazism, see Weinreich, *Hitler's Professors*; Hamilton, *Appeal of Fascism.*

16. Morgan, *Demon Lover,* 57.
17. Blackburn, *Education in Third Reich,* 6.
18. *S & P,* 1: 28. See also Nyomarky, *Charisma in Nazi Party,* 24; Maser, *Hitler's Mein Kampf,* 44.
19. Hanfstängl, *Unheard Witness,* 283.
20. Schacht, *Account Settled,* 85.
21. Speer, *Spandau,* 451.
22. Speer, *Slave State,* 305.
23. John Steiner, *Power Politics,* 317.
24. Rhodes, *Hitler Movement,* 31.
25. Ibid.
26. James, "Blaming the Germans," 44.
27. Toland, *Adolf Hitler,* 208.
28. Golo Mann in Calic, *Secret Conversations with Hitler,* 8.
29. Stern, *Hitler,* 35.
30. Feiling, *Life of Chamberlain,* 367.
31. Irving, *War Path,* 144.
32. Trevor-Roper, "Introduction" in Hitler, *Testament of Adolf Hitler,* 3; Feiling, *Life of Chamberlain,* 328.
33. Neumann, *Black March,* 42.
34. Baird, *Nazi War Propaganda,* 3.
35. Erikson, "Hitler's Imagery," 493.
36. Murray, *Personality of Hitler,* 176.
37. *MNO,* 42.
38. *Quotations,* 11.
39. Reichmann, *Hostages of Civilization,* 84.
40. Lewin, *Hitler's Mistakes,* 68.
41. Millett, *Sexual Politics,* 165.
42. Pryce-Jones, *Unity Mitford,* 102; Traudl Junge in Galante & Silianoff, *Voices from Bunker,* 76; Toland, *Adolf Hitler,* 192; Hoffmann, *Hitler My Friend,* 167; Fromm, *Blood and Banquets,* 211.
43. Pryce-Jones, *Unity Mitford,* 167; Schellenberg, *Labyrinth,* 94; Kersten, *Memoirs,* 195.
44. Schumann, *Being Present,* 41.

CHAPTER 11. TRANSFORMING THE NATION

1. *Trial,* 19: 443.
2. Siemson, *Hitler Youth,* 74.
3. Laffin, *Hitler Warned Us,* 102–103.
4. Tolischus, *They Wanted War,* 52.

5. Banse, *Germany Prepares War,* 350.
6. Pfeffer von Salomon in Höhne, *Order of Death's Head,* 70.
7. Grün, *Howl Like Wolves,* 76.
8. Schumann, *Being Present,* 24; Koehn, *Mischling, Second Degree,* 50; Brady, *Spirit of German Fascism,* 192.
9. Ziemer, *Education for Death,* Luther, *Blood and Honor,* 15.
10. *Trial,* 30: 537.
11. Siemson, *Hitler Youth,* 69.
12. Blackburn, *Education in Third Reich,* 43.
13. *Trial,* 30: 535.
14. Harwood Childs, "Preface" in Brennecke and Gierlichs, *Nazi Primer,* xxvii.
15. Neumann, *Black March,* 5.
16. Müller, *Hitler's Justice,* 295.
17. Crankshaw, *Gestapo,* 30. See also Kessel, *Miraculous Hands,* 149.
18. *Trial,* 29: 425.
19. Höhne, *Order of Death's Head,* 415; Koonz, *Mothers in Fatherland,* 405.
20. Pearlman, *Capture of Eichmann,* 420.
21. Neumann, *Black March,* 84.
22. Grün, *Howl Like Wolves,* 200–201.
23. Segev, *Soldiers of Evil,* 100–107.
24. Gerald Fleming, *Hitler and Final Solution,* 99–100.
25. Ibid., 54.
26. Conot, *Justice at Nuremberg,* 268–269.
27. Weiss, *Ideology of Death,* 109.
28. Rauschning, *Revolution of Nihilism,* 34; Rauschning, *Voice of Destruction,* 94; *Trial,* 33: 560; Schacht, *Account Settled,* 214.
29. Waite, *Psychopathic God,* 24.
30. Toland, *Adolf Hitler,* 144.
31. Schacht, *Account Settled,* 212.
32. Müller-Hill, *Murderous Science,* 39 ff; Weindling, *Health, Race and German Politics,* 546–549; Gallagher, *By Trust Betrayed,* 59; Burleigh & Wippermann, *Racial State,* 73.
33. Dawidowicz, *Holocaust Reader,* 15.
34. Speer, *Inside Third Reich,* 39.
35. Jean-François Steiner, *Treblinka,* 322 ff.
36. Loewenstein, *Hitler's Germany,* 36.
37. Shirer, *Rise and Fall,* 268.
38. Ibid.
39. Bleuel, *Sex and Race,* 39.
40. Calic, *Secret Conversations with Hitler,* 147.
41. Roland Freisler paraphrased by Roper & Leiser, *Skeleton of Justice,* 52.

42. Kogon, *Theory of Hell,* 23.
43. Ibid; Shirer, *Rise and Fall,* 271.
44. Bessel, *Life in Third Reich,* xv; Gallagher, *By Trust Betrayed,* 208.
45. Müller, *Hitler's Justice,* 47.
46. Judge Lothar Kreyssig to Minister Franz Gürtner in Gallagher, *By Trust Betrayed,* 216.
47. Grunberger, *12-Year Reich,* 120.
48. Otto Thierack in Burleigh & Wippermann, *Racial State,* 180.
49. Müller, *Hitler's Justice,* 79.
50. Dietrich, *Hitler,* 124–125; Bleuel, *Sex and Society,* 210.
51. Müller, *Hitler's Justice,* 75.
52. Grün, *Howl Like Wolves,* 90–91.
53. Müller, *Hitler's Justice,* 49.
54. *Trial,* 32: 26.
55. Franz Gürtner in Müller, *Hitler's Justice,* 75–76.
56. Ibid., 47–48.
57. Ibid., 146.
58. Ibid., 111.
59. *Trials,* 3: 854.
60. Ibid., 856.
61. Ibid., 858.
62. Ibid.
63. Ibid., 860.
64. Grunberger, *12-Year Reich,* 122.
65. Müller, *Hitler's Justice,* 181.
66. Grunberger, *12-Year Reich,* 124.
67. Broszat, *Hitler State,* 336; Grunberger, *12-Year Reich,* 124.
68. Oliner & Oliner, *Altruistic Personality,* 122. A general source on beneficiaries and accomplices is Simpson, *Splendid Blond Beast.*

CHAPTER 12. PURGING THE BLOOD

1. Gerald Fleming, *Hitler and Final Solution,* 17.
2. *MK-G,* 1: 64.
3. Heinz, *Germany's Hitler,* 45.
4. *MK-G,* 1: 64.
5. Ibid, 65.
6. Ibid., 66.
7. Ibid., 72–73.
8. Ibid., 60.
9. Toland, *Last 100 Days,* 251.
10. Waite, *Psychopathic God,* 99.

11. Ibid., 101.
12. Gerald Fleming, *Hitler and Final Solution,* 105.
13. Bezymenski, *Death of Adolf Hitler*; Petrova & Watson, *Death of Hitler.*
14. *MK-G,* 1: 252, 253.
15. Ibid., 246.
16. Ibid., 319.
17. Waite, "Hitler's Anti-Semitism," 205.
18. Snyder, *Encyclopedia of Third Reich,* 34.
19. *MK-G,* 2: 200.
20. Strom & Parsons, *Holocaust and Human Behavior,* 80.
21. Infield, *Eva and Adolf,* 94.
22. Rauschning, *Voice of Destruction,* 94.
23. Waite, *Psychopathic God,* 99.
24. Rauschning, *Voice of Destruction,* 230.
25. Bytwerk, *Julius Streicher,* 76.
26. *MK-G,* 1: 247.
27. Ibid., 1: 321.
28. *MK-G,* 2: 42.
29. Irving, *War Path,* xiii.

CHAPTER 13. SCAPEGOATING

1. Rauschning, *Voice of Destruction,* 232, 237.
2. *SC,* 193.
3. Flannery, *Anguish of Jews.* See also Weiss, *Ideology of Death,* 18.
4. Waite, *Psychopathic God,* 99.
5. Conot, *Justice at Nuremberg,* 265; Weinreich, *Hitler's Professors,* 164.
6. Harold Mattingly, "Introduction" in Tacitus, *Agricola and Germania,* 25; Burleigh & Wippermann, *Racial State,* 25.
7. Tacitus, *Agricola and Germania,* 104.
8. Goodricke-Clarke, *Occult Roots,* 90 ff; Waite, *Psychopathic God,* 104 ff.
9. Bormann, *Bormann Letters,* 192 ff. See also *MK-E,* 396 ff.
10. Mosse, *Crisis of German Ideology,* 52.
11. Ritchie, *German Literature,* 20.
12. Müller-Hill, *Murderous Science,* 81. The official commentary on the Nuremberg Laws said if an Aryan woman married a Jew, was widowed, and married an Aryan, descendants of the second marriage would be partly Jewish (Friedländer, *Nazi Germany and Jews,* 152).
13. *Trial,* 5: 95.
14. Neumann, *Black March,* 19.
15. *MK-G,* 1: 357.

16.   Kneller, *Educational Philosophy,* 15.

17.   A Nazi physician in Weiss, *Ideology of Death,* 311.

18.   *Words,* 79.

19.   Hoffmann, *Hitler My Friend,* facing 152, 193; Strasser, *Hitler and I,* 10.

20.   Pulzer, *Rise of Political Anti-Semitism,* 4; Flannery, *Anguish of Jews,* 96 ff.

21.   Gay, *Jews of Germany,* 221, 243; Flannery, *Anguish of Jews,* 197; Loewenstein, *Hitler's Germany,* 144.

22.   *MK-E,* 80; Müller, *Hitler's Justice,* 59.

23.   Schleunes, *Twisted Road,* 40 ff; Hamilton, *Appeal of Fascism,* 104.

24.   Hohne, *Order of Death's Head,* 33.

25.   Craig, *The Germans,* 126. See also Maltitz, *Evolution of Hitler's Germany*; Erikson, "Hitler's Imagery"; Fischer, *Nazi Germany,* 29. Hitler was struck by Jews' self-contempt (*MK-E,* 79): "I never understood their boundless hate towards their own nationality, how they despised their national greatness, soiled its history and abused its heroes. The fight against one's own race, against one's own nest and homeland, was as senseless as it was incomprehensible. It was unnatural." He seems not to have connected this idea with his own destructiveness toward Austria and Germany.

26.   Rauschning, *Voice of Destruction,* 136–137.

27.   *Quotations,* 37.

28.   Gottfried Feder in Baynes, *Germany Possessed,* 298.

29.   Rauschning, *Voice of Destruction,* 147–148.

30.   Ibid., 241, 238.

31.   Levin, *Holocaust,* 106; Arendt, *Eichmann in Jerusalem,* 28, 40, 41.

32.   Gay, *Jews of Germany,* 182.

33.   Craig, *The Germans,* 141.

34.   Bytwerk, *Julius Streicher,* 48.

35.   Pope, *Munich Playground,* 32–33.

36.   Observed by Erich Wolf (personal communication, 1993).

37.   Gustave Gilbert, *Nuremberg Diary,* 41.

38.   Bytwerk, *Julius Streicher,* 49.

39.   Fest, *Face of Third Reich,* 107. Graber; *Life of Heydrich,* 10.

40.   Fest, *Face of Third Reich,* 108; Kersten, *Totenkopf und Treue,* 128.

41.   Kelley, *22 Cells in Nuremberg,* 50. See also Roberts, *House that Hitler Built,* 49.

42.   Deuel, *People Under Hitler,* 126; Reitlinger, *The SS,* 35; Graber, *Life of Heydrich,* 109; Hagen, *Mark of Swastika,* 12.

43.   *Trial,* 22: 548.

CHAPTER 14. STRUGGLING WITH TEMPTATION

1.   Price, *I Knew These Dictators,* 15.

2.   Wagener, *Hitler,* 33.

3. Ibid.
4. Hoffmann, *Hitler My Friend,* 147; Infield, *Hitler's Secret Life,* 211; Eitner, *Der Führer,* 17.
5. Wagener, *Hitler,* 294.
6. *SC,* 247; Riefenstahl, *Leni Riefenstahl,* 228.
7. Kubizek, *Young Hitler,* 146–147.
8. Hanfstängl, *Unheard Witness,* 147; Irving, *War Path,* 111.
9. Waite, *Psychopathic God,* 5.
10. *NA-DC,* Record Group 226 (microfilm), 308.
11. Koonz, *Mothers in Fatherland,* 58–59.
12. Hanfstängl, *Unheard Witness,* 143.
13. Ibid.
14. Eitner, *Der Führer,* 228.
15. Hitler, *Hitler Close-Up,* 88.
16. Riefenstahl, *Leni Riefenstahl.,* 104.
17. Irving, *War Path,* 109. See also Hanfstängl, *Unheard Witness,* 169.
18. This section is based largely on Bridget Hitler, *Memoirs.* See also Hoffmann, *Hitler My Friend,* 150 ff; Hanfstaengl, *Unheard Witness,* 175; Toland, *Adolf Hitler,* 253; Infield, *Hitler's Secret Life,* 83; McKnight, *Loves of Hitler,* 122.
19. Hoffmann, *Hitler My Friend,* 150.
20. Ibid., 152. See also Strasser, *Hitler and I,* 71.
21. Infield, *Eva and Adolf,* 97. See also Bridget Hitler, *Memoirs,* 177–178. For similar stories, see Gustave Gilbert, *Psychology of Dictatorship,* 32; Jones, *Hitler in Vienna,* 282.
22. Bridget Hitler, *Memoirs,* 76.
23. Riefenstahl, *Leni Riefenstahl,* 228.
24. Wagener, *Hitler,* 222.
25. Rosenbaum, "Hitler's Doomed Angel," 181 ff.
26. Heiden, *Der Fuehrer,* 384–385; Langer, *Mind of Hitler,* 134, 168, 171; Bromberg & Small, *Hitler's Psychopathology,* 247; Heyst, *After Hitler,* 78.
27. This section is based on Janus & Bass & Saltus, *Sexual Profile*; Scott, *Erotic Power*; Shapiro, *Rigid Character*; Stoller, *Perversion*; and especially Baumeister, *Masochism and the Self.*
28. Ibid., x.
29. Laffin, *Hitler Warned Us,* 126.
30. Felix Gilbert, *Hitler Directs War,* 80.
31. Murray, *Personality of Hitler,* 18. See also Jones, *Hitler in Vienna,* 76.
32. Stoller, *Perversion,* 59.
33. Jones, *Hitler in Vienna,* 76.
34. Bromberg & Small, *Hitler's Psychopathology,* 119.
35. Hanfstängl, *Unheard Witness,* 290; Eitner, *Der Führer,* 240.

36. Infield, *Hitler's Secret Life,* 38; Gun, *Eva Braun,* 64.
37. Irving, *Secret Diaries,* 35; Maser, *Hitler,* 205. See also Trevor-Roper, *Last Days,* 69.
38. O'Donnell, *The Bunker,* 115, 124.

CHAPTER 15. CREATING THE MASTER RACE

1. *SB,* 215.
2. Stern, *Hitler,* 172.
3. Blackburn, *Education in Third Reich,* 12. See also Procktor, *Nazi Germany,* 42.
4. Stachura, *Youth Movement,* 145.
5. *MK-G,* 2: 331.
6. Blackburn, *Education in Third Reich,* 53 ff; Neumann, *Black March,* 15.
7. Ibid.
8. Ibid., 14. See also Schumann, *Being Present,* 62; Burleigh & Wippermann, *Racial State,* 154; Weindling, *Health, Race and German Politics,* 546.
9. Levin, *Holocaust,* 38; Grün, *Howl Like Wolves,* 112; Procktor, *Nazi Germany,* 73; Shirer, *Rise and Fall,* 250–251; Speer, *Inside Third Reich,* 273.
10. Levin, *Holocaust,* 47; Speer, *Inside Third Reich,* 273.
11. Burleigh & Wippermann, *Racial State,* 88.
12. Gustave Gilbert, *Nuremberg Diary,* 6.
13. Strom & Parsons, *Holocaust and Human Behavior,* 167.
14. Rempel, *Hitler's Children,* 297, 106. See also Stachura, *Youth Movement,* 148; Gellately, *Gestapo and German Society,* 129 ff.
15. Koonz, *Mothers in Fatherland,* 8.
16. Dodd, *Embassy Eyes,* 272–277; Engelmann, *In Hitler's Germany,* 31; Gellately, *Gestapo and German Society,* 129; Loewenstein, *Hitler's Germany,* 133.
17. Shirer, *Berlin Diary,* 288–289. For effects in daily life, see Engelmann, *In Hitler's Germany.*
18. Root, *Secret History,* 2: 28; *Trial,* 30: 529. See also *Trial,* 28: 237; Phillips, *Hitler and Third Reich,* 25.
19. Rempel, *Hitler's Children,* 51.
20. Hassell, *Diaries,* 48; Pope, *Munich Playground,* 236; Grunberger, *12-Year Reich,* 280.
21. Pope, *Munich Playground,* 240.
22. This section is based on Hillel & Henry, *Of Pure Blood.*
23. This section is also based on Hillel & Henry.
24. Lang, *The Secretary,* 229. See also Lewin, *Hitler's Mistakes,* 32.
25. Loewenstein, *Hitler's Germany,* 154.
26. Müller, *Hitler's Justice,* 91.
27. Adam, *Judenpolitik Dritten Reich,* 126.
28. Remak, *Nazi Years,* 149.

29. Deuel, *People Under Hitler,* 216; Ebenstein, *Nazi State,* 102.
30. Rich, *Hitler's War Aims,* 2, 8.
31. Deuel, *People Under Hitler,* 212–213; Johnson, *History of Jews,* 473.
32. Deuel, *People Under Hitler,* 211 ff.
33. Fest, *Face of Third Reich,* 274.
34. Ibid., 268; *MK-G,* 2: 40.
35. Binion, *Hitler Among Germans,* 132.
36. Kater, *Doctors Under Hitler,* 114, 236.
37. Davidson, "Introduction" in Speer, *Inside Third Reich,* xxi.
38. Deuel, *People Under Hitler,* 231–232.
39. Grunberger, *12-Year Reich,* 238.
40. Gallagher, *By Trust Betrayed,* 52.
41. Aycoberry, *The Nazi Question,* 6.
42. Arendt, *Eichmann in Jerusalem,* 108.
43. Grün, *Howl Like Wolves,* 176.
44. Ibid., 180.
45. Burleigh & Wippermann, *Racial State,* 148.
46. Gallagher, *By Trust Betrayed,* 119, 96.
47. Burleigh & Wippermann, *Racial State,* 164, 161–162.
48. Gasman, *Scientific Origins.* Hitler wrote (*SB,* 18): "[Sparta's] exposure of sick, weak, deformed children, in short their destruction, was more decent and in truth a thousand times more humane than the wretched insanity of our day which preserves the most pathological subject . . . to breed a race of degenerates burdened with illness."
49. Bock, *Zwangsterilisation,* 111; Zmarzlik, "Social Darwinism," 15.
50. Proctor, *Racial Hygiene,* 95.
51. Bock, *Zwangsterilisation.* See also Burleigh & Wippermann, *Racial State,* 46.
52. Bock, *Zwangsterilisation,* 112.
53. Ibid., 353.
54. Müller-Hill, *Murderous Science,* 29–30.
55. Müller, *Hitler's Justice,* 121–123; Röder & Kubillus & Burwell, *Psychiatrists,* 49.
56. Opitz & Oguntoye & Schultz, *Showing our Colors,* 47; Bock, *Zwangsterilisation,* 354.
57. Jeremy Noakes, "Social Outcasts in Third Reich" in Bessel, *Life in Third Reich,* 88.
58. Bock, *Zwangsterilisation,* 366.
59. Schleunes, *Twisted Road,* 129.
60. Müller-Hill, *Murderous Science,* 52.
61. Hilberg, *Destruction of European Jews,* 3: 944; Kogon, *Theory of Hell,* 156.
62. *Trials,* 1: 696, 720–721.
63. Ibid., 720. See also Müller-Hill, *Murderous Science,* 45.
64. *Trials,* 1: 696–701; *NA-DC,* Nuremberg War Crime Trials, Case I, Microfilm Pub. 887, Roll 16, Doc. 046a.

65. Ibid., Doc. 035; *Trials,* 1: 711.
66. Breitman, *Architect of Genocide,* 153.
67. Boelcke, *Conferences of Goebbels,* xiii; Smith, *Last Train from Berlin,* 182–183.
68. Aly & Roth, *Restlose Erfassung,* 12.
69. Brennecke & Gierlichs, *Nazi Primer,* 80; Schleunes, *Twisted Road.* 129; Friedländer, *Nazi Germany and Jews,* 150–151.
70. *Trials,* 1: 717–718.
71. Mitscherlich & Mielke, *Doctors of Infamy,* 133.
72. Müller-Hill, *Murderous Science,* 53.
73. Brennecke & Gierlichs, *Nazi Primer,* 80; Bergen, *Twisted Cross,* 83–84.

CHAPTER 16. CONQUEST AND ANNIHILATION

1. Rauschning, *Voice of Destruction,* 11.
2. Speer, *Inside Third Reich,* 85, 630; Robertson, *Hitler's Pre-War Policy,* 50 ff; Weinberg, *Germany, Hitler and World War II,* 43 ff.
3. Shirer, *End of Berlin Diary,* 219.
4. Baird, *Nazi War Propaganda,* 41.
5. Arendt, *Eichmann in Jerusalem,* 37.
6. Weinberg, *Germany, Hitler and World War II,* 72. See also Schmidt, *Hitler's Interpreter,* 153.
7. Shirer, *Rise and Fall,* 532.
8. Ciano, *Ciano Diaries,* 119, 582.
9. Hassell, *Diaries,* 71; Schmidt, *Hitler's Interpreter,* 153–154.
10. Shulman, *Defeat in West,* 34; Shirer, *End of Berlin Diary,* 217.
11. Haffner, *Meaning of Hitler,* 19. In 1937 Hitler said, "I shall not live much longer. I always counted on having enough time to realize my plans. I must carry them out my-self. None of my successors will have the force to." (Speer, *Inside Third Reich,* 127.) See also Guderian, *Panzer Leader,* 437.
12. Gustave Gilbert, *Nuremberg Diary,* 367.
13. Strawson, *Hitler's Battles,* 79.
14. Görlitz, *German General Staff,* 332.
15. Shirer, *End of Berlin Diary,* 233.
16. Speer, *Inside Third Reich,* 199.
17. Kessel, *Miraculous Hands,* 62–63; Fest, *Hitler,* 14; Trevor-Roper, *Last Days of Hitler,* 72; Schwaab, *Hitler's Mind,* 74.
18. Dawidowicz, *War Against Jews,* 142.
19. Strom & Parsons, *Holocaust and Human Behavior,* 97. After the invasion began, Gen. Eduard Wagner said (Irving, *Hitler's War,* 14, italics added): "It is the Führer's and Göring's intention to destroy and exterminate the Polish nation. *More than that cannot be even hinted at in writing.*" In 1941 a Nazi privy to plans for invading

the Soviet Union said (Root, *Secret History,* 2: 5): "Our plans do not include annexing any Russians. Those who don't take refuge on the other side of the Urals will be exterminated out of hand. Our Führer has decided to apply to these populations a process a hundred times quicker than he is using in Poland." He referred to a "Russian" population estimated at 133 million.

20. Strom & Parsons, *Holocaust and Human Behavior,* 97; Irving, *Hitler's War,* 617.

21. Conot, *Justice at Nuremberg,* 211.

22. Haffner, *Meaning of Hitler,* 19.

23. Strawson, *Hitler's Battles,* 95.

24. Speer, *Inside Third Reich,* 199.

25. Flower & Reeves, *Taste of Courage,* 48.

26. Ibid., 26.

27. Peter Fleming, *Operation Sea Lion,* 197 ff; Lewin, *Hitler's Mistakes,* 110; Halder, *War Diary,* 242; Gen. Siegfried Westphal in Freidin & Richardson, *Fatal Decisions,* 29–30.

28. Lukacs, *The Duel,* 187.

29. Kesselring, *Memoirs,* 62, 65.

30. Görlitz, *German General Staff,* 378.

31. Ciano, *Ciano Diaries,* 288.

32. Lukacs, *The Duel,* 88.

33. Johnson, *Modern Times,* 383; Irving, *Hitler's War,* 92–96; Dietrich, *Hitler,* 80.

34. Lukacs, *The Duel,* 88, 187.

35. Churchill, *Gathering Storm,* 318; Ciano, *Ciano Diaries,* 276.

36. Bullock, *Hitler and Stalin,* 682; Jäckel, *Hitler in History,* 33; Poliakov, *Harvest of Hate,* 109.

37. Warlimont, *Inside Hitler's Headquarters,* 111; Ciano, *Ciano Diaries,* 298.

38. Keitel, *Memoirs,* 116; Liddell Hart, *German Generals Talk,* 136.

39. Liddell Hart, *Other Side of Hill,* 199.

40. Shulman, *Defeat in West,* 51; Liddell Hart, *Second World War,* 82.

41. Liddell Hart, *Other Side of Hill,* 133.

42. Flower & Reeves, *Taste of Courage,* 91; Lord, *Miracle of Dunkirk,* 32; Liddell Hart, *German Generals Talk,* 134; Shirer, *Rise and Fall,* 734;

43. Liddell Hart, *Other Side of Hill,* 199.

44. Toland, *Adolf Hitler,* 611; Payne, *Life and Death,* 383; Lukacs, *The Duel,* 86; Liddell Hart, *Other Side of Hill,* 201.

45. Lukacs, *The Duel,* 86.

46. Payne, *Life and Death,* 384.

47. Lamb, "Kluge" in Barnett, *Hitler's Generals,* 400; Blumentritt, *Von Rundstedt,* 78; Liddell Hart, *Other Side of Hill,* 200.

48. Koehl, *Black Corps,* 234; Dawidowicz, *War Against Jews,* 191 ff.

49. Gerald Fleming, *Hitler and Final Solution,* 17.

50. Toland, *Adolf Hitler,* 200.
51. Jäckel, *Hitler in History,* 47.
52. Johnson, *Modern Times,* 472.
53. Lukacs, *Last European War,* 451.
54. Breitman, *Architect of Genocide,* 61–62. Much of the following is based on his book.
55. Dawidowicz, *Holocaust Reader,* 55.
56. Zeiger, *Case Against Eichmann,* 49.
57. Sydnor, *Executive Instinct,* 9–10.
58. Sydnor, *Soldiers of Destruction,* 17; Deschner, *Reinhard Heydrich,* 162; Kersten, *Totenkopf und Treue,* 201; Browning, *Final Solution,* 44; Weiss, *Ideology of Death,* 326. Jäckel (*Hitler in History,* 51) suggested Hitler reached his decision August 1940. See also Friedlander, *Origins of Genocide,* 286; Breitman, *Architect of Genocide,* 141.
59. Breitman, "Himmler," 82; Sydnor, *Soldiers of Destruction,* 29–30; oral statement by Sydnor accompanying *Executive Instinct.*
60. Frank, *Diensttagebuch,* 336.
61. Toland, *Last 100 Days,* 19.
62. Browning, *Ordinary Men,* 50; Browning, *Path to Genocide,* 111, 117; Kessel, *Miraculous Hands,* 140.
63. Grün, *Howl Like Wolves,* 188.
64. Gerald Fleming, *Hitler and Final Solution,* 31.
65. Dawidowicz, *War Against Jews,* 85.
66. Gerald Fleming, *Hitler and Final Solution,* 149–150.
67. Browning, *Path to Genocide,* 170.
68. Proch, *Poland's Cross;* Koehl, *Black Corps,* 234. Military resources were also allocated to less important projects. In approving the movie *Kolberg* in 1943, Goebbels authorized the director to use army personnel and 187,000 soldiers were taken out of active service to participate. The navy refused to lend men and equipment, and the director returned to Goebbels, who then ordered the navy to comply (Leiser, *Nazi Cinema,* 122 ff). See also Waite, *Psychopathic God,* 40.
69. Halder, *Hitler as Warlord,* 5.
70. Dietrich, *Hitler,* 67. "Hitler actually knew nothing about his enemies and even refused to use the information that was available to him." (Speer, *Inside Third Reich,* 198.)
71. Halder, *War Diary,* 245.
72. Irving, *Hitler's War,* 175; Jacobsen & Rohwer, *Decisive Battles,* 55.
73. Warlimont, *Inside Hitler's Headquarters,* 253.
74. On conditions and lack of supplies: Guderian, *Panzer Leader,* 248; Degrelle, *Campaign in Russia,* 32 ff; Haape, *Moscow Tram Stop,* 182 ff; Newton, *German Battle Tactics,* 35 ff; Lucas, *War on Eastern Front,* 97 ff; Sajer, *Forgotten Soldier.*
75. Strawson, *Hitler's Battles,* 144.

76. Sajer, *Forgotten Soldier,* 37 ff. See also Speer, *Inside Third Reich,* 272; Note 74 above, especially Degrelle, p. 147 on suicides.
77. Strawson, *Hitler's Battles,* 144.
78. Guderian, *Panzer Leader,* 266–267.
79. Weinberg, *World at Arms,* 302.
80. Warlimont, *Inside Hitler's Headquarters,* 189, 196; Schröter, *Stalingrad,* 44.
81. Guderian, *Panzer Leader*; Knappe & Brusaw, *Soldat,* 201.
82. Irving, *Hitler's War,* 351.
83. Fest, *Hitler,* 773.
84. Weizsäcker, *Memoirs,* 244; Gehlen, *The Service,* 29; Görlitz, *German General Staff,* 384.
85. *Trial,* 15: 329; Halder, *Hitler as Warlord,* 44; Irving, *Hitler's War,* 312 ff.
86. Grün, *Howl Like Wolves,* 202.
87. Collier, *Second World War,* 213; Halder, *Hitler as Warlord,* 41.
88. Halder, *War Diary,* 514. Gen. Blumentritt said (Deighton, *Blood, Tears and Folly,* 465): "Army Group Centre remained inactive . . . during the best months of July to September."
89. Lukacs, *Last European War,* 446.
90. Carell, *Stalingrad,* 101, 102.
91. Neumann, *Black March,* 137.
92. Gerald Fleming, *Hitler and Final Solution,* 122 ff; Irving, *Hitler's War,* xxix, 617.
93. Manstein, *Lost Victories,* 361.
94. Lucas, *Last Year of German Army,* 14.
95. Shirer, *Rise and Fall,* 879 ff; Irving, *Hitler's War,* 345–346; Boyd, *Hitler's Japanese Confidant,* 31.
96. Hofstadter, *American Political Tradition,* 450.
97. *Trial,* 2: 144; Weinberg, *Germany, Hitler and World War II,* 37.
98. Schellenberg, *Labyrinth,* 375–376.
99. Schramm, *Hitler,* 117 ff.
100. Schröter, *Stalingrad,* 45–46.
101. Ibid., 69.
102. Carell, *Hitler Moves East,* 590.
103. Speer, *Inside Third Reich,* 295.
104. Freidin & Richardson, *Fatal Decisions,* 163.
105. Schröter, *Stalingrad,* 110.
106. Haffner, *Meaning of Hitler,* 137.
107. Shirer, *Rise and Fall,* 930.
108. Görlitz, *Paulus and Stalingrad,* 83.
109. Strawson, *Hitler's Battles,* 162.
110. Shirer, *Rise and Fall,* 933.
111. Irving, *Hitler's War,* 806.

112. Felix Gilbert, *Hitler Directs War,* 20.
113. Irving, *Hitler's War,* 468. Similarly, before invading France, Hitler said (Weizsäcker, *Memoirs,* 219) the campaign "would cost me a million men, but it would cost the enemy that, too—and the enemy could not stand it."
114. Jukes, *Stalingrad,* 84; Carell, *Hitler Moves East,* 111.
115. Toland, *Last 100 Days,* 147, 200–201; Irving, *Hitler's War,* 425; Keitel, *Memoirs,* 185–186.
116. Warlimont, *Inside Hitler's Headquarters,* 277.
117. Felix Gilbert, *Hitler Directs War,* 95, 98.
118. Halder, *Hitler as Warlord,* 7.
119. Rauschning, *Voice of Destruction,* 20.
120. Waite, *Psychopathic God,* 444.
121. Eitner, *Der Führer,* 287.
122. Hoyt, *Hitler's War,* 354.
123. Halder, *Hitler as Warlord,* 67.
124. Toland, *Last 100 Days,* 244–246; Speer, *Inside Third Reich,* 526.
125. Haffner, *Meaning of Hitler,* 159; Speer, *Inside Third Reich,* 442.
126. Haffner, *Meaning of Hitler,* 159–160.
127. Goldston, *Life and Death,* 196.
128. Baur, *Hitler's Pilot,* 188, 190.
129. Sondern, "Hitler's Last Days," 518.
130. Baird, *Nazi War Propaganda,* 252.
131. O'Donnell, *The Bunker,* 174.
132. McKnight, *Strange Loves,* 24.

AFTERWORD

1. Fein, *Accounting for Genocide,* 8.
2. Gustave Gilbert, *Nuremberg Diary,* 281.
3. Morgan, *Demon Lover,* 62–63.
4. Ibid., 128.
5. Calic, *Conversations with Hitler,* 98.
6. *Trial,* 11: 25.
7. Chartok & Spencer, *Holocaust Years,* 128.
8. Milgram, *Obedience to Authority,* 3.
9. Harold Laski in Milgram, 189.
10. Papen, *Memoirs,* 582.
11. Rauschning, *Revolution of Nihilism,* xi.
12. Fritz, *Frontsoldaten,* 226.

REFERENCES

Adam, Uwe. *Judenpolitik im dritten Reich.* Düsseldorf: Droste, 1972.

Aly, Götz, and Karl Roth. *Die restlose Erfassung.* Berlin: Rotbuch, 1984.

Arendt, Hannah. *Eichmann in Jerusalem,* New York: Penguin, 1965.

———. *Men in Dark Times.* New York: Harcourt Brace & World, 1968.

Assault on the Arts. New York Public Library, Feb. 27, 1993 (pamphlet).

Aycoberry, Pierre. *The Nazi Question.* New York: Pantheon, 1981.

Baird, Jay. *To Die for Germany,* Bloomington: Indiana University Press, 1990.

———. *The Mythical World of Nazi War Propaganda.* Minneapolis: University of Minnesota Press, 1974.

Banse, Ewald. *Germany Prepares for War.* New York: Harcourt Brace, 1934.

Barnett, Correlli, ed. *Hitler's Generals.* New York: Grove Weidenfeld, 1989.

Baumeister, Roy. *Masochism and the Self.* Hillsdale, N.J.: Erlbaum, 1989.

Baur, Hans. *Hitler's Pilot.* London: Muller, 1958.

Baynes, Godwin. *Germany Possessed.* London: Cape, 1941.

Bellow, Saul. *Dangling Man.* New York: Vanguard, 1944.

Bergen, Doris. *Twisted Cross.* Chapel Hill: University of North Carolina Press, 1996.

Bessell, Richard. *Life in the Third Reich.* New York: Oxford University Press, 1987.

Bezymenski, Lev. *The Death of Adolf Hitler.* New York: Harcourt Brace & World, 1968.

Binion, Rudolph. *Hitler Among the Germans.* Amsterdam: Elsevier, 1976.

Blackburn, Gilmer. *Education in the Third Reich.* Albany: State University of New York Press, 1985.

Bleuel, Hans. *Sex and Society in Nazi Germany.* Philadelphia: Lippincott, 1973.

Bloch, Eduard. "My Patient Hitler" in *Colliers,* March 15, 1941, March 22, 1941.

Blumentritt, Günther. *Von Rundstedt.* London: Oldhams, 1952.

Bock, Gisela. *Zwangsterilisation im Nationalsozialismus.* Opladen: Westdeutcher, 1986.

Boelcke, Willi, ed. *The Secret Conferences of Dr. Goebbels.* New York: Dutton, 1970.

Bormann, Martin. *The Bormann Letters.* London: Weidenfeld & Nicolson, 1954.

Boyd, Carl. *Hitler's Japanese Confidant.* Lawrence: University of Kansas Press, 1993.

Brady, Robert. *The Spirit and Structure of German Fascism.* New York: Viking, 1937.

Breitman, Richard. *The Architect of Genocide.* New York: Knopf, 1991.

———. "Himmler" in Cesarini, David, ed. *The Final Solution.* London: Routledge, 1994.

Brennecke, Fritz, and Paul Gierlichs. *The Nazi Primer.* New York: Harper, 1938.

Bromberg, Norbert, and Verna Small. *Hitler's Psychopathology*. New York: International Universities Press, 1983.

Broszat, Martin. *German National Socialism*. Santa Barbara: Clio, 1966.

———. *The Hitler State*. London: Longman, 1981.

Browning, Christopher. *The Final Solution and the German Foreign Office*. New York: Holmes & Maier, 1978.

———. *Ordinary Men*. New York: HarperCollins, 1992.

———. *The Path to Genocide*. Cambridge: Cambridge University Press, 1992.

Bullock, Alan. *Hitler,* Rev. ed. New York: Harper, 1958; Bantam (paperback), 1961.

———. *Hitler and Stalin*. New York: Knopf, 1992.

Bunting, James. *Adolf Hitler*. Folkestone: Bailey Brothers & Swinton, 1973.

Burleigh, Michael, and Wolfgang Wippermann. *The Racial State*. Cambridge: Cambridge University Press, 1991.

Bytwerk, Randall. *Julius Streicher*. New York: Stein & Day, 1983.

Calic, Edouard, ed. *Secret Conversations with Hitler*. New York: Stein & Day, 1971.

Carell, Paul. *Hitler Moves East*. Boston: Little, Brown, 1964.

———. *Stalingrad*. Altglen, Pa.: Schiffer, 1993.

Chartok, Roselle, and Jack Spencer, eds. *The Holocaust Years*. New York: Bantam, 1978.

Churchill, Winston. *The Gathering Storm*. Boston: Houghton Mifflin, 1948.

Ciano, Galeazzo. *The Ciano Diaries*. New York: Garden City, 1947.

Collier, Basil. *The Second World War*. New York: Morrow, 1967.

Conger, Jay. *The Charismatic Leader*. San Francisco: Jossey-Bass, 1989.

Conot, Robert. *Justice at Nuremberg*. New York: Harper & Row, 1983.

Craig, Gordon. *The Germans*. New York: Meridian, 1983.

Crankshaw, Edward. *Gestapo*. London: Greenhill, 1990.

Dawidowicz, Lucy. *The Holocaust Reader*. New York: Behrmann House, 1976.

———. *The War Against the Jews*. New York: Bantam, 1976.

Degrelle, Leon. *Campaign in Russia*. Cosa Mesta, Calif.: Institute for Historical Review, 1985.

Deighton, Len. *Blood, Tears and Folly*. New York: HarperCollins, 1993.

Deschner, Günther. *Reinhard Heydrich*. New York: Stein & Day, 1981.

Deuel, Wallace. *People Under Hitler*. New York: Harcourt Brace, 1942.

Dietrich, Otto. *Hitler*. Chicago: Regnery, 1955.

Dodd, Martha. *Through Embassy Eyes*. New York: Harcourt Brace, 1939.

Dolan, Edward. *Adolf Hitler*. New York: Dodd, Mead, 1981.

Ebenstein, William. *The Nazi State*. New York: Farrar & Rinehart, 1943.

Eitner, Hans-Jürgen. *Der Führer*. Munich: Langen Müller, 1981.

Engelmann, Bernt. *In Hitler's Germany*. New York: Pantheon, 1986.

Erikson, Erik. "Hitler's Imagery and German Youth." In *Personality,* Clyde Kluckhohn and Henry Murray, eds. New York: Knopf, 1948.

Feiling, Keith. *The Life of Neville Chamberlain*. London: Macmillan, 1946.

Fein, Helen. *Accounting for Genocide*. New York: Free Press, 1979.

Fest, Joachim. *The Face of the Third Reich*. New York: Pantheon, 1970.

———. *Hitler*. New York: Harcourt Brace Jovanovich, 1974.

Fischer, Klaus. *Nazi Germany*. New York: Continuum, 1995.

Flannery, Edward. *The Anguish of the Jews*. New York: Macmillan, 1965.

Fleming, Gerald. *Hitler and the Final Solution*. Berkeley: University of California Press, 1984.

Fleming, Peter. *Operation Sea Lion*. New York: Simon & Schuster, 1957.

Flower, Desmond, and James Reeves. *The Taste of Courage*. New York: Harper, 1960.

Frank, Hans. *Im Angesicht des Galgens*. Munich: Beck, 1953.

———. *Das Diensttagebuch des deutschen Generalgouverneurs in Polen*. Stuttgart: Deutsche, 1975.

Freidin, Seymour, and William Richardson, eds. *The Fatal Decisions*. New York: Sloane, 1956.

Friedlander, Henry. *The Origins of Nazi Genocide*. Chapel Hill: University of North Carolina Press, 1995.

Friedländer, Saul. *Nazi Germany and the Jews*. New York: HarperCollins, 1997.

Fritz, Stephen. *Frontsoldaten*. Lexington: University Press of Kentucky, 1995.

Fromm, Bella. *Blood and Banquets*. New York: Birch Lane, 1990.

Gallagher, Hugh. *By Trust Betrayed*. New York: Holt, 1990.

Galante, Pierre, and Eugene Silianoff. *Voices from the Bunker*. New York: Putnam's, 1989.

Gasman, Daniel. *Scientific Origins of National Socialism*. London: Macdonald, 1971.

Gay, Ruth. *The Jews of Germany*. New Haven: Yale University Press, 1992.

Gehlen, Reinhard. *The Service*. New York: World, 1972.

Gellately, Robert. *The Gestapo and German Society*. New York: Oxford University Press, 1991.

Gervasi, Frank. *Adolf Hitler*. New York: Hawthorne, 1974.

Gilbert, Felix, ed. *Hitler Directs His War*. New York: Oxford University Press, 1951.

Gilbert, Gustave. *Nuremberg Diary*. New York: Farrar, Straus, 1947.

———. *The Psychology of Dictatorship*. New York: Ronald, 1950.

Gisevius, Hans. *To the Bitter End*. Boston: Houghton Mifflin, 1947.

Goebbels, Joseph. *The Goebbels Diaries: 1942–1943*. Garden City, N.Y.: Doubleday, 1948.

———. *Die Tagebücher von Joseph Goebbels*. Munich: Saur, 1987.

Goldston, Robert. *The Life and Death of Nazi Germany*. New York: Fawcett, 1969.

Goodricke-Clarke, Nicholas. *The Occult Roots of Nazism*. Willingborough, England: Aquarian, 1985.

Gordon, Mary. "The Fascination Begins in the Mouth," *The New York Times Book Review*, 13 June 1993.

Göring, Hermann. *Germany Reborn*. London: Matthews & Marrot, 1934.

Görlitz, Walter. *History of the German General Staff*. New York: Praeger, 1953.

———. *Paulus and Stalingrad*. New York: Citadel, 1963.

Graber, G.S. *The Life and Times of Reinhard Heydrich.* New York: McKay, 1980.

Grün, Max von der. *Howl Like the Wolves.* New York: Morrow, 1980.

Grunberger, Richard. *The 12-Year Reich.* New York: Holt Rinehart Winston, 1971.

Guderian, Heinz. *Panzer Leader.* London: Joseph, 1952.

Gun, Nerin. *Eva Braun.* New York: Meredith, 1968.

Haape, Heinrich. *Moscow Tram Stop.* London: Collins, 1957.

Haffner, Sebastian. *The Meaning of Hitler.* Cambridge: Harvard University Press, 1979.

―――. *Germany: Jekyll and Hyde.* New York: Dutton, 1941.

Hagen, Louis. *The Mark of the Swastika.* New York: Bantam, 1963.

Halder, Franz. *The Halder War Diary.* Novato, Calif.: Presidio, 1988.

―――. *Hitler as Warlord.* London: Putnam's, 1950.

Hamilton, Alistair. *The Appeal of Fascism.* New York: Macmillan, 1971.

Hanfstängl, Ernst. *Unheard Witness.* Philadelphia: Lippincott, 1957.

Hassell, Ulrich von. *The Von Hassell Diaries.* Garden City, N.Y.: Doubleday, 1947.

Heiden, Konrad. *Der Fuehrer.* Boston: Houghton Mifflin, 1944.

Heinz, Heinz. *Germany's Hitler.* London: Hurst & Blackett, 1934.

Heyst, Axel. *After Hitler.* London: Minerva, 1940.

Hilberg, Raul. *The Destruction of the European Jews,* Rev. ed. New York: Holmes & Maier, 1985.

―――. *Documents of Destruction.* Chicago: Quadrangle, 1971.

Hillel, Marc, and Clarissa Henry. *Of Pure Blood.* New York: McGraw-Hill, 1976.

Hitler, Adolf. *Adolf Hitler Quotations.* (n.l.): Hammer, 1990.

―――. *Hitler Close-Up.* New York: Macmillan, 1973.

―――. *Hitler's Letters and Notes.* New York: Bantam, 1976.

―――. *Hitler: Speeches and Proclamations.* Vol. 1, 1990, Vol. 2, 1992, London: Tauris.

―――. *Hitler's Secret Book.* New York: Evergreen, 1983.

―――. *Hitler's Secret Conversations.* New York: Farrar, Straus, 1953.

―――. *Hitler's Words.* Washington, D.C.: American Council on Public Affairs, 1944.

―――. *Mein Kampf.* New York: Reynal & Hitchcock, 1940.

―――. *Mein Kampf.* Munich: Eher, 1940.

―――. *My New Order.* New York: Octagon, 1973.

―――. *The Testament of Adolf Hitler.* London: Cassell, 1961.

Hitler, Bridget. *The Memoirs of Bridget Hitler.* London: Duckworth, 1979.

Hoffmann, Heinrich. *Hitler Was My Friend.* London: Burke, 1955.

Hofstadter, Richard. *The American Political Tradition.* New York: Vintage, 1974.

Hohne, Heinz. *The Order of the Death's Head.* New York: Coward McCann, 1970.

Holt, Winfield. *Command and Control in Nazi Germany.* Carlisle Barracks, Pa.: Army War College, 1973.

Hoyt, Edwin. *Hitler's War.* New York: McGraw-Hill, 1988.

Infield, Glenn. *Eva and Adolf.* New York: Grosset & Dunlap, 1974.

―――. *Hitler's Secret Life.* New York: Stein & Day, 1981.

Irving, David. *Hitler's War*. New York: Viking, 1977.

———. *The Secret Diaries of Hitler's Doctor*. New York: Macmillan, 1983.

———. *The War Path*. New York: Viking, 1978.

Jäckel, Eberhard. *Hitler in History*. Hanover, N.H.: University Press of New England, 1984.

Jacobsen, Hans-Adolf, and Jürgen Rohwer. *Decisive Battles of World War II*. New York: Putnam's, 1965.

James, Clive. "Blaming the Germans." in *The New Yorker*, 22 April 1996.

Janus, Sam, Barbara Bass, and Carol Saltus. *A Sexual Profile of Men in Power*. Englewood Cliffs, N.J.: Prentice-Hall, 1977.

Jenks, William. *Vienna and the Young Hitler*. New York: Columbia University Press, 1960.

Jetzinger, Franz. *Hitler's Youth*. Westport, Conn.: Greenwood, 1976.

Johnson, Paul. *A History of the Jews*. New York: Harper & Row, 1987.

———. *Modern Times*. New York: Perennial Library, 1985.

Jones, Sydney. *Hitler in Vienna*. New York: Stein & Day, 1983.

Jukes, Geoffrey. *Stalingrad the Turning Point*. New York: Ballantine, 1968.

Kater, Michael. *Doctors Under Hitler*. Chapel Hill: University of North Carolina Press, 1989.

Keitel, Wilhelm. *The Memoirs of Field-Marshal Keitel*. New York: Stein & Day, 1966.

Kelley, Douglas. *22 Cells in Nuremberg*. New York: Greenberg, 1947.

Kersten, Felix. *The Memoirs of Doctor Felix Kersten*. Garden City, N.Y.: Doubleday, 1947.

———. *Totenkopf und Treue*. Hamburg: Mölich, (n.d.).

Kessel, Joseph. *The Man with the Miraculous Hands*. New York: Dell, 1962.

Kesselring, Albert. *The Memoirs of Field Marshal Kesselring*. Novato, Calif.: Presidio, 1989.

Kitterman, David. "Those Who Said 'No!' " *German Studies Review* 11 (1988).

Knappe, Siegfried, and Ted Brusaw. *Soldat*. New York: Orion, 1992.

Kneller, George. *The Educational Philosophy of National Socialism*. New Haven: Yale University Press, 1941.

Koehl, Robert. *The Black Corps*. Madison: University of Wisconsin Press, 1983.

Koehler, Hansjürgen. *Inside Information*. London: Pallas, 1940.

Koehn, Ilse. *Mischling, Second Degree*. New York: Greenwillow, 1977.

Kogon, Eugen. *The Theory and Practice of Hell*. New York: Octagon, 1973.

Koonz, Claudia. *Mothers in the Fatherland*. New York: St. Martin's, 1987.

Krausnick, Helmut, Hans Buchheim, Martin Broszat, and Hans-Joseph Jacobson. *Anatomy of the SS State*. New York: Walker, 1968.

Kubizek, August. *The Young Hitler I Knew*. Westport, Conn.: Greenwood, 1976.

Laffin, John. *Hitler Warned Us*. London: Brassey's, 1995.

Lang, Jochen von. *The Secretary*. New York: Random House, 1979.

Langer, Walter. *The Mind of Adolf Hitler* (large ed.). New York: Basic, 1972.

Leiser, Erwin. *Nazi Cinema*. New York: Macmillan, 1975.

Levin, Nora. *The Holocaust*. New York: Thomas Crowell, 1968.

Lewin, Ronald. *Hitler's Mistakes*. London: Cooper, 1984.

Liddell Hart, B.H. *The German Generals Talk*. New York: Quill, 1979.

————. *History of the Second World War*. New York: Putnam's, 1970.

————. *The Other Side of the Hill*. London: Cassell, 1973.

Loewenstein, Karl. *Hitler's Germany*. 3d ed. New York: Macmillan, 1944.

Lord, Walter. *The Miracle of Dunkirk*. New York: Viking, 1982.

Lucas, James. *The Last Year of the German Army*. London: Arms & Armour, 1994.

————. *War on the Eastern Front*. New York: Bonanza, 1982.

Lüdecke, Kurt. *I Knew Hitler*. New York: Scribner's, 1937.

Lukacs, John. *The Duel*. New York: Ticknor & Fields, 1991.

————. *The Last European War*. Garden City, N.Y.: Anchor, 1976.

Luther, Craig. *Blood and Honor*. San Jose: Bender, 1987.

Maltitz, Horst von. *The Evolution of Hitler's Germany*. New York: McGraw-Hill, 1973.

Manstein, Erich von. *Lost Victories*. London: Methuen, 1958.

Manvell, Roger, and Heinrich Fraenkel. *Göring*. New York: Simon & Schuster, 1962.

————. *The Hundred Days to Hitler*. New York: St. Martin's, 1974.

Maser, Werner. *Hitler*. New York: Harper & Row, 1973.

————. *Hitler's Mein Kampf*. London: Faber & Faber, 1970.

McKnight, Gerald. *The Strange Loves of Adolf Hitler*. London: Sphere, 1978.

Milgram, Stanley. *Obedience to Authority*. New York: Harper & Row, 1974.

Millett, Kate. *Sexual Politics*. New York: Equinox, 1971.

Mitscherlich, Alexander, and Fred Mielke. *Doctors of Infamy*. New York: Schuman, 1949.

Morgan, Robin. *The Demon Lover*. New York: Norton, 1989.

Mosse, George. *The Crisis of German Ideology*. New York: Grosset & Dunlap, 1964.

Müller, Ingo. *Hitler's Justice*. Cambridge: Harvard University Press, 1991.

Müller-Hill, Benno. *Murderous Science*. Oxford: Oxford University Press, 1988.

Munch, Peter. *Norse Mythology*. New York: AMS, 1970.

Murray, Henry. *Analysis of the Personality of Adolf Hitler*. Roosevelt Library, Hyde Park, N.Y.: President's Secretary's File, Box 99, Oct. 1943.

Neumann, Peter. *The Black March*. New York: Bantam, 1960.

Newton, Steven, ed. *German Battle Tactics on the Russian Front*. Altglen, Pa.: Schiffer, 1994.

Nyomarky, Joseph. *Charisma and Factionalism in the Nazi Party*. Minneapolis: University of Minnesota Press, 1967.

O'Donnell, James. *The Bunker*. Boston: Houghton Mifflin, 1978.

Oliner, Samuel, and Pearl Oliner. *The Altruistic Personality*. New York: Free Press, 1988.

Opitz, May, Katherina Oguntoye, and Dagmar Schultz, eds. *Showing Our Colors*. Amherst: University of Massachusetts Press, 1992.

Padfield, Peter. *Himmler*. New York: Holt, 1990.

Papen, Franz von. *Memoirs*. New York: Dutton, 1953.

Pascal, Roy. *The German Novel*. Toronto: University of Toronto Press, 1956.

Payne, Robert. *The Life and Death of Adolf Hitler*. New York: Popular Library, 1973.

Pearlman, Moshe. *The Capture and Trial of Adolf Eichmann.* New York: Simon & Schuster, 1963.

Petrova, Ada, and Peter Watson. *The Death of Hitler.* New York: Norton, 1995.

Phillips, Leona. *Adolf Hitler and the Third Reich.* New York: Gordon, 1977.

Picard, Max. *Hitler in Our Selves.* Hinsdale, Ill.: Regnery, 1947.

Poliakov, Leon. *Harvest of Hate.* Syracuse, N.Y.: Syracuse University Press, 1954.

Pope, Ernest. *Munich Playground.* New York: Putnam's, 1941.

Price, Ward. *I Knew These Dictators.* New York: Holt, 1938.

Proch, Franciszek. *Poland's Way of the Cross.* New York: Polish Association of Former Political Prisoners of Nazi and Soviet Concentration Camps, (n.d.).

Procktor, Richard. *Nazi Germany.* New York: Holt, Rinehart, and Winston, 1970.

Proctor, Robert. *Racial Hygiene.* Cambridge: Harvard University Press, 1988.

Pryce-Jones, David. *Unity Mitford.* New York: Dial/Wade, 1977.

Pulzer, Peter. *The Rise of Political Anti-Semitism in Germany & Austria.* Rev. ed. Cambridge: Harvard University Press, 1988.

Rauschning, Hermann. *The Revolution of Nihilism.* New York: Alliance, 1939.

————. *The Voice of Destruction.* New York: Putnam's, 1940.

Reed, Douglas. *The Burning of the Reichstag.* New York: Covici-Friede, (n.d.).

Reichmann, Eva. *Hostages of Civilization.* Boston: Beacon, 1951.

Reichstag Fire Trial. London: Bodley Head, 1934.

Reimann, Viktor. *Goebbels.* New York: Doubleday, 1976.

Reitlinger, Gerald. *The Final Solution.* New York: Beechhurst, 1953.

————. *The SS.* New York: Viking, 1957.

Remak, Joachim, ed. *The Nazi Years.* Englewood Cliffs, N.J.: Spectrum, 1969.

Rempel, Gerhard. *Hitler's Children.* Chapel Hill: University of North Carolina Press, 1989.

Rhodes, James. *The Hitler Movement.* Stanford: Hoover Institute, 1980.

Ribbentrop, Joachim von. *The Ribbentrop Memoirs.* London: Weidenfeld & Nicolson, 1954.

Rich, Norman. *Hitler's War Aims.* New York: Norton, 1973.

Riefenstahl, Leni. *Leni Riefenstahl.* New York: St. Martin's, 1993.

Ritchie, J. M. *German Literature under National Socialism.* Totowa, N.J.: Barnes & Noble, 1983.

Roberts, Stephen. *The House that Hitler Built.* New York: Harpers, 1938.

Robertson, Esmonde. *Hitler's Pre-War Policy and Military Plans.* New York: Citadel, 1967.

Röder, Thomas, Volker Kubillus, and Anthony Burwell. *Psychiatrists—the Men Behind Hitler.* Los Angeles: Freedom, 1995.

Root, Waverly. *The Secret History of the War.* New York: Scribner's, 1945.

Roper, Edith, and Clara Leiser. *Skeleton of Justice.* New York: Dutton, 1941.

Rosenbaum, Ron. "Explaining Hitler." *The New Yorker,* 1 May 1995.

————. "Hitler's Doomed Angel." *Vanity Fair,* April 1992.

Sajer, Guy. *The Forgotten Soldier.* McLean, Va.: Brassey's, 1994.

Schacht, Hjalmar. *Account Settled*. London: Weidenfeld & Nicolson, 1949.

Schellenberg, Walter. *The Labyrinth*. New York: Harper, 1956.

Schenck, Ernst. *Patient Hitler*. Düsseldorf: Droste, 1989.

Schleunes, Karl. *The Twisted Road to Auschwitz*. Urbana: University of Illinois Press, 1970.

Schmidt, Paul. *Hitler's Interpreter*. New York: Macmillan, 1951.

Schramm, Percy. *Hitler*. Chicago: Quadrangle, 1971.

Schröter, Heinz. *Stalingrad*. New York: Dutton, 1958.

Schumann, Willy. *Being Present*. Kent, Ohio: Kent State University Press, 1991.

Schwaab, Edleff. *Hitler's Mind*. New York: Praeger, 1992.

Scott, Gini. *Erotic Power*. New York: Citadel, 1992.

Segev, Tom. *Soldiers of Evil*. New York: McGraw-Hill, 1988.

Seligman, Martin. *Helplessness*. New York: Freeman, 1975.

Shapiro, David. *Autonomy and Rigid Character*. New York: Basic, 1981.

Shirer, William. *Berlin Diary*. New York: Knopf, 1941.

———. *End of a Berlin Diary*. New York: Popular Library, (n.d.).

———. *The Nightmare Years*. Toronto: Bantam, 1984.

———. *The Rise and Fall of the Third Reich*. New York: Simon & Schuster, 1960.

Shulman, Milton. *Defeat in the West*. New York: Dutton, 1948.

Shuster, George. *Like a Mighty Army*. New York: Appleton-Century, 1935.

Siemson, Hans. *Hitler Youth*. London: Drummond, 1940.

Simpson, Christopher. *The Splendid Blond Beast*. New York: Grove, 1993.

Smith, Howard. *Last Train from Berlin,* New York: Knopf, 1942.

Snyder, Louis. *Encyclopedia of the Third Reich*. New York: Paragon House, 1989.

———. *Hitler's German Enemies*. New York: Berkley, 1992.

Sondern, Frederic. "Adolf Hitler's Last Days" in *Secrets & Spies*. Pleasantville, N.Y.: Reader's Digest Association, 1964.

Speer, Albert. *Inside the Third Reich*. New York: Macmillan, 1970.

———. *The Slave State*. London: Weidenfeld & Nicolson, 1981.

———. *Spandau*. New York: Pocket, 1977.

Stachura, Peter. *The German Youth Movement*. New York: St. Martin's, 1981.

Stein, George, ed. *Hitler*. Englewood Cliffs, N.J.: Prentice-Hall, 1968.

Steiner, Jean-François. *Treblinka*. New York: Simon & Schuster, 1967.

Steiner, John. *Power Politics and Social Change in National Socialist Germany*. The Hague: Mouton, 1976.

Stern, Joseph. *Hitler*. Berkeley: University of California Press, 1975.

Stierlin, Helm. *Adolf Hitler*. New York: Psychohistory Press, 1976.

Stoller, Robert. *Perversion*. New York: Dell, 1975.

Strasser, Otto. *Hitler and I*. Boston: Houghton Mifflin, 1940.

Strawson, John. *Hitler's Battles for Europe*. New York: Scribner's, 1971.

Strom, Margot, and William Parsons. *Holocaust and Human Behavior*. Watertown, Mass.: Intentional Publications, 1982.

Sydnor, Charles. *Executive Instinct*. Paper presented at U.S. Holocaust Memorial Museum, Washington, Dec. 6, 1993.

———. *Soldiers of Destruction*. Princeton: Princeton University Press, 1977.

Tacitus. *The Agricola and the Germania*. London: Penguin, 1970.

Tobias, Fritz. *The Reichstag Fire*. New York: Putnam's, 1964.

Toland, John. *Adolf Hitler*. Garden City, N.Y.: Doubleday, 1976.

———. *The Last 100 Days*. New York: Bantam, 1967.

Tolischus, Otto. *They Wanted War*. New York: Reynal & Hitchcock, 1940.

Trevor-Roper, Hugh. *The Last Days of Hitler*. New York: Macmillan, 1947.

Wagener, Otto. *Hitler*. New Haven: Yale University Press, 1985.

Waite, Robert. "Adolf Hitler's Anti-Semitism." In *The Psychoanalytic Interpretation of History*. Edited by Benjamin Wolman. New York: Basic, 1971.

———. *The Psychopathic God*. New York: Basic, 1977.

Walsh, Edmund. *Total Power*. Garden City, N.Y.: Doubleday, 1948.

Warlimont, Walter. *Inside Hitler's Headquarters*. New York: Praeger, 1964.

Weinberg, Gerhard. *Germany, Hitler, and World War II*. Cambridge: Cambridge University Press, 1995.

———. *A World at Arms*. Cambridge: Cambridge University Press, 1994.

Weindling, Paul. *Health, Race and German Politics between National Unification and Nazism*. Cambridge: Cambridge University Press, 1989.

Weinreich, Max. *Hitler's Professors*. New York: Yiddish Scientific Institute, 1946.

Weiss, John. *Ideology of Death*. Chicago: Dee, 1996.

Weizsäcker, Ernst von. *The Weizsäcker Memoirs*. Chicago: Regnery, 1951.

Wheeler-Bennett, John. *Knaves, Fools and Heroes*. New York: St. Martin's, 1974.

Willner, Ann. *The Spellbinders*. New Haven: Yale University Press, 1984.

Zeiger, Henry. *The Case Against Adolf Eichmann*. New York: Signet, 1960.

Ziemer, Gregor. *Education for Death*. London: Oxford University Press, 1941.

Zmarzlik, Hans-Günter. "Social Darwinism in Germany." In *The Nazi Holocaust*. Edited by Michael Marrus. Vol. 2. Westport, Conn.; Meckler, 1969.

INDEX

THE AUTHOR

A psychologist and psychotherapist for over thirty years, George Victor, Ph.D., was educated at Columbia, Harvard, and New York universities. His previous books are *Invisible Men* and *The Riddle of Autism*. He lives in West Orange, N.J.